STANLEY KUBRICK

INTERVIEWS

CONVERSATIONS WITH FILMMAKERS SERIES

PETER BRUNETTE, GENERAL EDITOR

D0999226

Courtesy of the Kubrick Collection

STANLEY KUBRICK

INTERVIEWS

EDITED BY GENE D. PHILLIPS

UNIVERSITY PRESS OF MISSISSIPPI / JACKSON

www.upress.state.ms.us

09   08   07   06   05   04   03   02   01   4   3   2   1

∞

Library of Congress Cataloging-in-Publication Data

Kubrick, Stanley.
    Stanley Kubrick : interviews / edited by Gene D. Phillips.
        p.   cm. — (Conversations with filmmakers series)
    Includes index.
    ISBN 1-57806-296-9 (cloth : alk. paper) — ISBN 1-57806-297-7 (pbk. :
alk. paper)
    1. Kubrick, Stanley—Interviews.   2. Motion picture producers and
directors—United States—Interviews.   I. Phillips, Gene D.   II. Title.
III. Series.
PN1998.3.K83 A5 2000
791.43'0233'092—dc21   00-038186

British Library Cataloging-in-Publication Data available

CONTENTS

INTRODUCTION

VARIOUS BOOKS ON FILM directors in recent years have each hazarded that the subject of that particular volume was the greatest living American director. That statement could be fully justified about a filmmaker other than Stanley Kubrick only after Kubrick's death in 1999. Indeed, a host of obituaries and memorial articles by movie critics and film historians did in fact proclaim him the greatest American director of his era.

Few directors were able to work within the studio system of the American film industry with the independence that Stanley Kubrick achieved. By steadily building a reputation as a filmmaker of international importance, he gained full artistic control over his films, guiding the production of each of them from the earliest stages of planning and scripting through post-production. Kubrick was able to capitalize on the wide artistic freedom accorded him by the major studios because he learned his craft from the ground up. He is almost unique among directors in that he taught himself the techniques of filmmaking and did not serve the usual apprenticeship by working lesser jobs in a movie studio. By the time he began directing films for the major studios, he was able to command a degree of independence rare in motion-picture history. Consequently, his earliest interviewers in the late 1950s and early 1960s focus on Kubrick's status as an independent filmmaker who—while still in his early thirties—was already a role model for aspiring young directors.

In these first interviews Kubrick was reticent about his background and private life. He did mention to journalists, however, his lonely childhood, adding that his youth was spent in local movie houses like the cavernous

Loew's Paradise just off the Grand Concourse in the Bronx. He further indicated that seeing a number of mediocre Hollywood films convinced him that he could not make a film worse than the ones he was seeing — indeed, he could, in fact make one that was better. From childhood he was obsessed with the motion-picture medium. Once he had become a director, movies continued to be a passion — not merely a profession, much less a job. Even at the beginning of his career, Kubrick's more perceptive interviewers noted that he had already displayed more imagination with the camera than Hollywood had witnessed since Orson Welles went riding out of town. They may have been picking up Welles's oft-repeated observation that "among the younger generation Kubrick strikes me as a giant."[1]

The young filmmaker's working habits were already firmly established by the time he began to grant interviews. In an article not included in this book, one of Kubrick's earliest interviewers, after noting his fascination with film techniques, added, "Kubrick is fiercely concerned with the accuracy of the small details that make up the background of his films, because he feels that helps the audience to believe what they see on the screen."[2] This penchant for detail resulted in his guiding the production of each of his films from the preliminary stages of planning and composing the script up to the final snap of the editor's shears. In fact, when Jeremy Bernstein visited the set of 2001, he noticed that, in the course of a single day, Kubrick dropped in on "Santa's workshop" (the special effects department) to check on the design of a spacecraft, examined the costume designer's sketches of the astronauts' space suits, and studied a scale model of the moon constructed by the art department. Bernstein's descriptions of Kubrick's working methods help to establish that he was a premier auteur among film directors. He was the controlling force who synthesized and supervised the work of the technicians and creative artists who collaborated with him on a film.

The interviews collected here contain references to pet projects early in their inception, demonstrating that Kubrick sometimes nursed ideas over long periods before he was able to bring them to fruition. In a 1971 interview with Michael Hofsess, Kubrick mentioned that he planned to do an adaptation of *Traumnovelle* (*Dream Story*), which Viennese novelist Arthur Schnitzler (*La Ronde*) published in 1926. Nearly three decades later the novella, which deals with sexual obsession and jealousy, became Kubrick's final film, *Eyes Wide Shut*.

Another project, which got off the ground much sooner, was *Journey Beyond the Stars* (the working title of *2001: A Space Odyssey*). Although Kubrick spent four years making the movie with great care, from co-authoring the screenplay to overseeing the complicated special effects, the picture opened to mixed reviews. In interviews immediately following the premiere, Kubrick attempted to analyze the indifferent notices that the film initially received. He told Maurice Rapf that the crucial first New York preview on April 1, 1968, was an unmitigated disaster because the audience, which included several New York critics, was not prepared for the unprecedented visual experience to which they were treated. Many did not know what to make of *2001*, as the first reviews of the film indicate. Subsequent reviewers, of course, began to realize that here was a film that needed discussion and deliberation before the breadth of its meaning could be grasped. Early notices, written for newspapers and weekly magazines with immediate deadlines to meet, tended to judge *2001* more harshly than the reviews composed by critics for monthly magazines, who had more time to reflect on the picture.

In the interest of precision, Kubrick customarily asked an interviewer for the opportunity to read the transcript before it was published. He read the text of an interview with pen in hand, making marginal comments along the way. In my interview with him, I had written, "*2001* opened to indifferent and even hostile reviews." He added, "reviews which subsequent critical opinion has completely overwhelmed." He was obviously very gratified that his faith in the film was ultimately vindicated.

As *2001* caught on with audiences and garnered more favorable reviews in its release across the country, Kubrick ceased to be defensive with interviewers, confidently stressing the film's strong points. Its visual dimension, he explained, was more important than the plot. *2001* was not a film about space travel; it *was* space travel. By the time I interviewed him, some three years after the film's opening, he was pleased by the high grosses that the movie had achieved at the box office. As the interviews show, this film, which was released a year before the first moon landing, presents a fully realized vision of outer space. As such it is the yardstick by which subsequent sci-fi pictures are judged.

For my interview with Kubrick, I was invited to "Castle Kubrick," a huge, rambling old house in rural England where the director lived with his family and where he did much of the pre- and post-production work on his films. The mansion had the unmistakable air of an English manor house about it, but its owner was just as unmistakably American as the Bronx section of New York where he grew up. As a matter of fact, Kubrick kept his Bronx accent to the end of his days, despite his living in England.

Kubrick moved to there to shoot *Lolita* (1962) because financing for that film was easier to come by. He found living and working near London so congenial that he decided to settle in England permanently. Penelope Houston and Philip Strick noted, when they visited Kubrick's home for their *Sight and Sound* interview, that it was a casual collection of offices and living rooms in which family life and filmmaking overlapped as though the one were unthinkable without the other. For a man like Kubrick, for whom filmmaking was a whole way of life, this was probably true.

Shortly after the release of *A Clockwork Orange*, some critics attacked the movie for its moral stance. Kubrick insisted that the film reflected a strong moral vision and told Houston and Strick so when they interviewed him. Some of his comments on that occasion are echoed in his observations about the picture in my interview with him. Kubrick, who was sensitive to criticism, felt that *A Clockwork Orange* had been misunderstood in some quarters. Because his films were body and soul to him, Kubrick was hurt by hostile reactions to the picture. He consequently went to great pains to defend it to interviewers. The movie was denounced in Britain, particularly by the religious right for allegedly inspiring copycat crimes by youth gangs who apparently modeled themselves on Alex and his gang of delinquents. Deeply shocked by these allegations, Kubrick withdrew the film from distribution in Britain in 1974. (The film was given a theatrical re-release in Britain in 2000, a year after Kubrick's death.)

A remarkable consistency is obvious in the opinions that Kubrick voiced throughout his career. When asked by various journalists over the years how he went about choosing a property for filming, his answer was invariably the same. He would read voraciously in search of a suitable subject for filming and not relent until he finally found a story that gripped his imagination. Hence, when he was looking for a subject dealing with the preternatural, he perused stacks of horror novels, flinging each one across the office and against the wall when it failed to please him. One day he came upon a story that intrigued him, and he exclaimed, "This is it." He was reading Stephen King's *The Shining*.[3]

After he made an adaptation of *The Shining,* Kubrick told interviewers that he would not apologize for making a genre film. He was interested in giving his audience a real scare. Although the picture was a huge popular success, critical reaction to it was mixed. In a letter to me at the time, he mentioned, "Despite the usual critical love-hate it syndrome, I believe audiences like it a lot." His rather casual dismissal of reviewers was quite typical of the attitude toward critics that he expressed in interviews.

Kubrick customarily gave interviews to publicize the opening of his films. He commented on his working methods, elaborating on cinematic techniques and describing how he supervised the cinematography, editing, and even the choice of music for a film's underscore. He had planned to follow that procedure with *Eyes Wide Shut* in 1999; indeed, he had already arranged with Michael Herr, who had co-scripted *Full Metal Jacket,* to do an interview before the film opened in July. Because of Kubrick's death on March 7, only four days after delivering the final cut of the movie to Warner Bros., he was unable to give interviews about *Eyes Wide Shut,* to Herr or to anyone else.

Kubrick's last film, derived from the controversial Schnitzler novella, focuses on Dr. William Harford (Tom Cruise). He jeopardizes his marriage to Alice (Nicole Kidman) by making a foray into the unsavory netherworld of the decadent rich in New York City. As this final film indicates, Kubrick was still intent on taking the temperature of a sick society.

Kubrick virtually reinvented each genre in which he worked, whether it was horror or science-fiction. With *Eyes Wide Shut* he chose to redefine psychological drama. Since he worked in so many areas, each of his films was different from the one before, and they were, as the *London Times* has put it, marked with rare distinction "in an industry that gorges on mediocrity."[4] As the interviews collected in this book demonstrate, Kubrick found this versatility stimulating.

Kubrick long ago earned a place in the front rank of American auteurs as a director whose films are characterized by preoccupation with moral and social issues, coupled with consummate technical artistry that remains unsurpassed. Hence many accolades have been bestowed on him and his films. In 1997, he received both the D. W. Griffith Award from the Directors Guild of American and a Life Achievement Award from the Venice Film Festival. In accepting the Griffith Award, Kubrick stated, "Anyone who has ever been privileged to direct a film also knows that, although it can be like trying to write *War and Peace* in a bumper car at an amusement part, when you finally get it right, there are not many joys in life that can equal that feeling."

In an earlier tribute, *Dr. Strangelove* and *2001* were selected by the Library of Congress as among those American motion pictures to be preserved in the permanent collection of the National Film Registry as film classics that remain culturally, historically, and aesthetically important works. Although he lived for more than three decades in Britain, Kubrick never ceased to consider himself an American filmmaker, and rightly so. The bulk of his movies have American subjects and American settings. (He even transplanted his last film from Vienna, the original story location, to New York City.) Furthermore, the official recognition accorded Kubrick by the Directors Guild of America, the American Film Institute, and the Library of Congress attests to his enduring contribution to American film.

In keeping with the policy of the University Press of Mississippi regarding this series of Conversations with Filmmakers, the interviews in this book have not been edited in any substantial fashion. Therefore, the reader will at times observe Kubrick repeating himself. Still, the redundancies are meaningful in that these ideas were clearly concepts that were important to Kubrick and that he accordingly wished to emphasize.

The Kubrick Estate very kindly granted their permission to reprint certain selections in this book that would otherwise not have been available. The cooperation of Playboy Enterprises is also acknowledged.

This book is for Anthony Frewin, who served as Stanley Kubrick's production assistant from 1965 to 1968, and from 1979 through 1999, and now represents the Kubrick Estate.

Endnotes

1. Vincent LoBrutto, *Stanley Kubrick: A Biography* (New York: Da Capo, 1999).

2. Joanne Stang, "Stanley Kubrick," *New York Times Magazine,* 12 October 1958.

3. Harlan Kennedy, "Kubrick Goes Gothic," *American Film,* June 1980.

4. "Stanley on a Knife-edge," *London Times,* 1 November 1997.

CHRONOLOGY

1928   Born July 26, in the Bronx, New York, to Jacques and Gertrude Kubrick.

1945   Graduates from William Howard Taft High School and becomes a staff photographer for *Look* magazine at age sixteen.

1950   Expands a picture story he had done for *Look* on a boxer into a documentary short entitled, "Day of the Fight," and sells it to RKO.

1951   Makes "Flying Padre," a short documentary about a priest in New Mexico, which RKO likewise acquires.

1953   Directs his first feature, *Fear and Desire,* a low-budget movie which briefly plays the art house circuit.

1955   Makes another B picture, *Killer's Kiss,* which is distributed by a major studio, United Artists.

1956   Begins a three-film partnership with producer James B. Harris with *The Killing,* his first important film.

1957   His first big budget film, *Paths of Glory,* shot on location in Munich, with superstar Kirk Douglas.

1958   Fired as director of a Western, *One-Eyed Jacks,* when the star, Marlon Brando, decides to direct it himself; the film, released in 1961, is a disaster.

1960   Takes over as director of *Spartacus,* after another director is fired; his first commercial success.

1962   *Lolita,* the first of his films to be shot entirely in England; he then makes Britain the permanent base of his filmmaking operation.

1964   *Dr. Strangelove or: How I Learned to Stop Worrying and Love the Bomb,* the first film in his science fiction trilogy, wins him a Best Director Award from the New York Film Critics.

1968   *2001: A Space Odyssey,* a groundbreaking science fiction movie, celebrated for its ingenious use of state-of-the-art special effects; it wins an Academy Award for Special Visual Effects.

1972   The controversial *A Clockwork Orange,* a nightmarish fantasy about England in the near future, wins him a second Best Director Award from the New York Film Critics.

1975   *Barry Lyndon,* a historical epic derived from the Thackeray novel, garners him a British Academy Award as Best Director.

1980   *The Shining,* based on a horror tale by Stephen King, becomes a major box office triumph; a documentary about the making of the film, directed by Kubrick's daughter Vivian, is screened by BBC-TV.

1987   *Full Metal Jacket,* Kubrick's depiction of the war in Vietnam.

1995   After considering a series of possible film projects, including *AI,* a science fiction scenario about artificial intelligence, he finally opts to make *Eyes Wide Shut,* from the Arthur Schnitzler novella, "Dream Story."

1996   "The Invisible Man," a documentary about his career, is shown on Britain's Channel 4 to introduce a retrospective of his films.

1997   Recipient of the D. W. Griffith Award, the highest honor that can be bestowed by the Directors Guild of America; accorded a special Golden Lion at the Venice Film Festival for his contribution to the art of the cinema.

1999   Dies on March 7, four days after delivering the final print of *Eyes Wide Shut* to Warner Bros.; release on video cassette of the Kubrick

Collection, including his films from *The Killing* through *Full Metal Jacket.*

2000   Full-scale theatrical re-release of *Dr. Strangelove,* theatrical re-release in England of *A Clockwork Orange,* which Kubrick had withdrawn from distribution in Britain in 1974, when it was denounced for allegedly fomenting violence among teenage delinquents.

Major Kubrick Retrospective held at New York's Film Forum. Feature-length documentary about Kubrick is produced by veteran members of his production staff.

FILMOGRAPHY

Short Films

1951
Day of the Fight
Photography, Editing, Sound: **Stanley Kubrick**
Assistant: Alexander Singer
Music: Gerald Fried
Commentary: Douglas Edwards
Length: 16 minutes
Distributor: RKO Radio

1952
Flying Padre
Photography, Editing, Sound: **Stanley Kubrick**
Music: Nathaniel Shilkret
Length: 9 minutes
Distributor: RKO Radio

1953
The Seafarers
Photographed in color and directed by **Stanley Kubrick.** Written by Will
Chasan. Narrated by Don Hollenbeck. Technical advice by the staff of
the *Seafarers Log.* Produced by Lester Cooper. Presented by Seafarers International Union, Atlantic and Gulf Coast District, AFL. Running time:
30 minutes.

FEATURE FILMS

1953
Fear and Desire
Producer: **Stanley Kubrick**
Director, Photography, Editing: **Stanley Kubrick**
Screenplay: Howard O. Sackler
Music: Gerald Fried
Cast: Frank Silvera (Mac), Kenneth Harp (Corby), Virginia Leith (the girl), Paul Mazursky (Sidney), Steve Coit (Fletcher), David Allen (Narrator)
Length: 68 minutes
Distributor: Joseph Burstyn

1955
Killer's Kiss
Production Company: Minotaur
Producers: **Stanley Kubrick** and Morris Bousel
Director, Photography, Editing: **Stanley Kubrick**
Screenplay: **Stanley Kubrick**, Howard O. Sackler
Music: Gerald Fried
Choreography: David Vaughan
Cast: Jamie Smith (Davy Gordon), Frank Silvera (Vincent Rapallo), Irene Kane (Gloria), Jerry Jarret (Albert), Ruth Sobotka (Iris)
Length: 67 minutes
Distributor: United Artists

1956
The Killing
Production Company: Harris-Kubrick Productions
Producer: James B. Harris
Director: **Stanley Kubrick**
Screenplay: **Stanley Kubrick,** based on the novel *Clean Break* by Lionel White
Additional Dialogue: Jim Thompson
Photography: Lucien Ballard
Music: Gerald Fried
Editor: Betty Steinberg
Sound: Earl Snyder

Art Director: Ruth Sobotka Kubrick
Costumes: Rudy Harrington
Cast: Sterling Hayden (Johnny Clay), Colleen Gray (Fay), Jay C. Flippen
(Marv Unger), Marie Windsor (Sherry Peatty), Elisha Cook (George Peatty),
Ted de Corsia (Randy Kennan), Joe Sawyer (Mike O'Reilly), James Edwards
(parking lot attendant), Timothy Carey (Nikki), Vince Edwards (Val),
Joseph Turkel (Tiny), Kola Kwariani (Maurice)
Length: 83 minutes
Distributor: United Artists

1957
Paths of Glory
Production Company: Harris-Kubrick Productions
Producer: James B. Harris
Director: **Stanley Kubrick**
Screenplay: **Stanley Kubrick,** Jim Thompson, Calder Willingham, based
on the novel by Humphrey Cobb
Photography: George Krause
Music: Gerald Fried
Editor: Eva Kroll
Sound: Martin Muller
Art Director: Ludwig Reiber
Cast: Kirk Douglas (Colonel Dax), Ralph Meeker (Captain Paris), Adolphe
Menjou (General Broulard), George Macready (General Mireau), Wayne
Morris (Lieutenant Roget), Richard Anderson (Major Saint-Aubain), Joseph
Turkel (Private Arnaud), Timothy Carey (Private Ferol), Peter Cappel (Judge),
Susanne Christian (German girl), Bert Freed (Sergeant Boulanger), Emile
Meyer (priest), John Stein (Captain Rousseau)
Length: 86 minutes
Distributor: United Artists (Presented by Bryna Productions)

1960
Spartacus
Production Company: Bryna Productions
Producer: Edward Lewis
Executive Producer: Kirk Douglas
Director: **Stanley Kubrick**

Screenplay: Dalton Trumbo, from the novel by Howard Fast
Photography: Russell Metty
Additional Photography: Clifford Stine
Process: Super Technirama, 70 mm. Technicolor
Editors: Robert Lawrence, Robert Schultz, Fred Chulack
Second Unit: Irving Lerner
Music: Alex North
Music Director: Joseph Gershenson
Production Designer: Alexander Golitzen
Set Decoration: Russell Gausman, Julia Heron
Art Director: Eric Orbom
Costumes: Peruzzi, Valles, Bill Thomas
Titles: Saul Bass
Sound: Waldo Watson, Joe Lapis, Murray Spivack, Ronald Pierce
Cast: Kirk Douglas (Spartacus), Laurence Olivier (Marcus Crassus), Jean
Simmons (Varinia), Charles Laughton (Gracchus), Peter Ustinov (Batiatus),
Tony Curtis (Antoninus), John Gavin (Julius Caesar), Nina Foch (Helena),
Herbert Lom (Tiogranes), John Ireland (Crixus), John Dall (Glabrus),
Charles McGraw (Marcellus), Harold J. Stone (David), Woody Strode
(Draba)
Length: 196 minutes
Distributor: Universal Pictures

1962
Lolita
Production Companies: Seven Arts/Anya/Transworld
Producer: James B. Harris
Director: **Stanley Kubrick**
Screenplay: Vladimir Nabokov, based on his novel (**Stanley Kubrick,**
uncredited)
Photography: Oswald Morris
Editor: Anthony Harvey
Art Director: Bill Andrews
Associate Art Director: Sid Cain
Costumes: Gene Coffin, Elsa Fennell
Music: Nelson Riddle
Lolita theme: Bob Harris

Orchestrations: Gil Grau
Production Supervisor: Raymond Anzarut
Sound Recordists: H. L. Bird, Len Shilton
Cast: James Mason (Humbert Humbert), Peter Sellers (Clare Quilty),
Shelley Winters (Charlotte Haze), Sue Lyon (Lolita), Marianne Stone
(Vivian Darkbloom), Jeff Stovin (John Farlow), Diana Decker (Jean Farlow),
Gary Cockrell (Dick Schiller), Suzanne Gibbs (Mona Farlow), William
Greene (Mr. Swine), Cec Linder (physician), Lois Maxwell (Nurse Lord),
John Harrision (Tom)
Length: 152 minutes
Distributor: Metro Goldwyn Mayer

1964
Dr. Strangelove or: How I Learned to Stop Worrying and Love the Bomb
Production Company: Hawk Films
Producer/Director: **Stanley Kubrick**
Screenplay: **Stanley Kubrick,** Terry Southern, Peter George, based on the
book *Red Alert* by Peter George
Photography: Gilbert Taylor
Editor: Anthony Harvey
Production Designer: Ken Adam
Music: Laurie Johnson
Art Director: Peter Murton
Special Effects: Wally Veevers
Sound Recordist: Richard Bird
Assistant Editor: Ray Lovejoy
Associate Producer: Victor Lyndon
Cast: Peter Sellers (Group Captain Mandrake, President Muffley, Dr.
Strangelove), George C. Scott (General "Buck" Turgidson), Sterling Hayden
(General Jack D. Ripper), Keenan Wynn (Colonel "Bat" Guano), Slim
Pickens (Major T. J. "King" Kong), Peter Bull (Ambassador de Sadesky),
James Earl Jones (Lieutenant Lothar Zogg), Tracy Reed (Miss Scott), Jack
Creley (Mr. Staines), Frank Berry (Lieutenant Dietrich), Glenn Beck
(Lieutenant Kivel), Shane Rimmer (Captain Ace Owens), Paul Tamarin
(Lieutenant Goldberg)
Length: 94 minutes
Distributor: Columbia Pictures

1968

2001: A Space Odyssey

Production Company: Metro Goldwyn Mayer

Producer/Director: **Stanley Kubrick**

Screenplay: **Stanley Kubrick**, Arthur C. Clarke, based on Clarke's short story "The Sentinel."

Photography: Geoffrey Unsworth

Process: Super Panavision

Additional Photography: John Alcott

Production Designers: Tony Masters, Harry Lange, Ernie Archer

Editor: Ray Lovejoy

Special Photographic Effects Designer/Director: **Stanley Kubrick**

Special Photographic Effects Supervisors: Wally Veevers, Douglas Trumbell, Con Pederson, Tom Howard

Music: Richard Strauss, Johann Strauss, Aram Khachaturian, Gyorgy Ligeti

Costumes: Hardy Amies

Cast: Keir Dullea (Dave Bowman), Gary Lockwood (Frank Poole), William Sylvester (Dr. Heywood Floyd), Douglas Rain (voice of HAL), Daniel Richter (Moonwatcher), Leonard Rossiter (Smylov), Margaret Tyzack (Elena), Robert Beatty (Halvorsen)

Length: 141 minutes (originally 160 minutes)

Distributor: Metro Goldwyn Mayer

1971

A Clockwork Orange

Production Company: Warner Bros./Hawk Films

Producer/Director: **Stanley Kubrick**

Executive Producers: Max Raab, Si Litvinoff

Screenplay: **Stanley Kubrick,** based on the novel by Anthony Burgess

Photography: John Alcott

Editor: Bill Butler

Production Design: John Barry

Art Directors: Russell Hagg, Peter Shields

Electronic Music: Walter (Wendy) Carlos

Music: Ludwig von Beethoven, Edward Elgar, Gioacchino Rossini, Nikolai Rimsky-Korsakov, Henry Purcell, Terry Tucker, Arthur Freed, Nacio Herb Brown, James Yorkston, Erica Eigen

Costumes: Milena Canonero
Assistant to Producer: Jan Harlan
Cast: Malcolm McDowell (Alex), Patrick Magee (Mr. Alexander), Michael
Bates (Chief Guard), Anthony Sharp (Minister of the Interior), Godfrey
Quigley (Prison Chaplain), Adrienne Corri (Mrs. Alexander), Warren Clarke
(Dim), Miriam Karlin (Cat Lady), Paul Farrell (tramp), Philip Stone (Dad),
Sheila Raynor (Mum), Aubrey Morris (Mrs. Deltoid), Carl Duering (Dr.
Brodsky), John Clive (stage actor), Madge Ryan (Dr. Branom), Pauline
Taylor (psychiatrist), Margaret Tyzack (conspirator), John Savident (con-
spirator), Steven Berkoff (Constable), David Prowse (Julian), Michael Tarn
(Peter)
Length: 137 minutes
Distributor: Warner Bros.

1975
Barry Lyndon
Production Company: Hawk/Peregrine Films for Warner Bros.
Producer/Director: **Stanley Kubrick**
Executive Producer: Jan Harlan
Screenplay: **Stanley Kubrick**, based on the novel *The Luck of Barry Lyndon*
by William Makepeace Thackary
Photography: John Alcott
Editor: Tony Lawson
Production Designer: Ken Adam
Art Director: Roy Walker
Costumes: Ulla-Britt Soderlund, Milena Canonero
Music: J. S. Bach, Frederick the Great, W. A. Mozart, G. F. Handel, Franz
Schubert, Giovanni Paisiello, Antonio Vivaldi, traditional irish music
played by The Chieftains
Music Adaptation: Leonard Rosenman
Cast: Ryan O'Neal (Redmond Barry/Barry Lyndon), Marisa Berenson (Lady
Lyndon), Patrick Magee (Chevalier de Balibari), Hardy Kruger (Captain
Potzdorf), Steven Berkoff (Lord Ludd), Gay Hamilton (Nora Brady), Marie
Kean (Mrs. Barry), Murray Melvin (Reverend Runt), Godfrey Quigley (Cap-
tain Grogan), Leon Vitali (Lord Bullington), Diana Koerner (Lischen), Frank
Middlemass (Sir Charles Lyndon), André Morell (Lord Wendover), Philip
Stone (Graham), Anthony Sharp (Lord Hallum), Michael Hordern (Narrator)

Length: 185 minutes
Distributor: Warner Bros.

1980
The Shining
Production Company: Hawk/Peregrine Films (in association with The Producer Circle Company) for Warner Bros.
Producer/Director: **Stanley Kubrick**
Executive Producer: Jan Harlan
Screenplay: **Stanley Kubrick**, Diane Johnson, based on the novel by Stephen King
Photography: John Alcott
Steadicam Operator: Garrett Brown
Editor: Ray Lovejoy
Production Designer: Roy Walker
Art Director: Les Tompkins
Music: Béla Bartók, Gyorgy Ligeti, Krzysztof Penderecki, Wendy Carlos, Rachel Elkind, Henry Hall
Costumes: Milena Canonero
Sound: Ivan Sharrock
Second Unit Photography: Douglas Milsome, Gregg Macgillivray
Personal Assistant to Stanley Kubrick: Leon Vitali
Cast: Jack Nicholson (Jack Torrance), Shelley Duvall (Wendy Torrance), Danny Lloyd (Danny Torrance), Scatman Crothers (Halloran), Philip Stone (Delbert Grady), Joe Turkel (Lloyd), Barry Nelson (Ullman), Anne Jackson (Doctor), Lia Beldam (young woman in bath), Billie Gibson (old woman in bath), Lisa and Louise Burns (the Grady girls)
Length: 144 minutes
Distributor: Warner Bros.

1987
Full Metal Jacket
Production Company: Puffin Films for Warner Bros.
Executive Producer: Jan Harlan
Producer/Director: **Stanley Kubrick**
Screenplay: **Stanley Kubrick**, Michael Herr, Gustav Hasford, based on Hasford's novel *The Short-Timers*

Lighting Cameraman: Douglas Milsome
Production Designer: Anton Furst
Costumes: Keith Denny
Editor: Martin Hunter
Original Music: Abigail Nead (plus songs: "Hello Vietnam," performed by
Johnny Wright; "The Marines Hymn," performed by the Goldman Band;
"These Boots Are Made for Walking," performed by Nancy Sinatra; "Chapel
of Love," performed by the Dixie Cups, "Wooly Bully," performed by Sam
the Sham and the Pharaohs, and "Paint It Black," performed by the Rolling
Stones).
Sound Recording: Edward Tise
Special Effects Supervisor: John Evans
Production Assistant: Anthony Frewin
Cast: Matthew Modine (Private Joker), Lee Ermey (Sergeant Hartman),
Vincent D'Onofrio (Private Pyle), Adam Baldwin (Animal Mother), Arliss
Howard (Private Cowboy), Dorian Harewood (Eightball), Kevyn Major
Howard (Rafterman), Ed O'Ross (Lt. Touchdown), John Terry (Lt. Lockhart),
Ngoc Le (V. C. Sniper)
Length: 118 minutes
Distributor: Warner Bros.

1999
Eyes Wide Shut
Production Company: Hobby Films, Warner Bros.
Executive Producer: Jan Harlan
Producer/Director: **Stanley Kubrick**
Screenplay: **Stanley Kubrick**, Frederic Raphael, based on "Traumnovelle"
("Dream Story") by Arthur Schnitzler
Lighting Cameraman: Larry Smith
Production Designers: Leslie Tomkins, Roy Walker
Costumes: Marit Allen
Editor: Nigel Galt
Original Music: Jocelyn Pook (plus "Musica Ricercata II" by Gyorgy Liget;
"Waltz 2" from "Jazz Suite" by Dmitri Shostakovich; "Baby Did a Bad
Thing" performed by Chris Isaak)
Sound Recording: Edward Tise
Art Director: John Fenner

Production Assistant to Stanley Kubrick: Anthony Frewin
Cast: Tom Cruise (Dr. William Harford), Nicole Kidman (Alice Harford),
Sydney Pollack (Victor Ziegler), Todd Field (Nick Nightingale), Sky Dumont
(Sandor Szavost), Marie Richardson (Marion), Thomas Gibson (Carl),
Vinessa Shaw (Domino), Rade Sherbedgia (Milich), Leelee Sobieski
(Milich's Daughter)
Length: 155 minutes
Distributor: Warner Bros.

S T A N L E Y   K U B R I C K

I N T E R V I E W S

The Hollywood War of Independence

COLIN YOUNG/1959

IN THE UNITED STATES a studio must hope to recover most or all of its costs within the domestic market. This represents the least specialized audience in the world (as we all know there is nothing special about being an American) and there is a constant temptation, almost always succumbed to, to level everything down to the lowest common denominator. In such conditions there is little chance that an individual filmmaker will produce a personal work. Almost always an American film is edited, not by the director, but by the studio—often in committee. It is not difficult to understand why. When several million dollars are at stake a responsible business will rarely rely on the opinion of one man. Other opinions, often outside opinions, will be sought. And each time such an opinion is applied to a film, it becomes to that extent less and less the director's personal statement. The Screen Directors' Guild in Hollywood in recent years has added a clause to its standard contract requiring a producer to grant the director right of first cut. But this is often no more than a formality. (There was a recent case in which the director's version of a film was seen only by him and his editor before it was taken apart again to be run, uncut, for the producers.) And with the current trend to larger budgets, based on the hypothesis that a larger investment is less risky than a smaller one, it is likely that less and less control will be left in the hands of a director, unless he is by age or experience or perhaps

From *Film Quarterly,* vol. 12 no. 3, Spring 1959, 4–15. © 1959 by The Regents of the University of California. Reprinted by permission.

by financial participation powerful enough to have a controlling interest.

This is all very discouraging for the young filmmaker trying to bore his way into films through the porthole eye of television, or to make the long hard jump from shorts or the repertory theater into features. And for many European directors this is reason enough for not working in Hollywood. Their financing problems are usually solved film by film, whenever they persuade a backer to support their latest speculation — frequently for a budget which would have been consumed by one elephant charge in a film by the late Cecil B. DeMille. . . .

The freedom to make the films of their own choosing, in their own way, is not even the goal of most Hollywood directors, who seem quite content to be parts of a large organic whole. It is only a small hard-core minority which chases these freedoms, each in his own way, perhaps known to each other, but not united by anything more than interest. Some of them play poker together but they solve their problems in different ways, some choosing to remain independent of a major studio entirely (like Stanley Kubrick), others already in possession of a more or less safe Hollywood studio contract but waiting for their chance to be free of studio control. Others again, not yet so far advanced, are serving a hopeful, waiting apprenticeship in the theater or in live television, or have started by making some shorts — usually documentary, but occasionally dramatic. In each case the mechanical problems are different — there is no single happy road to independence. But in each case the goal is the same — freedom to make a personal film, as free as possible from compromise. The fear that they will fail is a real one, and is responsible yearly for no one knows how many defections. And the thought that when they earn their freedom they will have lost the will to use it is a constant threat. . . .

Stanley Kubrick is perhaps the most widely discussed of the postwar Hollywood newcomers, with four independent features behind him — *Fear and Desire, Killer's Kiss, The Killing,* and *Paths of Glory.* He recently withdrew from the unit about to start shooting *One-Eyed Jacks,* Marlon Brando's independent production, ostensibly to begin work on *Lolita,* with his producer (since *The Killing*) James Harris. They bought the film rights about a month after the novel appeared and since then have had several bids from other producers — the highest for $650,000. This offer, like the others, was refused.

All this gives an impression of typically inflated Hollywood economics. But it is curiously untypical of the manner in which Kubrick and Harris work. *Paths of Glory* was made for $900,000–$350,000 of which went to Kirk Douglas, its star. Thus, apart from Douglas's slice, the film was comparatively inexpensive—certainly a bargain for its distributors, United Artists. (It has to date grossed two and a half million dollars, worldwide.)

Kubrick is certain that genuine independence is possible only if the director stays clear of the major studios as long as possible. By this he means that a director should have a completed script, and if possible have a cast selected and signed, before going to a major studio for money. Anything less is inviting interference and a loss of control. It must include at least one "name" star, and the list of possibles is quite small—Kubrick mentioned about fifteen men and only seven women. "What this implies," he summarized, "is that you require the means to remain independent until the script is finished, until you have a star, and until the deal is set up properly." (By "properly" he means that the director's control will not prove to be illusory.)

A system so inexorably tied to a box-office list of actors and actresses obviously imposes severe limitations on a director's freedom of choice with material. But this does not distress Kubrick. "There is still a large enough number of good properties to permit you to do what you want— and remain independent."

The only time he has ever worked with a major studio was after *Paths of Glory,* when, with a forty-week contract from Dore Schary, he was let loose in the MGM library of story properties. It took him a long time to find anything to interest him, but before he left (in the wake of Schary's fall from grace) he had turned Stefan Zweig's touching short story *The Burning Secret* into a screenplay.

Employed by *Look* as a still photographer, he turned to film, making two shorts for RKO before stepping up to features with two hurly-burly films which he would rather not talk about now—*Fear and Desire* and *Killer's Kiss.* But when they came out film critics did talk about them and saw the kind of promise which, it is generally agreed, Kubrick honored in his next two films. The money for his first two came from family and friends. Without this support, which must at times have seemed like blind devotion, he might never have reached his present position; it would be hard to estimate the number of aspirants who have never solved the problem of how to raise that first $50,000.

When he came to make *Paths of Glory,* United Artists was the only financing organization in Hollywood which would touch it, and then only after Kirk Douglas agreed to play in it. The majors might have balked, Kubrick thinks, at the thought of offending their interests in France (through theater holdings, etc.). But United Artists is not committed in this way and, Kubrick added, perhaps has a more realistic view of the contemporary world market. In his experience they have been very good with scripts about which there is general apathy or, as in this case, antagonism.

Kubrick's two later films have received widespread critical attention—almost all of it favorable. *The Killing* is thoroughly manufactured, but the script goes out of its way to give motivation to all of the central characters and this alone would distinguish it from run-of-the-mill gunslingers if it did not anyway have considerable style and impact; it holds up well when reseen today. *Paths of Glory* is in almost every way a more important work—not only because it was almost three times as expensive. It is obviously *about something*—when we remember that this dramatization of an incident of military deceit in the French Army of World War I has still to be shown publicly in France.

What will probably be Kubrick's next film is also a war story. Presently titled *The German Lieutenant,* it is by a new writer, Richard Adams, formerly a paratrooper in Korea and more recently a Fulbright scholar to Europe, where he studied with Carl Dreyer. The story is based partially on his experiences, but has been switched to Germany in World War II.

I asked Kubrick at this point in our conversation why he wanted to make another war film—was there nothing about the contemporary scene which interested him? His reply is crucial and must be given in full.

"To begin with," he said, "one of the attractions of a war or crime story is that it provides an almost unique opportunity to contrast an individual of our contemporary society with a solid framework of accepted value, which the audience becomes fully aware of, and which can be used as a counterpoint to a human, individual, emotional situation. Further, war acts as a kind of hothouse for forced, quick breeding of attitudes and feelings. Attitudes crystallize and come out into the open. Conflict is natural, when it would in a less critical situation have to be introduced almost as a contrivance, and would thus appear forced, or—even worse—false.

Eisenstein, in his theoretical writings about dramatic structure, was often guilty of oversimplification. The black and white contrasts of *Alexander Nevsky* do not fit all drama. But war *does* permit this basic kind of contrast—and spectacle. And within these contrasts you can begin to apply some of the possibilities of film—of the sort explored by Eisenstein."

He said somewhat wistfully, however, that he hoped to be able to deal some day with a more straightforward contemporary scene. To some extent he might do so of course with *Lolita,* but here his primary interest is to explore the development of Humbert's character, and the varieties of his love for his moppet—ending, ironically enough, with what Kubrick takes to be an almost selfless love for Lolita when, now seventeen, she is stuck with a humdrum pregnancy, and husband, and life. He does not plan to change the ages of the principals, nor the nature of their relationship, but he says they have a way of handling the subject which allows them to consider making the film at all.

Kubrick stands much closer to his material than almost any other director currently working in Hollywood. In each of his films to date he has been the principal or sole author of the screenplay (he did the original draft of *Paths of Glory,* and Calder Willingham came in for the second), and he is at least the supervising if not the actual editor of his filmed material. On *Killer's Kiss* he carried credit for photography as well as direction, and he operated one of the cameras during the attack sequence in *Paths of Glory* (one fitted with a Zoomar lens). Thus it is not surprising that there should be a strong feeling of unity and single-mindedness in his films. Such a result is not guaranteed by one man's control of the material—he could be undecided about it. But it is rarely achieved in committee films. "A camel," as the recent proverb has it, "is a mule made by a committee."

There is an unconventionally intellectual air about Kubrick's films, but this may be more a by-product of style than an intentional ingredient. Certainly he does not mean his films to be intellectual in the sense of making a clear-cut statement about something. "I cannot give a precise *verbal* summary of the philosophical meaning of, for example, *Paths of Glory.* It is intended to involve the audience in an experience. Films deal with the emotions and reflect the fragmentation of experience. It is thus misleading to try to sum up the meaning of a film verbally." However, it is precisely his very evident style, praised by an eagerly perceptive band of professional film critics, which for some commentators (although not myself) prevents their involvement in Kubrick's characters and situations.

Kubrick has already given ample evidence of his strong grasp of *mise en scène* and the extension of character which an actor can be encouraged to bring to the pauses between lines of dialogue. On a second viewing of *Paths of Glory*, Douglas causes some uneasiness, but the film is otherwise beautifully performed, staged, photographed, cut, and scored—using, for example, a rasping, alarming staccato of drums during the battle scenes. It is a disappointment that Kubrick was not able to continue with Brando. Their relationship could not have been an easy one, but the result could have been fascinating. . . .

This, then, is the "growing edge" of Hollywood. It is a different story than the one which might be told of Bergman, Ray, or Bresson, and it is perhaps not as heartening. But Kubrick is American, trying to work in or through Hollywood. If there is to be any "native" cinema in this country at all, it is as well that Kubrick and other gentlemen who pursue artistic freedom are there, making the attempt.

Stanley Kubrick and *Dr. Strangelove*

ELAINE DUNDY/1963

AT FIRST THE IDEA of making a funny film of the inherently tragic H-bomb situation is beset with danger and except for Chaplin's attempt to laugh Hitler and Mussolini out of existence in *The Great Dictator,* without precedent; yet judging from its script at least, the new Stanley Kubrick picture *Dr. Strangelove or: How I Learned to Stop Worrying and Love the Bomb* bids fair to being the black comedy of all time. You do laugh — at moments you laugh out loud reading it, but all time it never lets you stop thinking, "Yes, this could happen." ("Wait till the audiences see this one," said Sterling Hayden, "they'll have nightmares." "That's what we're here for, isn't it?" asked Keenan Wynn quietly.) And it is possible under the tense and concentrated conditions of the actual shooting, to have to stifle giggles while listening to plausible lunatic telephone exchanges between Top Brass Security, without having one's awareness dimmed that these men are muddling themselves onto the verge of the end of the world:

> General Ripper (Sterling Hayden): Do you recognize my voice, Captain?
>
> Captain Mandrake (Peter Sellers): Certainly, General. Why do you ask?
>
> General Ripper: Why do you think I ask, Captain?
>
> Captain Mandrake: Well, I really don't know, sir. I mean we just spoke a few minutes ago, didn't we?

From *The Queen Magazine,* 13 March 1963. Reprinted by permission of the author.

General Ripper: You don't think I'd ask if you recognized my
   voice unless it was important, do you Captain?
Captain Mandrake: No sir, I'm sure you wouldn't.
General Ripper: O.K. Let's see if we can stay on the ball then....

"This is a picture, not a war," the First Assistant was hired to say re-
assuringly to the intense ulcerated movie director every morning. Stanley
Kubrick would not find that remark amusing. Nor would he have taken
any comfort in it. For him, filmmaking is a war and a war he intends to
win...against laziness, goofing off, passing the buck, playing at Who's
in Charge, wasting time, wasting energy—anything, in short, that prevents him from getting the best working conditions for himself and his
actors. At first glance the set at Shepperton, where he is now shooting *Dr.
Strangelove,* looks like any other British film set. The same depressing endless mugs of tea in everybody's hands; a sound man totally uninterested in
the proceedings reads the *Guardian* under his sound board, a scriptgirl is
slow and vague about prompting the actors in their lines. It is cold and
uncomfortable and there is no place to sit. But after five minutes of watching Stanley Kubrick at work the feeling becomes quite different. For one
thing Kubrick is not asking the questions ("Can we get that shot, Joe?"
"How's that for a level?" "Did he have his cigar in his mouth then?");
he is giving the orders. "Get out of the way," he will say casually and inof-
fensively to anyone who is in it. For another, the set itself, the office of
General Ripper at SAC headquarters, looks different. More realistic. It has
a ceiling (as will all the sets). And a great absence of all those cables and
wires to trip you up. The lighting—which incidentally Kubrick does himself—is simpler, what they call "natural lighting," i.e., coming only from
what would be the real sources of light in the situation instead of the complicated series of arc lamps hung from above that give most interior shots
in films their unnatural quality. And no boom mikes. The actors often
wear tiny concealed mikes on their persons. All technical aspects have
been streamlined; stripped for action. I watch them shoot the scene in
which Sterling Hayden (playing with deep, exquisite square-ness and maximum comic effect), having set off a chain of reactions which may lead to
a nuclear war, takes time off to explain his theory of fluoridation to Peter
Sellers.

Captain, I have been following this thing very carefully for years ever since the commies introduced it. Did you know that, in addition to fluoridating water, there are studies under way to fluoridate salt, flour, fruit juices, milk, and ice-cream — ice-cream, Captain — children's *ice*-cream? Do you know when fluoridation first began? It began in 1946, Captain. How does that coincide with your post-war communist conspiracy? Incredibly obvious, isn't it? A foreign substance is introduced into the precious bodily fluids without the knowledge of the individual and certainly without any choice. That's the way your commies work...

Laughing helplessly, I wander off the set and speak to Victor Lyndon, the Associate Producer.

Is it different working with Kubrick than with other directors?
"Is it not!"

How?
"Well, for one thing, my mind is working at twice the speed it generally does. It's no good just saying to Kubrick such and such will or won't work. You've got to prove it to him to his satisfaction and that means you've got to have all your arguments lined up very logically and precisely. Not that he doesn't leave you alone to get on with it — he delegates power but only on the noncreative side of the film and even then he checks and double checks. The creative side is entirely in his hands. He even designs his own posters. A most stimulating man to work with. The mind of a crack chess player — which he is."

Of all the film directors you've worked with, who do you think would make the best general?
He thinks for a moment. "Bob Aldrich." I am a little disappointed.

And Kubrick, I ask. What rank would you give him?
Lyndon smiles. "Field marshal," he says promptly.

Ken Adam the art director (who did such remarkable work on *The Trials of Oscar Wilde* and *Dr. No*) joins us:

"Stanley's been doing research on this film for two years now. He's so steeped in his material that when we first met to discuss it his conversation was full of fail-safe points, gyro-headings, strobe markings, and CRM-114s— I didn't know what he was talking about. You learn fast though. You have to, working with him. I like him. He's a funny combination of coldness and hypersensitivity. He walked by my wife on the set the other day as if totally unaware of her existence and then rang her that evening to apologize. When he's working, he just doesn't take in anything else. It registers in the back of his mind, though, and essentially he's a very kind person. There was a friend of his, a scriptwriter he's suggested for a job here in England, but before the man went to be interviewed for it Stanley had him over to the house and rehearsed him thoroughly on what to say and how to behave. His love of strategy extends to his liking to plan strategy for others. What else can I say about him personally? He loves his children. No I mean that. He really loves them. I think he's more passionately concerned with them than with anyone else."

Does he have any other interest outside making films? Any hobbies?
"No, I don't think so. Not really."

A mat of black hair, a white complexion, a high forehead and dramatically arched black eyebrows: from a distance the face of Stanley Kubrick at thirty-four seems to be settling into a Harlequin mask. Closer to, he resembles one of those just-off-the-street non-actors De Sica stars for a single film, so that the very American voice, the soft normal contemporary tones of the bright Big City boy (none of your loud-mouthed tycoonery around here) comes as a shock when you hear it.

After lunch he suddenly comes towards me taking my arm. "I have a few minutes before they set up again. What do you want to ask me?" Taken by surprise, I try to frame a question that will help me discover what kind of a person he is.

What do you do with your money? I blurt out.
"What do I do?" The Harlequin eyebrows knit.

With your money. Yes. What do you buy?
A slight laugh and a blank.

What do you indulge in? I persist.
Indulge in?" (What kind of a nut question is this?)

You know—like clothes. Do you buy clothes?
Sheepishly he looks down at his dark blue suit and zipper-collared jersey (he owns a total of three other suits, I am told later). "No . . . I don't spend money on clothes."

We are getting nowhere fast. *Where is your home?*
"Nowhere. Wherever I work. I have a flat in New York, though," he adds with what appears to be a notable lack of enthusiasm for it. He leans forward. "Look, I don't think the point of money is spending it. The point of money is to *have* it so that you don't have to make a film unless you really want to. You raise your standard of living and suddenly you're broke and some studio forces you to do a picture you don't want to and . . . it's a lot of trouble making a picture, you know . . . it can be very boring. I don't make many films. Maybe one every two years. I spend my money buying the film rights of books I like. And I save it so that if I do find a book I like I'll have the money to buy it."

Whom do you identify with among your contemporaries?
(Very quickly) "Nobody. I'm a loner."

But don't you like to work with people you've worked with before—actors and technicians building up a repertory company?
"Well, it's really who's free at the time, isn't it? Of course, I like working with people I've gotten on with. I've worked with both Sterling Hayden and Peter Sellers before but usually if one person isn't free at the time I have to use someone else."

Why Peter Sellers in three parts? In Lolita *he was Clare Quilty in various disguises. But in this film none of his roles seem to have anything to do with each other—or is this your way of saying that they have?*
"Not at all. I happen to think Peter Sellers is one of the great film actors working today. And I don't think anyone else can play these roles as well. To me it's like having three different great actors." (For the price of one, I was on the verge of saying—though for the price of six is a probably more accurate estimate.)

What interests you in the minutiæ of the social scene?
"What interests me about making a film," he said (not answering the question as is so often the case), "is the impact the original idea makes on me in the first place. That's what I hang on to. That's what I try to remember all through the shooting and cutting and editing. Because films are all in bits and pieces and you can easily lose track of the main objective and that's where you go wrong. I don't really explain to myself why it has such an impact. It's like a girl you're in love with—" I look at him quickly. It seems so unexpected—the word love dropped into the conversation. His face hasn't changed; nor has his voice. "—I try to remember the emotional impact it made on me initially. After that it's what the actors do to it."

But what interests you in the minutiæ of the social scene? Three out of your seven films: Paths of Glory, Spartacus, *and* Dr. Strangelove, *have war as the main theme. The others:* The Day of the Fight, Killer's Kiss, The Killing, *have been about the strategic planning of murder and violence. That leaves* Lolita.
"Well, what about *Lolita*? That was a comment on the social scene."

Umm—a bit grotesque—not really a normal social situation.
"There are lots of things I'm interested in that I haven't yet made films about. Like I felt in the past about women—that I could be in love with a lot of them. And live with them for a while. Separately." (Still the same boyish tones: Stanley Kubrick has been married three times.)

What was the turning point in your life? When did you decide to be the person you are or have the career you have?
"I was a photographer for *Look* Magazine during the '40s and I used to go and see movies all the time."

Which ones did you like?
Harlequin eyebrows again. "You mean the foreign ones?"

Did you only see foreign ones?
"No. I saw all the movies."

Which ones do you remember?
None in particular. But the bad ones encouraged me more than the good ones because I could say, 'I don't know much about making a film but I

can see where I could have made this one better.' And then I got some money together and I made my first film. It wasn't very good, but having done it, I was able to promote enough money to make my second film . . . and that was a little better and then — "

And then Hollywood sent for you?
Nobody ever sent for me."

Again I look at him. Any bitterness in the remark? Just the opposite. "And I'll see to it that nobody ever does," was its unsaid finish. "And then," he continued calmly, "I went to Hollywood to do *The Killing* because that's where it was set up. I have to get back now, they're ready for me." And smoothly he disappeared.

Later on I have a drink with the American novelist Terry Southern, author of *Flash and Filigree* and *The Magic Christian*. In collaboration (script by Peter George and Stanley Kubrick, additional dialogue by Terry Southern) it is impossible to know who did what. But connoisseurs of Terry Southern's style — his odd use of *italics* and quirky punctuation — will understand what I mean when I note that, for instance, it is the *only* film script I have ever read with two *question marks* at the end of a bit of dialogue. Terry, new to the movie game, enjoying himself immensely at the studio, creeping up behind Ken Adam murmuring, "Nice set there, Ken, but will it *dress?*" and chatting away in jargonese about "faking-out" an audience — which turns out to mean simply casting against type. He discusses Kubrick: "Well, It was great working with him; he's a very pure cat. He had his telephone number changed because too many people were calling me up there."

Does he really not spend money on things? I mean there must be something . . .
"Well, tape recorders. He likes tape recorders."

But, how many of those can you buy?
"Exactly."

Things around the house. Doesn't he drink at least?
"He forgets to. You know what I mean? He'll pour himself a drink and then begin talking about something and just forget to drink it. Here's a

scene that happened the other night: I was over there, see, and started to get myself a drink—he forgets to offer you one too—and there was no glass. So I asked him about a glass and he said we'll drink out of the bottle then. But that was all right. Inessentials don't bother him. No, he's something else; probably a genius. Have you talked to him about the concerns of being a filmmaker as opposed to a mere director? That's what he's about. It means doing it all yourself. As a matter of fact, I was fascinated by this new thing of director as God . . . like Fellini and Bergman. It's a new breed. In the old days of the big studios it used to be that working in films would hurt your creativity. Now—because of people like Kubrick—it *is* your creativity. I'm going to write a novel about this. Modelling my hero on Stanley."

Does he know you are?
"Yes I told him."

What did he say?
"He said it might make a great movie."

Beyond the Stars

JEREMY BERNSTEIN/1965

TO MOST PEOPLE, INCLUDING us, the words "science-fiction movie" bring up visions of super-monsters who have flames shooting out of at least one eye while an Adonislike Earthman carries Sylvanna, a stimulating blonde, to a nearby spaceship. It is a prospect that has often kept us at home. However, we are happy to report, for the benefit of science-fiction buffs—who have long felt that, at its best, science fiction is a splendid medium for conveying the poetry and wonder of science— that there will soon be a movie for *them*. We have this from none other than the two authors of the movie, which is to be called *Journey Beyond the Stars*—Stanley Kubrick and Arthur C. Clarke. It is to be based on a forthcoming novel called *Journey Beyond the Stars,* by Arthur C. Clarke and Stanley Kubrick. [*Journey Beyond the Stars* was the working title of *2001.*—*Ed.*]

Mr. Clarke and Mr. Kubrick, who have been collaborating on the two projects for over a year, explained to us that the order of the names in the movie and the novel was reversed to stress Mr. Clarke's role as a science-fiction novelist (he has written dozens of stories, many of them regarded as modern science-fiction classics) and Mr. Kubrick's role as a moviemaker (his most recent film was *Dr. Strangelove*).

Our briefing session took place in the living room of Mr. Kubrick's apartment. When we got there, Mr. Kubrick was talking on a telephone in the next room, Mr. Clarke had not yet arrived, and three lively Kubrick

From *New Yorker,* 24 April 1965. Reprinted by permission of the author.

daughters—the eldest is eleven—were running in and out with several young friends. We settled ourselves in a large chair, and a few minutes later the doorbell rang. One of the little girls went to the door and asked, "Who is it?" A pleasantly English-accented voice answered, through the door, "It's Clarke," and the girls began jumping up and down and saying, "It's Clark Kent!"—a reference to another well-known science-fiction personality. They opened the door, and in walked Mr. Clarke, a cheerful-looking man in his forties. He was carrying several manila envelopes, which, it turned out, contained parts of *Journey Beyond the Stars*. Mr. Kubrick then came into the room carrying a thick pile of diagrams and charts, and looking like the popular conception of a nuclear physicist, who has been interrupted in the middle of some difficult calculations. Mr. Kubrick and Mr. Clarke sat down side by side on a sofa, and we asked them about their joint venture.

Mr. Clarke said that one of the basic problems they've had to deal with is how to describe what they are trying to do. "Science-fiction films have always meant monsters and sex, so we have tried to find another term for our film," said Mr. C.

"About the best we've been able to come up with is a space odyssey—comparable in some ways to the Homeric *Odyssey*," said Mr. K. "It occurred to us that for the Greeks the vast stretches of the sea must have had the same sort of mystery and remoteness that space has for our generation, and that the far-flung islands Homer's wonderful characters visited were no less remote to them than the planets our spacemen will soon be landing on are to us. *Journey* also shares with *The Odyssey* a concern for wandering, exploration, and adventure."

Mr. Clarke agreed, and went on to tell us that the new film is set in the near future, at a time when the moon will have been colonized and space travel, at least around the planetary system, will have become commonplace. "Since we will soon be visiting the planets, it naturally occurs to one to ask whether, in the past, anybody has come to Earth to visit us," he said. "In *Journey Beyond the Stars*, the answer is definitely yes, and the odyssey unfolds as our descendants attempt to make contact with some extra-terrestrial explorers. There will be no women among those who make the trip, although there will be some on Earth, some on the moon, and some working in space."

Relieved, we asked where the film was to be made, and were told that it would be shot in the United States and several foreign countries.

"How about the scenes Out There?" we inquired.

Mr. Kubrick explained that they would be done with the aid of a vast assortment of cinematic tricks, but he added emphatically that everything possible would be done to make each scene completely authentic and to make it conform to what is known to physicists and astronomers. He and Mr. Clarke feel that while there will be dangers in space, there will also be wonder, adventure, and beauty, and that space is a source of endless knowledge, which may transform our civilization in the same way that the voyages of the Renaissance transformed the Dark Ages. They want all these elements to come through in the film. Mr. Kubrick told us that he has been a reader of science fiction and popular-science books, including Mr. Clarke's books on space travel, for many years, and that he has become increasingly disturbed by the barrier between scientific knowledge and the general public. He has asked friends basic questions like how many stars there are in our galaxy, he went on, and has discovered that most people have no idea at all. "The answer is a hundred billion, and sometimes they stretch their imaginations and say maybe four or five million," he said.

Speaking almost simultaneously, Mr. Clarke and Mr. Kubrick said that they hoped their film would give people a real understanding of the facts and of the overwhelming implications that the facts have for the human race.

We asked when the film will be released.

Mr. Kubrick told us that they are aiming for December 1966, and explained that the longest and hardest part of the job will be designing the "tricks," even though the ones they plan to use are well within the range of modern cinematic technology.

When we had been talking for some time, Mr. Clarke said he had to keep another appointment, and left. After he had gone, we asked Mr. Kubrick how *Dr. Strangelove* had been received abroad. It had been shown all over the world, he told us, and had received favorable criticism everywhere except, oddly, in Germany. He was not sure why this was, but thought it might reflect the German reliance on our nuclear strength and a consequent feeling of uneasiness at any attempt to make light of it. He said that his interest in the whole question of nuclear weapons had come upon him suddenly, when it struck him that here he was, actually in the same world with the hydrogen bomb, and he didn't know how he was learning to live with that fact. Before making *Dr. Strangelove,* he read widely in the literature dealing with atomic warfare.

We said goodbye shortly afterward, and on our way out a phrase of J. B. S. Haldane's came back to us: "The Universe is not only stranger than we imagine; it is stranger than we *can* imagine."

Profile: Stanley Kubrick

JEREMY BERNSTEIN/1966

ON PLEASANT AFTERNOONS, I often go into Washington Square Park to watch the Master at work. The Master is a professional chess player—a chess hustler, if you will. He plays for fifty cents a game; if you win, you get the fifty, and if he wins, he gets it. In case of a draw, no money changes hands. The Master plays for at least eight hours a day, usually seven days a week; in the winter he plays indoors in one or another of the Village coffeehouses. It is a hard way to make a living, even if you win all your games; the Master wins most of his, although I have seen him get beaten several games straight. It is impossible to cheat in chess, and the only hustle that the Master perpetrates is to make his opponents think they are better than they are. When I saw him one day recently, he was at work on what in the language of the park is called a "potzer"—a relatively weak player with an inflated ego. A glance at the board showed that the Master was a rook and a pawn up on his adversary—a situation that would cause a rational man to resign the game at once. A potzer is not rational (otherwise, he would have avoided the contest in the first place), and this one was determined to fight it out to the end. He was moving pawns wildly, and his hands were beginning to tremble. Since there is no one to blame but yourself, nothing is more rankling than a defeat in chess, especially if you are under the illusion that you are better than your opponent. The Master, smiling as seraphically as his hawklike, angular features would allow, said, "You always were a good pawn player—especially when

From *New Yorker,* 12 November 1996. Reprinted by permission of the author.

it comes to pushing them," which his deluded opponent took to be a compliment. At a rook and four pawns down, the potzer gave up, and a new game began.

My acquaintance with the Master goes back several years, but it was only recently that I learned of a connection between him and another man I know—the brilliant and original filmmaker Stanley Kubrick, who has been responsible for such movies as *Paths of Glory, Lolita,* and *Dr. Strangelove.* The Master is not much of a moviegoer—his professional activities leave little time for it—and, as far as I know, he has never seen one of Kubrick's pictures. But his recollection of Kubrick is nonetheless quite distinct, reaching back to the early nineteen-fifties, when Kubrick, then in his early twenties (he was born in New York City on July 26, 1928), was also squeezing out a small living (he estimates about three dollars a day, "which goes a long way if all you are buying with it is food") by playing chess for cash in Washington Square. Kubrick was then living on Sixteenth Street, off Sixth Avenue, and on nice days in the spring and summer he would wander into the park around noon and take up a position at one of the concrete chess tables near Macdougal and West Fourth Streets. At nightfall, he would change tables to get one near the street light. "If you made the switch the right way," he recalls, "you could get a table in the shade during the day and one nearer the fountain, under the lights, at night." There was a hard core of perhaps ten regulars who came to play every day and, like Kubrick, put in about twelve hours at the boards, with interruptions only for food. Kubrick ranked himself as one of the stronger regulars. When no potzers or semi-potzers were around, the regulars played each other for money, offering various odds to make up for any disparities in ability. The best player, Arthur Feldman, gave Kubrick a pawn—a small advantage—and, as Kubrick remembers it, "he didn't make his living off me." The Master was regarded by the regulars as a semi-potzer—the possessor of a flashy but fundamentally unsound game that was full of pseudo traps designed to enmesh even lesser potzers and to insure the quickest possible win, so that he could collect his bet and proceed to a new customer.

At that time, Kubrick's nominal non-chess-playing occupation (when he could work at it) was what it is now—making films. Indeed, by the time he was twenty-seven he had behind him a four-year career as a staff photographer for *Look,* followed by a five-year career as a filmmaker, during which he had made two short features and two full-length films—*Fear and Desire* (1953) and *Killer's Kiss* (1955). By all sociological odds, Kubrick should never have got into the motion-picture business in the first place. He comes from an American Jewish family of Austro-Hungarian ancestry. His father is a doctor, still in active practice, and he grew up in comfortable middleclass surroundings in the Bronx. If all had gone according to form, Kubrick would have attended college and probably ended up as a doctor or a physicist—physics being the only subject he showed the slightest aptitude for in school. After four desultory years at Taft High School, in the Bronx, he graduated, with a sixty-seven average, in 1945, the year in which colleges were flooded with returning servicemen. No college in the United States would even consider his application. Apart from everything else, Kubrick had failed English outright one year, and had had to make it up in the summer. In his recollection, high-school English courses consisted of sitting behind a book while the teacher would say, "Mr. Kubrick, when Silas Marner walked out of the door, what did he see?," followed by a prolonged silence caused by the fact that Kubrick hadn't read *Silas Marner*, or much of anything else.

When Kubrick was twelve, his father taught him to play chess, and when he was thirteen, his father, who is something of a camera bug, presented him with his first camera. At the time, Kubrick had hopes of becoming a jazz drummer and was seriously studying the technique, but he soon decided that he wanted to be a photographer, and instead of doing his schoolwork he set out to teach himself to become one. By the time he left high school, he had sold *Look* two picture stories—one of them, ironically, about an English teacher at Taft, Aaron Traister, who had succeeded in arousing Kubrick's interest in Shakespeare's plays by acting out all the parts in class. After high school, Kubrick registered for night courses at City College, hoping to obtain a B average so that he could transfer to regular undergraduate courses, but before he started going to classes, he was back at *Look* with some more pictures. The picture editor there, Helen O'Brian, upon hearing of his academic troubles, proposed that he come to *Look* as an apprentice photographer. "So I backed into a fantastically good job at the age of seventeen," Kubrick says. Released from the bondage of schoolwork, he also began to read everything that he could lay his hands on. In retrospect, he feels that not going to college and having had the four years to practice photography at *Look* and to read on his own was probably the most fortunate thing that ever happened to him.

It was while he was still at *Look* that Kubrick became a filmmaker. An incessant moviegoer, he had seen the entire film collection of the Museum of Modern Art at least twice when he learned from a friend, Alex Singer (now also a movie director), that there was apparently a fortune to be made in producing short documentaries. Singer was working as an office boy at the March of Time and had learned—or thought he had learned—that his employers were spending forty thousand dollars to produce eight or nine minutes of film. Kubrick was extremely impressed by the number of dollars being spent per foot, and even more impressed when he learned, from phone calls to Eastman Kodak and various equipment-rental companies, that the cost of buying and developing film and renting camera equipment would allow him to make nine minutes of film, complete with an original musical score, for only about a thousand dollars. "We assumed," Kubrick recalls, "that the March of Time must have been selling their films at a profit, so if we could make a film for a thousand dollars, we couldn't lose our investment." Thus bolstered, he used his savings from the *Look* job to make a documentary about the middleweight boxer Walter Cartier, about whom he had previously done a picture story for *Look*. Called "Day of the Fight," it was filmed with a rented spring-wound thirty-five millimeter Eyemo camera and featured a musical score by Gerald Fried, a friend of Kubrick's who is now a well-known composer for the movies. Since Kubrick couldn't afford any professional help, he took care of the whole physical side of the production himself; essentially, this consisted of screwing a few ordinary photofloods into existing light fixtures. When the picture was done—for thirty-nine hundred dollars—Kubrick set out to sell it for forty thousand. Various distributing companies liked it, but, as Kubrick now says ruefully, "we were offered things like fifteen hundred dollars and twenty-five hundred dollars. We told one distributor that the March of Time was getting forty thousand dollars for *its* documentaries, and he said, 'You must be crazy.' The next thing we knew, the March of Time went out of business." Kubrick was finally able to sell his short to RKO Pathé for about a hundred dollars more than it had cost him to make it.

Kubrick, of course, got great satisfaction out of seeing his documentary at the Paramount Theatre, where it played with a Robert Mitchum-Ava

Gardner feature. He felt that it had turned out well, and he figured that he would now instantly get innumerable offers from the movie industry — "of which," he says, "I got none, to do anything." After a while, however, he made a second short for RKO (which put up fifteen hundred dollars for it, barely covering expenses), this one about a flying priest who travelled through the Southwest from one Indian parish to another in a Piper Cub. To work on the film, Kubrick quit his job at *Look,* and when the film was finished, he went back to waiting for offers of employment, spending his time playing chess for quarters in the park. He soon reached the reasonable conclusion that there simply wasn't any money to be made in producing documentaries and that there were no film jobs to be had. After thinking about the millions of dollars that were being spent on making feature films, he decided to make one himself. "I felt that I certainly couldn't make one worse than the ones I was seeing every week," he says. On the assumption that there were actors around who would work for practically nothing, and that he could act as the whole crew, Kubrick estimated that he could make a feature film for something like ten thousand dollars, and he was able to raise this sum from his father and an uncle, Martin Perveler. The script was put together by an acquaintance of Kubrick's in the Village, and, as Kubrick now describes it, it was an exceedingly serious, undramatic, and pretentious allegory. "With the exception of Frank Silvera, the actors were not very experienced," he says, "and I didn't know anything about directing *any* actors. I totally failed to realize what I didn't know." The film *Fear and Desire,* was about four soldiers lost behind enemy lines and struggling to regain their identities as well as their home base, and it was full of lines like, "We spend our lives looking for our real names, our permanent addresses." "Despite everything, the film got an art-house distribution," Kubrick says. "It opened at the Guild Theatre, in New York, and it even got a couple of fairly good reviews, as well as a compliment from Mark Van Doren. There were a few good moments in it. It never returned a penny on its investment."

Not at all discouraged, Kubrick decided that the mere fact that a film of his was showing at a theatre at all might be used as the basis for raising money to make a second one. In any case, it was not otherwise apparent how he was going to earn a living. "There were still no offers from anybody to do anything," he says. "So in about two weeks a friend and I wrote another script. As a contrast to the first one, this one, called *Killer's Kiss,* was nothing but action sequences, strung together on a mechanically constructed gangster plot."

Killer's Kiss was co-produced by Morris Bousel, a relative of Kubrick's who owned a drugstore in the Bronx. Released in September, 1955, it, too, failed to bring in any revenue (in a retrospective of his films at the Museum of Modern Art two summers ago, Kubrick would not let either of his first two films be shown, and he would probably be just as happy if the prints were to disappear altogether), so, broke and in debt to Bousel and others, Kubrick returned to Washington Square to play chess for quarters.

The scene now shifts to Alex Singer. While serving in the Signal Corps during the Korean War, Singer met a man named James B. Harris, who was engaged in making Signal Corps training films. The son of the owner of an extremely successful television-film-distribution company, Flamingo Films (in which he had a financial interest), Harris wanted to become a film producer when he returned to civilian life. As Harris recalls it, Singer told him about "some guy in the Village who was going around all by himself making movies," and after they got out of the Army, introduced him to Kubrick, who had just finished *Killer's Kiss*. Harris and Kubrick were both twenty-six, and they got on at once, soon forming Harris-Kubrick Pictures Corporation. From the beginning, it was an extremely fruitful and very happy association. Together they made *The Killing, Paths of Glory,* and *Lolita.* They were going to do *Dr. Strangelove* jointly, but before work began on it, Harris came to the conclusion that being just a movie producer was not a job with enough artistic fulfillment for him, and he decided to both produce and direct. His first film was *The Bedford Incident,* which Kubrick considers very well directed. For his part, Harris regards Kubrick as a cinematic genius who can do anything.

The first act of the newly formed Harris-Kubrick Pictures Corporation was to purchase the screen rights to *Clean Break,* a paperback thriller by Lionel White. Kubrick and a writer friend named Jim Thompson turned it into a screenplay, and the resulting film, *The Killing,* which starred Sterling Hayden, was produced in association with United Artists, with Harris putting up about a third of the production cost. While *The Killing,* too, was something less than a financial success, it was sufficiently impressive to catch the eye of Dore Schary, then head of production for MGM. For the first time, Kubrick received an offer to work for a major studio, and he and Harris were invited to look over all the properties owned by MGM and pick out something to do. Kubrick remembers being astounded by the mountains of stories that MGM owned. It took the pair of them two weeks simply to go through the alphabetical synopsis cards. Finally, they selected *The Burning Secret,* by Stefan Zweig, and Kubrick and Calder Willingham turned it into a screenplay—only to find that Dore Schary had lost his job as a result of a major shuffle at MGM. Harris and Kubrick left soon afterward. Sometime during the turmoil, Kubrick suddenly recalled having read *Paths of Glory,* by Humphrey Cobb, while still a high-school student. "It was one of the few books I'd read for pleasure in high school," he says. "I think I found it lying around my father's office and started to read it while waiting for him to get finished with a patient." Harris agreed that it was well worth a try. However, none of the major studios took the slightest interest in it. Finally, Kubrick and Harris's agent, Ronnie Lubin, managed to interest Kirk Douglas in doing it, and this was enough to persuade United Artists to back the film, provided it was done on a very low budget in Europe. Kubrick, Calder Willingham, and Jim Thompson wrote the screenplay, and in January of 1957 Kubrick went to Munich to make the film.

Seeing *Paths of Glory* is a haunting experience. The utter desolation, cynicism, and futility of war, as embodied in the arbitrary execution of three innocent French soldiers who have been tried and convicted of cowardice during a meaningless attack on a heavily fortified German position, comes through with simplicity and power. Some of the dialogue is imperfect, Kubrick agrees, but its imperfection almost adds to the strength and sincerity of the theme. The finale of the picture involves a young German girl who has been captured by the French and is being forced to sing a song for a group of drunken French soldiers about to be sent back into battle. The girl is frightened, and the soldiers are brutal. She begins to sing, and the humanity of the moment reduces the soldiers to silence, and then to tears. In the film, the girl was played by a young and pretty German actress, Suzanne Christiane Harlan (known in Germany by the stage name Suzanne Christian), and a year after the film was made, she and Kubrick were married. Christiane comes from a family of opera singers and stage personalities, and most of her life has been spent in the theatre; she was a ballet dancer before she became an actress, and currently she is a serious painter, in addition to managing the sprawling Kubrick household, which now includes three daughters. Later this month, she will have an exhibition at the Grosvenor Gallery in London.

Paths of Glory was released in November, 1957, and although it received excellent critical notices and broke about even financially, it did not lead to any real new opportunities for Kubrick and Harris. Kubrick returned to Hollywood and wrote two new scripts, which were never used, and worked for six months on a Western for Marlon Brando, which he left before it went into production. (Ultimately, Brando directed it himself, and it became *One-Eyed Jacks*.) It was not until 1960 that Kubrick actually began working on a picture again. In that year, Kirk Douglas asked him to take over the direction of *Spartacus*, which Douglas was producing and starring in. Shooting had been under way for a week, but Douglas and Anthony Mann, his director, had had a falling out. On *Spartacus*, in contrast to all his other films, Kubrick had no legal control over the script or the final form of the movie. Although Kubrick did the cutting on *Spartacus*, Kirk Douglas had the final say as to the results, and the consequent confusion of points of view produced a film that Kubrick thinks could have been better.

While *Spartacus* was being edited, Kubrick and Harris bought the rights to Vladimir Nabokov's novel *Lolita*. There was immense pressure from all sorts of public groups not to make *Lolita* into a film, and for a while it looked as if Kubrick and Harris would not be able to raise the money to do it. In the end, though, the money was raised, and the film was made in London. Kubrick feels that the weakness of the film was its lack of eroticism, which was inevitable. "The important thing in the novel is to think at the outset that Humbert is enslaved by his 'perversion,'" Kubrick says. "Not until the end, when Lolita is married and pregnant and no longer a nymphet, do you realize—along with Humbert—that he loves her. In the film, the fact that his sexual obsession could not be portrayed tended to imply from the start that he was in love with her."

It was the building of the Berlin Wall that sharpened Kubrick's interest in nuclear weapons and nuclear strategy, and he began to read everything he could get hold of about the bomb. Eventually, he decided that he had about covered the spectrum, and that he was not learning anything new. "When you start reading the analyses of nuclear strategy, they seem so thoughtful that you're lulled into a temporary sense of reassurance," Kubrick has explained. "But as you go deeper into it, and become more involved, you begin to realize that every one of these lines of thought leads to a paradox." It is this constant element of paradox in all the nuclear strategies and in the conventional attitudes toward them that Kubrick transformed into the principal theme of *Dr. Strangelove.* The picture was a new departure for Kubrick. His other films had involved putting novels on the screen, but *Dr. Strangelove,* though it did have its historical origins in *Red Alert,* a serious nuclear suspense story by Peter George, soon turned into an attempt to use a purely intellectual notion as the basis of a film. In this case, the intellectual notion was the inevitable paradox posed by following any of the nuclear strategies to their extreme limits. "By now, the bomb has almost no reality and has become a complete abstraction, represented by a few newsreel shots of mushroom clouds," Kubrick has said. "People react primarily to direct experience and not to abstractions; it is very rare to find anyone who can become emotionally involved with an abstraction. The longer the bomb is around without anything happening, the better the job that people do in psychologically denying its existence. It has become as abstract as the fact that we are all going to die someday, which we usually do an excellent job of denying. For this reason, most people have very little interest in nuclear war. It has become even less interesting as a problem than, say, city government, and the longer a nuclear event is postponed, the greater becomes the illusion that we are constantly building up security, like interest at the bank. As time goes on, the danger increases, I believe, because the thing becomes more and more remote in people's minds. No one can predict the panic that suddenly arises when all the lights go out—that indefinable something that can make a leader abandon his carefully laid plans. A lot of effort has gone into trying to imagine possible nuclear accidents and to protect against them. But whether the human imagination is really capable of encompassing all the subtle permutations and psychological variants of these possibilities, I doubt. The nuclear strategists who make up all those war scenarios are never as inventive as reality, and political and military leaders are never as sophisticated as they think they are."

Such limited optimism as Kubrick has about the long-range prospects of the human race is based in large measure on his hope that the rapid development of space exploration will change our views of ourselves and our world. Most people who have thought much about space travel have arrived at the somewhat ironic conclusion that there is a very close correlation between the ability of a civilization to make significant space voyages and its ability to learn to live with nuclear energy. Unless there are sources of energy that are totally beyond the ken of modern physics, it is quite clear that the only source at hand for really elaborate space travel is the nucleus. The chemical methods of combustion used in our present rockets are absurdly inefficient compared to nuclear power. A detailed study has been made of the possibilities of using nuclear explosions to propel large spaceships, and, from a technical point of view, there is no reason that this cannot be done; indeed, if we are to transport really large loads to, say, the planets, it is essential that it be done. Thus, any civilization that operates on the same laws of nature as our own will inevitably reach the point where it learns to explore space and to use nuclear energy about simultaneously. The question is whether there can exist any society with enough maturity to peacefully use the latter to perform the former. In fact, some of the more melancholy thinkers on this subject have come to the conclusion that the earth has never been visited by beings from outer space because no civilization has been able to survive its own technology. That there *are* extraterrestrial civilizations in some state of development is firmly believed by many astronomers, biologists, philosophers, physicists, and other rational people — a conclusion based partly on the vastness of the cosmos, with its billions of stars. It is presumptuous to suppose that we are its only living occupants. From a chemical and biological point of view, the processes of forming life do not appear so extraordinary that they should not have occurred countless times throughout the universe. One may try to imagine what sort of transformation would take place in human attitudes if intelligent life should be discovered elsewhere in our universe. In fact, this is what Kubrick has been trying to do in his latest project, *2001: A Space Odyssey,* which, in the words of Arthur C. Clarke, the co-author of its screenplay, "will be about the first contact" — the first human contact with extraterrestrial life.

It was Arthur Clarke who introduced me to Kubrick. A forty-eight-year-old Englishman who lives in Ceylon most of the time, Clarke is, in my opinion, by all odds the best science-fiction writer now operating. (He is also an accomplished skin diver, and what he likes about Ceylon, apart from the climate and the isolation, is the opportunities it affords him for underwater exploration.) Clarke, who is highly trained as a scientist, manages to combine scientific insights with a unique sense of nostalgia for worlds that man will never see, because they are so far in the past or in the future, or are in such a distant part of the cosmos. In his hands, inanimate objects like the sun and the moon take on an almost living quality. Personally, he is a large, good-natured man, and about the only egoist I know who makes conversation about himself somehow delightful. We met in New York a few years back, when he was working on a book about the future of scientific ideas and wanted to discuss some of the latest developments in physics, which I teach. Now I always look forward to his occasional visits, and when he called me up one evening two winters ago, I was very happy to hear from him. He lost no time in explaining what he was up to. "I'm working with Stanley Kubrick on the successor to *Dr. Strangelove*," he said. "Stanley is an amazing man, and I want you to meet him." It was an invitation not to be resisted, and Clarke arranged a visit with Kubrick soon afterward.

Kubrick was at that time living, on the upper East Side, in a large apartment whose décor was a mixture of Christiane's lovely paintings, the effects of three rambunctious young children, and Kubrick's inevitable collection of cameras, tape recorders, and hi-fi sets. (There was also a short-wave radio, which he was using to monitor broadcasts from Moscow, in order to learn the Russian attitude toward Vietnam. Christiane once said that "Stanley would be happy with eight tape recorders and one pair of pants.") Kubrick himself did not conform at all to my expectations of what a movie mogul would look like. He is of medium height and has the bohemian look of a riverboat gambler or a Rumanian poet. (He has now grown a considerable beard, which gives his broad features a somewhat Oriental quality.) He had the vaguely distracted look of a man who is simultaneously thinking about a hard problem and trying to make everyday conversation. During our meeting, the phone rang incessantly, a messenger arrived at the door with a telegram or an envelope every few minutes, and children of various ages and sexes ran in and out of the living room. After a few attempts at getting the situation under control, Kubrick abandoned the place to the children, taking me into a small breakfast room near the kitchen. I was immediately impressed by Kubrick's immense intellectual curiosity. When he is working on a subject, he becomes completely immersed in it and appears to absorb information from all sides, like a sponge. In addition to writing a novel with Clarke, which was to be the basis of the script for *2001*, he was reading every popular and semi-popular book on science that he could get hold of.

During our conversation, I happened to mention that I had just been in Washington Square Park playing chess. He asked me whom I had been playing with, and I described the Master. Kubrick recognized him immediately. I had been playing a good deal with the Master, and my game had improved to the point where I was almost breaking even with him, so I was a little stunned to learn that Kubrick had played the Master on occasion, and that in his view the Master was a potzer. Kubrick went on to say that he loved playing chess, and added, "How about a little game right now?" By pleading another appointment, I managed to stave off the challenge.

I next saw Kubrick at the end of the summer in London, where I had gone to a physicists' meeting and where he was in the process of organizing the actual filming of *2001*. I dropped in at his office in the MGM studio in Boreham Wood, outside London, one afternoon, and again was confronted by an incredible disarray—papers, swatches of materials to be used for costumes, photographs of actors who might be used to play astronauts, models of spaceships, drawings by his daughters, and the usual battery of cameras, radios, and tape recorders. Kubrick likes to keep track of things in small notebooks, and he had just ordered a sample sheet of every type of notebook paper made by a prominent paper firm—about a hundred varieties—which were spread out on a large table. We talked for a while amid the usual interruptions of messengers and telephone calls, and then he got back to the subject of chess: How about a little game right now? He managed to find a set of chessmen—it was missing some pieces, but we filled in for them with various English coins—and when he couldn't find a board he drew one up on a large sheet of paper. Sensing the outcome, I remarked that I had never been beaten five times in a row—a number that I chose more or less at random, figuring that it was unlikely that we would ever get to play five games.

I succeeded in losing two rapid games before Kubrick had to go back to London, where he and his family were living in a large apartment in the Dorchester Hotel. He asked me to come along and finish out the five games—the figure appeared to fascinate him—and as soon as he could get the girls off to bed and order dinner for Christiane, himself, and me sent up to the apartment, he produced a second chess set, with all the pieces and a genuine wooden board.

Part of the art of the professional chess player is to unsettle one's opponent as much as possible by small but legitimate annoying incidental activities, such as yawning, looking at one's watch, and snapping one's fingers softly—at all of which Kubrick is highly skilled. One of the girls came into the room and asked, "What's the matter with your friend?"

"He's about to lose another game," said Kubrick.

I tried to counter these pressures by singing "Moon River" over and over, but I lost the next two games. Then came the crucial fifth game, and by some miracle I actually won it. Aware that this was an important psychological moment, I announced that I had been hustling Kubrick and had dropped the first four games deliberately. Kubrick responded by saying that the poor quality of those games had lulled him into a temporary mental lapse. (In the course of making *Dr. Strangelove,* Kubrick had all but hypnotized George C. Scott by continually beating him at chess while simultaneously attending to the direction of the movie.) We would have played five more games on the spot, except that it was now two in the morning, and Kubrick's working day on the *2001* set began very early.

"The Sentinel," a short story by Arthur Clarke in which *2001* finds its genesis, begins innocently enough: "The next time you see the full moon high in the south, look carefully at its right-hand edge and let your eye travel upward along the curve of the disk. Round about two o'clock you will notice a small dark oval; anyone with normal eyesight can find it quite easily. It is the great walled plain, one of the finest on the moon, known as the Mare Crisium—the Sea of Crises." Then Clarke adds, unobtrusively, "Three hundred miles in diameter, and almost completely surrounded by a ring of magnificent mountains, it had never been explored until we entered it in the late summer of 1996." The story and the style are typical of Clarke's blend of science and fantasy. In this case, an expedition exploring the moon uncovers, on the top of a mountain, a little pyramid set on a carefully hewed-out terrace. At first, the explorers suppose it to be a trace left behind by a primitive civilization in the moon's past. But the terrain around it, unlike the rest of the moon's surface, is free of all debris and craters created by falling meteorites—the pyramid, they discover, contains a mechanism that sends out a powerful force that shields it from external disturbances and perhaps signals to some distant observer. When the explorers finally succeed in breaking through the shield and studying the pyramid, they become convinced that its origins are as alien to the moon as they are themselves. The astronaut telling the story says, "The mystery haunts us all the more now that the other planets have been reached and we know that only Earth has ever been the home of intelligent life in our universe. Nor could any lost civilization of our own world have built that machine.... It was set there upon its mountain before life had emerged from the seas of Earth."

But suddenly the narrator realizes the pyramid's meaning. It was left by some far-off civilization as a sentinel to signal that living beings had finally reached it:

> Nearly a hundred thousand million stars are turning in the circle of the Milky Way, and long ago other races on the worlds of other suns must have scaled and passed the heights that we have reached. Think of such civilizations, far back in time against the fading afterglow of Creation, masters of a universe so young that life as yet had come only to a handful of worlds. Theirs would have been a loneliness we cannot imagine, the loneliness of gods looking out across infinity and finding none to share their thoughts.
>
> They must have searched the star-clusters as we have searched the planets. Everywhere there would be worlds, but they would be empty or peopled with crawling, mindless things. Such was our own Earth, the smoke of the great volcanoes still staining the skies, when that first ship of the peoples of the dawn came sliding in from the abyss beyond Pluto. It passed the frozen outer worlds, knowing that life could play no part in their destinies. It came to rest among the inner planets, warming themselves around the fire of the sun and waiting for their stories to begin.
>
> These wanderers must have looked on Earth, circling safely in the narrow zone between fire and ice, and must have guessed that it was the favorite of the sun's children. Here, in the distant future, would be intelligence; but there were countless stars before them still, and they might never come this way again.
>
> So they left a sentinel, one of millions they have scattered throughout the universe, watching over all worlds with the promise of life. It was a beacon that down the ages has been patiently signalling the fact that no one had discovered it.

The astronaut concludes:

I can never look now at the Milky Way without wondering from which of those banked clouds of stars the emissaries are coming. If you will pardon so commonplace a simile, we have set off the fire alarm and have nothing to do but to wait.

I do not think we will have to wait for long.

Clarke and Kubrick spent two years transforming this short story into a novel and then into a script for *2001,* which is concerned with the discovery of the sentinel and a search for traces of the civilization that put it there—a quest that takes the searchers out into the far reaches of the solar system. Extraterrestrial life may seem an odd subject for a motion picture, but at this stage in his career Kubrick is convinced that any idea he is really interested in, however unlikely it may sound, can be transferred to film. "One of the English science-fiction writers once said, 'Sometimes I think we're alone, and sometimes I think we're not. In either case, the idea is quite staggering,'" Kubrick once told me, "I must say I agree with him."

By the time the film appears, early next year, Kubrick estimates that he and Clarke will have put in an average of four hours a day, six days a week, on the writing of the script. (This works out to about twenty-four hundred hours of writing for two hours and forty minutes of film.) Even during the actual shooting of the film, Kubrick spends every free moment reworking the scenario. He has an extra office set up in a blue trailer that was once Deborah Kerr's dressing room, and when shooting is going on, he has it wheeled onto the set, to give him a certain amount of privacy for writing. He frequently gets ideas for dialogue from his actors, and when he likes an idea he puts it in. (Peter Sellers, he says, contributed some wonderful bits of humor for *Dr. Strangelove.*)

In addition to writing and directing, Kubrick supervises every aspect of his films, from selecting costumes to choosing the incidental music. In making *2001,* he is, in a sense, trying to second-guess the future. Scientists planning long-range space projects can ignore such questions as what sort of hats rocket-ship hostesses will wear when space travel becomes common (in *2001* the hats have padding in them to cushion any collisions with the ceiling that weightlessness might cause), and what sort of voices computers will have if, as many experts feel is certain, they learn to talk and to respond to voice commands (there is a talking computer in *2001* that arranges for the astronauts' meals, gives them medical treatments,

and even plays chess with them during a long space mission to Jupiter—
"Maybe it ought to sound like Jackie Mason," Kubrick once said), and
what kind of time will be kept aboard a spaceship (Kubrick chose Eastern
Standard, for the convenience of communicating with Washington). In
the sort of planning that NASA does, such matters can be dealt with as
they come up, but in a movie everything is immediately visible and
explicit, and questions like this must be answered in detail. To help him
find the answers, Kubrick has assembled around him a group of thirty-five
artists and designers, more than twenty special-effects people, and a staff
of scientific advisers. By the time the picture is done, Kubrick figures that
he will have consulted with people from a generous sampling of the leading aeronautical companies in the United States and Europe, not to
mention innumerable scientific and industrial firms. One consultant, for
instance, was Professor Marvin Minsky, of MIT, who is a leading authority
on artificial intelligence and the construction of automata. (He is now
building a robot at MIT that can catch a ball.) Kubrick wanted to learn
from him whether any of the things that he was planning to have his
computers do were likely to be realized by the year *2001*; he was pleased
to find out that they were.

Kubrick told me he had seen practically every science-fiction film ever
made, and any number of more conventional films that had interesting
special effects. One Saturday afternoon, after lunch and two rapid chess
games, he and Christiane and I set out to see a Russian science-fiction
movie called *Astronauts on Venus,* which he had discovered playing somewhere in North London. Saturday afternoon at a neighborhood movie
house in London is like Saturday afternoon at the movies anywhere; the
theatre was full of children talking, running up and down the aisles, chew-
ing gum, and eating popcorn. The movie was in Russian, with English
subtitles, and since most of the children couldn't read very well, let alone
speak Russian, the dialogue was all but drowned out by the general babble.
This was probably all to the good, since the film turned out to be a terrible
hodgepodge of pseudo-science and Soviet propaganda. It featured a talking
robot named John and a talking girl named Masha who had been left in a
small spaceship orbiting Venus while a party of explorers—who thought,
probably correctly, that she would have been a nuisance below—went off
to explore. Although Kubrick reported that the effects used were crude, he
insisted that we stick it out to the end, just in case.

Before I left London, I was able to spend a whole day with Kubrick, starting at about eight-fifteen, when an MGM driver picked us up in one of the studio cars. (Kubrick suffers automobiles tolerably well, but he will under almost no circumstances travel by plane, even though he holds a pilot's license and has put in about a hundred and fifty hours in the air, principally around Teterboro Airport; after practicing landings and takeoffs, flying solo cross-country to Albany, and taking his friends up for rides, he lost interest in flying.) Boreham Wood is a little like the area outside Boston that is served by Route 128, for it specializes in electronics companies and precision industry, and the MGM studio is hardly distinguishable from the rather antiseptic-looking factories nearby. It consists of ten enormous sound stages concealed in industrial-looking buildings and surrounded by a cluster of carpenter shops, paint shops, office units, and so on. Behind the buildings is a huge lot covered with bits and pieces of other productions—the facade of a French provincial village, the hulk of a Second World War bomber, and other debris. Kubrick's offices are near the front of the complex in a long bungalow structure that houses, in addition to his production staff, a group of youthful model-makers working on large, very detailed models of spacecraft to be used in special-effects photography; Kubrick calls their realm "Santa's Workshop." When we walked into his private office, it seemed to me that the general disorder had grown even more chaotic since my last visit. Tacked to a bulletin board were some costume drawings showing men dressed in odd-looking, almost Edwardian business suits. Kubrick said that the drawings were supposed to be of the business suit of the future and had been submitted by one of the innumerable designers who had been asked to furnish ideas on what men's clothes would look like in thirty-five years. "The problem is to find something that looks different and that might reflect new developments in fabrics but that isn't so far out as to be distracting," Kubrick said. "Certainly buttons will be gone. Even now, there are fabrics that stick shut by themselves."

Just then, Victor Lyndon, Kubrick's associate producer (he was also the associate producer of *Dr. Strangelove* and, most recently, of *Darling*), came in. A trim, athletic-looking man of forty-six, he leans toward the latest "mod" styling in clothes, and he was wearing an elegant green buttonless, self-shutting shirt. He was followed by a young man wearing hair down to his neck, a notably non-shutting shirt, and boots, who was introduced as a brand-new costume designer. (He was set up at a drawing table in Santa's Workshop, but that afternoon he announced that the atmosphere was too distracting for serious work, and left; the well-known British designer Hardy Amies was finally chosen to design the costumes.) Lyndon fished from a manila envelope a number of shoulder patches designed to be worn as identification by the astronauts. (The two principal astronauts in the film were to be played by Keir Dullea, who has starred in *David and Lisa* and *Bunny Lake Is Missing*, and Gary Lockwood, a former college-football star and now a television and movie actor.) Kubrick said that the lettering didn't look right, and suggested that the art department make up new patches using actual NASA lettering. He then consulted one of the small notebooks in which he lists all the current production problems, along with the status of their solutions, and announced that he was going to the art department to see how the drawings of the moons of Jupiter were coming along.

The art department, which occupies a nearby building, is presided over by Tony Masters, a tall, Lincolnesque man who was busy working on the Jupiter drawings when we appeared. Kubrick told me that the department, which designs and dresses all sets, was constructing a scale model of the moon, including the back side, which had been photographed and mapped by rocket. Looking over the Jupiter drawings, Kubrick said that the light in them looked a little odd to him, and suggested that Masters have Arthur Clarke check on it that afternoon when he came out from London.

Our next stop was to pick up some papers in the separate office where Kubrick does his writing—a made-over dressing room in a quiet part of the lot. On our way to it, we passed an outbuilding containing a number of big generators; a sign reading "DANGER!—11,500 VOLTS!" was nailed to its door. "Why eleven thousand five *hundred*?" Kubrick said. "Why not twelve thousand? If you put a sign like that in a movie, people would think it was a fake." When we reached the trailer, I could see that it was used as much for listening as for writing, for in addition to the usual battery of tape recorders (Kubrick writes rough first drafts of his dialogue by dictating into a recorder, since he finds that this gives it a more natural flow) there was a phonograph and an enormous collection of records, practically all of them of contemporary music. Kubrick told me that he thought he had listened to almost every modern composition available on records in an effort to decide what style of music would fit the film. Here,

again, the problem was to find something that sounded unusual and dis-
tinctive but not so unusual as to be distracting. In the office collection
were records by the practitioners of *musique concrète* and electronic music
in general, and records of works by the contemporary German composer
Carl Orff. In most cases, Kubrick said, film music tends to lack originality,
and a film about the future might be the ideal place for a really striking
score by a major composer.

We returned to the main office, and lunch was brought in from the
commissary. During lunch, Kubrick signed a stack of letters, sent off several cables, and took a long-distance call from California. "At this stage
of the game, I feel like the counterman at Katz's delicatessen on Houston
Street at lunch hour," he said. "You've hardly finished saying 'Half a
pound of corned beef' when he says 'What else?,' and before you can
say 'A sliced rye' he's saying 'What else?' again."

I asked whether he ever got things mixed up, and he said rarely, adding
that he thought chess playing had sharpened his naturally retentive memory and gift for organization. "With such a big staff, the problem is for
people to figure out what they should *not* come to see you about," he went
on. "You invariably find your time taken up with questions that aren't
important and could have easily been disposed of without your opinion.
To offset this, decisions are sometimes taken without your approval that
can wind up in frustrating dead ends."

As we were finishing lunch, Victor Lyndon came in with an almanac
that listed the average temperature and rainfall all over the globe at every
season of the year. "We're looking for a cool desert where we can shoot
some sequences during the late spring," Kubrick said. "We've got our eye
on a location in Spain, but it might be pretty hot to work in comfortably,
and we might have trouble controlling the lighting. If we don't go to
Spain, we'll have to build an entirely new set right here. More work for
Tony Masters and his artists." (Later, I learned that Kubrick did decide to
shoot on location.)

After lunch, Kubrick and Lyndon returned to a long-standing study of
the space-suit question. In the film, the astronauts will wear space suits
when they are working outside their ships, and Kubrick was very anxious
that they should look like the space suits of thirty-five years from now.
After numerous consultations with Ordway and other NASA experts, he
and Lyndon had finally settled on a design, and now they were studying a

vast array of samples of cloth to find one that would look right and photo-graph well. While this was going on, people were constantly dropping into the office with drawings, models, letters, cables, and various props, such as a model of a lens for one of the telescopes in a spaceship. (Kubrick rejected it because it looked too crude.) At the end of the day, when my head was beginning to spin, someone came by with a wristwatch that the astronauts were going to use on their Jupiter voyage (which Kubrick rejected) and a plastic drinking glass for the moon hotel (which Kubrick thought looked fine). About seven o'clock, Kubrick called for his car, and by eight-thirty he had returned home, put the children to bed, discussed the day's events with his wife, watched a news broadcast on television, telephoned Clarke for a brief discussion of whether nuclear-powered spacecraft would pollute the atmosphere with their exhausts (Clarke said that they certainly would today but that by the time they actually come into use somebody will have figured out what to do about poisonous exhausts), and taken out his chess set. "How about a little game?" he said in a seductive tone that the Master would have envied.

On December 29, 1965, shooting of the film began, and in early March the company reached the most intricate part of the camerawork, which was to be done in the interior of a giant centrifuge. One of the problems in space travel will be weightlessness. While weightlessness has, because of its nov-elty, a certain glamour and amusement, it would be an extreme nuisance on a long trip, and probably a health hazard as well. Our physical systems have evolved to work against the pull of gravity, and it is highly probable that all sorts of unfortunate things, such as softening of the bones, would result from exposure to weightlessness for months at a time. In addition, of course, nothing stays in place without gravity, and no normal activity is possible unless great care is exercised; the slightest jar can send you hurtling across the cabin. Therefore, many spacecraft designers figure that some sort of artificial gravity will have to be supplied for space travellers. In principle, this is very easy to do. An object on the rim of a wheel rotat-ing at a uniform speed is subjected to a constant force pushing it away from the center, and by adjusting the size of the wheel and the speed of its rotation this centrifugal force can be made to resemble the force of gravity. Having accepted this notion, Kubrick went one step further and commis-sioned the Vickers Engineering Group to make an actual centrifuge, large

enough for the astronauts to live in full time. It took six months to build
and cost about three hundred thousand dollars. The finished product
looks from the outside like a Ferris wheel thirty-eight feet in diameter and
can be rotated at a maximum speed of about three miles an hour. This is
not enough to parallel the force of gravity—the equipment inside the centrifuge has to be bolted to the floor—but it has enabled Kubrick to achieve
some remarkable photographic effects. The interior, eight feet wide, is fitted out with an enormous computer console, an electronically operated
medical dispensary, a shower, a device for taking an artificial sunbath, a
recreation area, with a ping-pong table and an electronic piano, and five
beds with movable plastic domes—hibernacula, where astronauts who
are not on duty can, literally, hibernate for months at a time. (The trip to
Jupiter will take two hundred and fifty-seven days.)

I had seen the centrifuge in the early stages of its construction and very
much wanted to observe it in action, so I was delighted when chance sent
me back to England in the early spring. When I walked through the door
of the *2001* set one morning in March, I must say that the scene that presented itself to me was overwhelming. In the middle of the hangarlike
stage stood the centrifuge, with cables and lights hanging from every available inch of its steel-girdered superstructure. On the floor to one side of its
frame was an immense electronic console (not a prop), and, in various
places, six microphones and three television receivers. I learned later that
Kubrick had arranged a closed-circuit-television system so that he could
watch what was going on inside the centrifuge during scenes being filmed
when he could not be inside himself. Next to the microphone was an
empty canvas chair with "Stanley Kubrick" painted on its back in fading
black letters. Kubrick himself was nowhere to be seen, but everywhere I
looked there were people, some hammering and sawing, some carrying
scripts, some carrying lights. In one corner I saw a woman applying
makeup to what appeared to be an astronaut wearing blue coveralls and
leather boots. Over a loudspeaker, a pleasantly authoritative English
voice—belonging, I learned shortly, to Derek Cracknell, Kubrick's first
assistant director—was saying, "Will someone bring the Governor's
Polaroid on the double?" A man came up to me and asked how I would
like my tea and whom I was looking for, and almost before I could reply
"One lump with lemon" and "Stanley Kubrick," led me, in a semi-daze, to
an opening at the bottom of the centrifuge. Peering up into the dazzlingly

illuminated interior, I spotted Kubrick lying flat on his back on the floor of the machine and staring up through the viewfinder of an enormous camera, in complete concentration. Keir Dullea, dressed in shorts and a white T shirt, and covered by a blue blanket, was lying in an open hibernaculum on the rising curve of the floor. He was apparently comfortably asleep, and Kubrick was telling him to wake up as simply as possible. "Just open your eyes," he said. "Let's not have any stirring, yawning, and rubbing."

One of the lights burned out, and while it was being fixed, Kubrick unwound himself from the camera, spotted me staring openmouthed at the top of the centrifuge, where the furniture of the crew's dining quarters was fastened to the ceiling, and said, "Don't worry—that stuff is bolted down." Then he motioned to me to come up and join him.

No sooner had I climbed into the centrifuge than Cracknell, who turned out to be a cheerful and all but imperturbable youthful-looking man in tennis shoes (all the crew working in the centrifuge were wearing tennis shoes, not only to keep from slipping but to help them climb the steeply curving sides; indeed, some of them were working while clinging to the bolted-down furniture halfway up the wall), said, "Here's your Polaroid, Guv," and handed Kubrick the camera. I asked Kubrick what he needed the Polaroid for, and he explained that he used it for checking subtle lighting effects for color film. He and the director of photography, Geoffrey Unsworth, had worked out a correlation between how the lighting appeared on the instantly developed Polaroid film and the settings on the movie camera. I asked Kubrick if it was customary for movie directors to participate so actively in the photographing of a movie, and he said succinctly that he had never watched any other movie director work.

The light was fixed, and Kubrick went back to work behind the camera. Keir Dullea was reinstalled in his hibernaculum and the cover rolled shut. "You better take your hands from under the blanket," Kubrick said. Kelvin Pike, the camera operator, took Kubrick's place behind the camera, and Cracknell called for quiet. The camera began to turn, and Kubrick said, "Open the hatch." The top of the hibernaculum slid back with a whirring sound, and Keir Dullea woke up, without any stirring, yawning, or rubbing. Kubrick, playing the part of the solicitous computer, started feeding him lines.

"Good morning," said Kubrick. "What do you want for breakfast?"

"Some bacon and eggs would be fine," Dullea answered simply.

Later, Kubrick told me that he had engaged an English actor to read the computer's lines in the serious dramatic scenes, in order to give Dullea and Lockwood something more professional to play against, and that in the finished film he would dub in an American-accented voice. He and Dullea went through the sequence four or five times, and finally Kubrick was satisfied with what he had. Dullea bounced out of his hibernaculum, and I asked him whether he was having a good time. He said he was getting a great kick out of all the tricks and gadgets, and added, "This is a happy set, and that's something."

When Kubrick emerged from the centrifuge, he was immediately surrounded by people. "Stanley, there's a black pig outside for you to look at," Victor Lyndon was saying. He led the way outside, and, sure enough, in a large truck belonging to an animal trainer was an enormous jet-black pig. Kubrick poked it, and it gave a suspicious grunt.

"The pig looks good," Kubrick said to the trainer.

"I can knock it out with a tranquilizer for the scenes when it's supposed to be dead," the trainer said.

"Can you get any tapirs or anteaters?" Kubrick asked.

The trainer said that this would not be an insuperable problem, and Kubrick explained to me, "We're going to use them in some scenes about prehistoric man."

At this point, a man carrying a stuffed lion's head approached and asked Kubrick whether it would be all right to use.

"The tongue looks phony, and the eyes are only marginal," Kubrick said, heading for the set. "Can somebody fix the tongue?"

Back on the set, he climbed into his blue trailer. "Maybe the company can get back some of its investment selling guided tours of the centrifuge," he said. "They might even feature a ride on it." He added that the work in the machine was incredibly slow, because it took hours to rearrange all the lights and cameras for each new sequence. Originally, he said, he had planned on a hundred and thirty days of shooting for the main scenes, but the centrifuge sequences had slowed them down by perhaps a week. "I take advantage of every delay and breakdown to go off by myself and think," he said. "Something like playing chess when your opponent takes a long time over his next move."

At one o'clock, just before lunch, many of the crew went with Kubrick to a small projection room near the set to see the results of the previous day's shooting. The most prominent scene was a brief one that showed Gary Lockwood exercising in the centrifuge, jogging around its interior and shadow-boxing to the accompaniment of a Chopin waltz—picked by Kubrick because he felt that an intelligent man in *2001* might choose Chopin for doing exercise to music. As the film appeared on the screen, Lockwood was shown jogging around the complete interior circumference of the centrifuge, which appeared to me to defy logic as well as physics, since when he was at the top he would have needed suction cups on his feet to stay glued to the floor. I asked Kubrick how he had achieved this effect, and he said he was definitely, absolutely not going to tell me. As the scene went on, Kubrick's voice could be heard on the sound track, rising over the Chopin: "Gain a little on the camera, Gary! . . . Now a flurry of lefts and rights! . . . A little more vicious!" After the film had run its course, Kubrick appeared quite pleased with the results, remarking, "It's nice to get two minutes of usable film after two days of shooting."

Later that afternoon, I had a chance to see a publicity short made up of some of the most striking material so far filmed for *2001*. There were shots of the space station, with people looking out of the windows at the earth wheeling in the distance; there was an incredible sequence, done in red, showing a hostess on a moon rocket appearing to walk on the ceiling of the spaceship; there was a solemn procession of astronauts trudging along on the surface of the moon. The colors and the effects were extremely impressive.

When I got back to the set, I found Kubrick getting ready to leave for the day. "Come around to the house tomorrow," he said. "I'll be working at home, and maybe we can get in a little game. I still think you're a complete potzer. But I can't understand what happens every fifth game."

He had been keeping track of our games in a notebook, and the odd pattern of five had indeed kept reappearing. The crucial tenth game had been a draw, and although I had lost the fifteenth, even Kubrick admitted that he had had an amazingly close call. As for the games that had not been multiples of five, they had been outright losses for me. We had now completed nineteen games, and I could sense Kubrick's determination to break the pattern.

The next morning, I presented myself at the Kubricks's house, in Hertfordshire, just outside London, which they have rented until *2001* is finished. It is a marvellous house and an enormous one, with two suits of armor in one of the lower halls, and rooms all over the place, including a panelled billiard room with a big snooker table. Christiane has fixed up one room as a painting studio, and Kubrick has turned another into an office, filled with the inevitable tape recorders and cameras. They moved their belongings from New York in ninety numbered dark-green summer-camp trunks bought from Boy Scout headquarters—the only sensible way of moving, Kubrick feels. The house is set in a lovely bit of English countryside, near a rest home for horses, where worthy old animals are sent to live out their declining years in tranquility. Heating the house poses a major problem. It has huge picture windows, and Arthur Clarke's brother Fred, who is a heating engineer, has pointed out to Kubrick that glass conducts heat so effectively that he would not be much worse off (except for the wind) if the glass in the windows were removed entirely. The season had produced a tremendous cold spell, and in addition to using electric heaters in every corner of the rooms, Kubrick had acquired some enormous thick blue bathrobes, one of which he lent me. Thus bundled up, we sat down at the inevitable chessboard at ten in the morning for our twentieth game, which I proceeded to win on schedule. "I can't understand it," Kubrick said. "I know you are a potzer, so why are you winning these fifth games?"

A tray of sandwiches was brought in for lunch, and we sat there in our blue bathrobes like two figures from Bergman's *The Seventh Seal,* playing on and taking time out only to munch a sandwich or light an occasional cigar. The children, who had been at a birthday party, dropped in later in the day in their party dresses to say hello, as did Christiane, but the games went on. I lost four in a row, and by late afternoon it was time for the twenty-fifth game, which, Kubrick announced, would settle the matter once and for all. We seesawed back and forth until I thought I saw a marvellous chance for a coup. I made as if to take off one of Kubrick's knights, and Kubrick clutched his brow dramatically, as though in sharp pain. I then made the move ferociously, picking off the knight, and Kubrick jumped up from the table.

"I knew you were a potzer! It was a trap!" he announced triumphantly, grabbing my queen from the board.

"I made a careless mistake," I moaned.

"No, you didn't," he said. "You were hustled. You didn't realize that I'm an actor, too."

It was the last chess game we have had a chance to play, but I did succeed in beating him once at snooker.

Playboy Interview: Stanley Kubrick

ERIC NORDERN / 1968

PLAYBOY: *Much of the controversy surrounding 2001 deals with the meaning of the metaphysical symbols that abound in the film—the polished black monoliths, the orbital conjunction of Earth, Moon and Sun at each stage of the monoliths' intervention in human destiny, the stunning final kaleidoscopic mael-strom of time and space that engulfs the surviving astronaut and sets the stage for his rebirth as a "star child" drifting toward Earth in a translucent placenta. One critic even called 2001 "the first Nietzschean film," contending that its essential theme is Nietzsche's concept of man's evolution from ape to human to superman. What was the metaphysical message of 2001?*

KUBRICK: It's not a message that I ever intend to convey in words. *2001* is a nonverbal experience; out of two hours and nineteen minutes of film, there are only a little less than forty minutes of dialog. I tried to create a *visual* experience, one that bypasses verbalized pigeonholing and directly penetrates the subconscious with an emotional and philosophic content. To convolute McLuhan, in *2001* the message is the medium. I intended the film to be an intensely subjective experience that reaches the viewer at an inner level of consciousness, just as music does; to "explain" a Beethoven symphony would be to emasculate it by erecting an artificial barrier be-tween conception and appreciation. You're free to speculate as you wish about the philosophical and allegorical meaning of the film—and such speculation is one indication that it has succeeded in gripping the audience at a deep level—but I don't want to spell out a verbal road map for *2001* that every viewer will feel obligated to pursue or else fear he's missed the point. I think that if *2001* succeeds at all, it is in reaching a wide spectrum of people who would not often give a thought to man's destiny, his role in the cosmos and his relationship to higher forms of life. But even in the case of someone who is highly intelligent, certain ideas found in *2001* would, if presented as abstractions, fall rather lifelessly and be automatically assigned to pat intellectual categories; experienced in a moving visual and emotional context, however, they can resonate within the deepest fibers of one's being.

PLAYBOY: *Without laying out a philosophical road map for the viewer, can you tell us your own interpretation of the meaning of the film?*
KUBRICK: No, for the reasons I've already given. How much would we appreciate *La Gioconda* today if Leonardo had written at the bottom of the canvas: "This lady is smiling slightly because she has rotten teeth"— or "because she's hiding a secret from her lover"? It would shut off the viewer's appreciation and shackle him to a "reality" other than his own. I don't want that to happen to *2001.*

PLAYBOY: *Arthur Clarke has said of the film, "If anyone understands it on the first viewing, we've failed in our intention." Why should the viewer have to see a film twice to get its message?*
KUBRICK: I don't agree with that statement of Arthur's, and I believe he made it facetiously. The very nature of the visual experience in *2001* is to give the viewer an instantaneous, visceral reaction that does not—and should not—require further amplification. Just speaking generally, however, I would say that there are elements in any good film that would increase the viewer's interest and appreciation on a second viewing; the momentum of a movie often prevents every stimulating detail or nuance from having a full impact the first time it's seen. The whole idea that a movie should be seen only once is an extension of our traditional conception of the film as an ephemeral entertainment rather than as a visual work of art. We don't believe that we should hear a great piece of music only once, or see a great painting once, or even read a great book just once. But the film has until recent years been exempted from the category of art—a situation I'm glad is finally changing.

PLAYBOY: *Some prominent critics—including Renata Adler of* The New York Times, *John Simon of* The New Leader, *Judith Crist of* New York *magazine and Andrew Sarris of the* Village Voice—*apparently felt that* 2001 *should be among those films still exempted from the category of art; all four castigated it as dull, pretentious, and overlong. How do you account for their hostility?*

KUBRICK: The four critics you mention all work for New York publications. The reviews across America and around the world have been ninety-five percent enthusiastic. Some were more perceptive than others, of course, but even those who praised the film on relatively superficial grounds were able to get something of its message. New York was the only really hostile city. Perhaps there is a certain element of the lumpen literati that is so dogmatically atheist and materialist and Earth-bound that it finds the grandeur of space and the myriad mysteries of cosmic intelligence anathema. But film critics, fortunately, rarely have any effect on the general public; houses everywhere are packed and the film is well on its way to becoming the greatest moneymaker in MGM's history. Perhaps this sounds like a crass way to evaluate one's work, but I think that, especially with a film that is so obviously *different,* record audience attendance means people are saying the right things to one another after they see it—and isn't this really what it's all about?

PLAYBOY: *Speaking of what it's all about—if you'll allow us to return to the philosophical interpretation of* 2001—*would you agree with those critics who call it a profoundly religious film?*

KUBRICK: I will say that the God concept is at the heart of *2001*—but not any traditional, anthropomorphic image of God. I don't believe in any of Earth's monotheistic religions, but I do believe that one can construct an intriguing *scientific* definition of God, once you accept the fact that there are approximately 100 billion stars in our galaxy alone, that each star is a life-giving sun and that there are approximately 100 billion galaxies in just the *visible* universe. Given a planet in a stable orbit, not too hot and not too cold, and given a few billion years of chance chemical reactions created by the interaction of a sun's energy on the planet's chemicals, it's fairly certain that life in one form or another will eventually emerge. It's reasonable to assume that there must be, in fact, countless *billions* of such planets where biological life has arisen, and the odds of some proportion of such life developing intelligence are high. Now, the sun is by no means an old star, and its planets are mere children in cosmic age, so it seems likely that there are billions of planets in the universe not only where intelligent life is on a lower scale than man but other billions where it is approximately equal and others still where it is hundreds of thousands of millions of years in advance of us. When you think of the giant technological strides that man has made in a few millennia—less than a microsecond in the chronology of the universe—can you imagine the evolutionary development that much older life forms have taken? They may have progressed from biological species, which are fragile shells for the mind at best, into immortal machine entities—and then, over innumerable eons, they could emerge from the chrysalis of matter transformed into beings of pure energy and spirit. Their potentialities would be limitless and their intelligence ungraspable by humans.

PLAYBOY: *Even assuming the cosmic evolutionary path you suggest, what has this to do with the nature of God?*
KUBRICK: Everything—because these beings would *be* gods to the billions of less advanced races in the universe, just as man would appear a god to an ant that somehow comprehended man's existence. They would possess the twin attributes of all deities—omniscience and omnipotence. These entities might be in telepathic communication throughout the cosmos and thus be aware of everything that occurs, tapping every intelligent mind as effortlessly as we switch on the radio; they might not be limited by the speed of light and their presence could penetrate to the farthest corners of the universe; they might possess complete mastery over matter and energy; and in their final evolutionary stage, they might develop into an integrated collective immortal consciousness. They would be incomprehensible to us except as gods; and if the tendrils of their consciousness ever brushed men's minds, it is only the hand of God we could grasp as an explanation.

PLAYBOY: *If such creatures do exist, why should they be interested in man?*
KUBRICK: They may not be. But why should man be interested in microbes? The motives of such beings would be as alien to us as their intelligence.

PLAYBOY: *In 2001, such incorporeal creatures seem to manipulate our destinies and control our evolution, though whether for good or evil—or both, or neither—remains unclear. Do you really believe it's possible that man is a cosmic plaything of such entities?*

KUBRICK: I don't really *believe* anything about them; how can I? Mere speculation on the possibility of their existence is sufficiently overwhelming, without attempting to decipher their motives. The important point is that all the standard attributes assigned to God in our history could equally well be the characteristics of biological entities who billions of years ago were at a stage of development similar to man's own and evolved into something as remote from man as man is remote from the primordial ooze from which he first emerged.

PLAYBOY: *In this cosmic phylogeny you've described, isn't it possible that there might be forms of intelligent life on an even higher scale than these entities of pure energy—perhaps as far removed from them as they are from us?*

KUBRICK: Of course there could be; in an infinite, eternal universe, the point is that *anything* is possible, and it's unlikely that we can even begin to scratch the surface of the full range of possibilities. But at a time [1968] when man is preparing to set foot on the Moon, I think it's necessary to open up our Earth bound minds to such speculation. No one knows what's waiting for us in the universe. I think it was a prominent astronomer who wrote recently, "Sometimes I think we are alone, and sometimes I think we're not. In either case, the idea is quite staggering."

PLAYBOY: *You said there must be billions of planets sustaining life that is considerably more advanced than man but has not yet evolved into non- or suprabiological forms. What do you believe would be the effect on humanity if the Earth were contacted by a race of such ungodlike but technologically superior beings?*

KUBRICK: There's a considerable difference of opinion on this subject among scientists and philosophers. Some contend that encountering a highly advanced civilization—even one whose technology is essentially comprehensible to us—would produce a traumatic cultural shock effect on man by divesting him of his smug ethnocentrism and shattering the delusion that he is the center of the universe. Carl Jung summed up this position when he wrote of contact with advanced extraterrestrial life that the "reins would be torn from our hands and we would, as a tearful old medicine man once said to me, find ourselves 'without dreams' . . . we would find our intellectual and spiritual aspirations so outmoded as to leave us completely paralyzed." I personally don't accept this position, but it's one that's widely held and can't be summarily dismissed.

In 1960, for example, the Committee for Long Range Studies of the Brookings Institution prepared a report for the National Aeronautics and Space Administration warning that even indirect contact—i.e., alien artifacts that might possibly be discovered through our space activities on the Moon, Mars, or Venus or via radio contact with an interstellar civilization—could cause severe psychological dislocations. The study cautioned that "Anthropological files contain many examples of societies, sure of their place in the universe, which have disintegrated when they have had to associate with previously unfamiliar societies espousing different ideas and different life ways; others that survived such an experience usually did so by paying the price of changes in values and attitudes and behavior." It concluded that since intelligent life might be discovered at any time, and that since the consequences of such a discovery are "presently unpredictable," it was advisable that the government initiate continuing studies on the psychological and intellectual impact of confrontation with extraterrestrial life. What action was taken on this report I don't know, but I assume that such studies are now under way. However, while not discounting the possible adverse emotional impact on some people, I would personally tend to view such contact with a tremendous amount of excitement and enthusiasm. Rather than shattering our society, I think it could immeasurably enrich it.

Another positive point is that it's a virtual certainty that all intelligent life at one stage in its technological development must have discovered nuclear energy. This is obviously the watershed of any civilization; does it find a way to use nuclear power without destruction and harness it for peaceful purposes, or does it annihilate itself? I would guess that any civilization that has existed for a thousand years after its discovery of atomic energy has devised a means of accommodating itself to the bomb, and this could prove tremendously reassuring to us—as well as give us specific guidelines for our own survival. In any case, as far as cultural shock is concerned, my impression is that the attention span of most people is quite brief; after a week or two of great excitement and over-saturation in newspapers and on television, the public's interest would drop off and the

United Nations, or whatever world body we then had, would settle down to discussions with the aliens.

PLAYBOY: *You're assuming that extraterrestrials would be benevolent. Why?*
KUBRICK: Why should a vastly superior race *bother* to harm or destroy us? If an intelligent ant suddenly traced a message in the sand at my feet reading, "I am sentient; let's talk things over," I doubt very much that I would rush to grind him under my heel. Even if they weren't superintelligent, though, but merely more advanced than mankind, I would tend to lean more toward the benevolence, or at least indifference, theory. Since it's most unlikely that we would be visited from within our own solar system, any society capable of traversing light-years of space would have to have an extremely high degree of control over matter and energy. Therefore, what possible motivation for hostility would they have? To steal our gold or oil or coal? It's hard to think of any nasty intention that would justify the long and arduous journey from another star.

PLAYBOY: *You'll admit, though, that extraterrestrials are commonly portrayed in comic strips and cheap science-fiction films as bug-eyed monsters scuttling hungrily after curvaceous Earth maidens.*
KUBRICK: This probably dates back to the pulp science-fiction magazines of the twenties and thirties and perhaps even to the Orson Welles Martian-invasion broadcast in 1938 and the resultant mass hysteria, which is always advanced in support of the hypothesis that contact would cause severe cultural shock. In a sense, the lines with which Welles opened that broadcast set the tone for public consideration of extraterrestrial life for years to come. I've memorized them: "Across an immense ethereal gulf, minds that are to our minds as ours are to the beasts in the jungle—intellects vast, cool, and unsympathetic—regarded this Earth with envious eyes and slowly and surely drew their plans against us. . . ." Anything we can imagine about such other life forms is possible, of course. You could have psychotic civilizations, or decadent civilizations that have elevated pain to an aesthetic and might covet humans as gladiators or torture objects, or civilizations that might want us for zoos, or scientific experimentation, or slaves or even for food. While I am appreciably more optimistic, we just can't be sure *what* their motivations will be.

I'm interested in the argument of Professor Freeman Dyson of Princeton's Institute for Advanced Study, who contends that it would be a mistake to expect that all potential space visitors will be altruistic, or to believe that they would have *any* ethical or moral concepts comparable to mankind's. Dyson writes, if I remember him correctly, that "Intelligence may indeed be a benign influence creating isolated groups of philosopher kings far apart in the heavens," but it's just as likely that "Intelligence may be a cancer of purposeless technological exploitation, sweeping across a galaxy as irresistibly as it has swept across our own planet." Dyson concludes that it's "just as unscientific to impute to remote intelligence wisdom and serenity as it is to impute to them irrational and murderous impulses. We must be prepared for either possibility and conduct our searches accordingly."

This is why some scientists caution, now that we're attempting to intercept radio signals from other solar systems, that if we do receive a message we should wait awhile before answering it. But we've been transmitting radio and television signals for so many years that any advanced civilization could have received the emissions long ago. So in the final analysis, we really don't have much choice in this matter; they're either going to contact us or they're not, and if they do we'll have nothing to say about their benevolence or malevolence.

Even if they prove to be malevolent, their arrival would have at least one useful by-product in that the nations of the Earth would stop squabbling among themselves and forge a common front to defend the planet. I think it was André Maurois who suggested many years ago that the best way to realize world peace would be to stage a false threat from outer space; it's not a bad idea. But I certainly don't believe we should view contact with extraterrestrial life forms with foreboding, or hesitate to visit other planets for fear of what we may find there. If others don't contact us, we must contact them; it's our destiny.

PLAYBOY: *You indicated earlier that intelligent life is extremely unlikely elsewhere within our solar system. Why?*

KUBRICK: From what we know of the other planets in this system, it appears improbable that intelligence exists, because of surface temperatures and atmospheres that are inhospitable to higher life forms. Improbable, but not impossible. I will admit that there are certain tantalizing clues pointing in the other direction. For example, while the consensus of scientific opinion dismisses the possibility of intelligent life on Mars — as opposed to plant or low orders of organic life — there are some eminently respectable dissenters. Dr. Frank B. Salisbury, professor of plant physiology at Utah State University, has contended in a study in *Science* magazine that if vegetation exists on a planet, then it is logical that there will be higher orders of life to feed on it. "From there," he writes, "it is but one more step — granted, a big one — to intelligent beings."

Salisbury also points out that a number of astronomers have observed strange flashes of light, possibly explosions of great magnitude, on Mars's surface, some of which emit clouds; and he suggests that these could actually be nuclear explosions. Another intriguing facet of Mars is the peculiar orbits of its twin satellites, Phobos and Deimos, first discovered in 1877 — the same year, incidentally, that Schiaparelli discovered his famous but still elusive Martian "canals." One eminent astronomer, Dr. Josif Shklovsky, chairman of the department of radio astronomy at the Shternberg Astronomical Institute in Moscow, has propounded the theory that both moons are artificial space satellites launched by the Martians thousands of years ago in an effort to escape the dying surface of their planet. He bases this theory on the unique orbits of the two moons, which, unlike the thirty-one other satellites in our solar system, orbit *faster* than the revolution of their host planet. The orbit of Phobos is also deteriorating in an inexplicable manner and dragging the satellite progressively closer to Mars's surface. Both of these circumstances, Shklovsky contends, make sense only if the two moons are *hollow*.

Shklovsky believes that the satellites are the last remnants of an extinct ancient Martian civilization; but Professor Salisbury goes a step further and suggests that they were launched within the past hundred years. Noting that the moons were discovered by a relatively small power telescope in 1877 and not detected by a much more powerful telescope observing Mars in 1862 — when the planet was appreciably nearer Earth — he asks: "Should we attribute the failure of 1862 to imperfections in the existing telescope, or may we imagine that the satellites were launched into orbit between 1862 and 1877?" There are no answers here, of course, only questions, but it is fascinating speculation. On balance, however, I would have to say that the weight of available evidence dictates against intelligent life on Mars.

PLAYBOY: *How about possibilities, if not the probabilities, of intelligent life on the other planets?*

KUBRICK: Most scientists and astronomers rule out life on the outer planets since their surface temperatures are thousands of degrees either above or below zero and their atmospheres would be poisonous. I suppose it's possible that life could evolve on such planets with, say, a liquid ammonia or methane base, but it doesn't appear too likely. As far as Venus goes, the Mariner probes indicate that the surface temperature of the planet is approximately eight hundred degrees Fahrenheit, which would deny the chemical basis for molecular development of life. And there could be no indigenous intelligent life on the Moon, because of the total lack of atmosphere—no life as we know it, in any case; though I suppose that intelligent rocks or crystals, or statues, with a silicone life base are not really impossible, or even conscious gaseous matter or swarms of sentient electric particles. You'd get no technology from such creatures, but if their intelligence could control matter, why would they need it? There could be nothing about them, however, even remotely humanoid—a form that would appear to be an eminently practicable universal life prototype.

PLAYBOY: *What do you think we'll find on the Moon?*

KUBRICK: I think the most exciting prospect about the Moon is that if alien races have ever visited Earth in the remote past and left artifacts for man to discover in the future, they probably chose the arid, airless lunar vacuum, where no deterioration would take place and an object could exist for millennia. It would be inevitable that as man evolved technologically, he would reach his nearest satellite and the aliens would then expect him to find their calling card—perhaps a message of greeting, a cache of knowledge or simply a cosmic burglar alarm signaling that another race had mastered space flight. This, of course, was the central situation of *2001*.

But an equally fascinating question is whether there could be another race of intelligent life on Earth. Dr. John Lilly, whose research into dolphins has been funded by the National Aeronautics and Space Administration, has amassed considerable evidence pointing to the possibility that the bottle-nosed dolphin may be as intelligent as or more intelligent than man. [See *Deep Thinkers* in *Playboy,* August 1968—Ed.] He bases this not only on its brain size—which is larger than man's and with a more complex cortex—but on the fact that dolphins have evolved an extensive language.

Lilly is currently attempting, with some initial success, to decipher this language and establish communication with the dolphins. NASA's interest in this is obvious, because learning to communicate with dolphins would be a highly instructive precedent for learning to communicate with alien races on other planets. Of course, if the dolphins are really intelligent, theirs is obviously a nontechnological culture, since without an opposable thumb, they could never create artifacts. Their intelligence might also be on a totally different order than man's, which could make communication additionally difficult. Dr. Lilly has written that, "It is probable that their intelligence is comparable to ours, though in a very strange fashion... they may have a new class of large brain so dissimilar to ours that we cannot within our lifetime possibly understand its mental processes." Their culture may be totally devoted to creating works of poetry or devising abstract mathematical concepts, and they could conceivably share a telepathic communication to supplement their high-frequency underwater language.

What is particularly interesting is that dolphins appear to have developed a concept of altruism; the stories of shipwrecked sailors rescued by dolphins and carried to shore, or protected by them against sharks, are by no means all old wives' tales. But I'm rather disturbed by some recent developments that indicate not only how we may treat dolphins but also how we may treat intelligent races on other planets. The Navy, impressed by the dolphin's apparent intelligence, is reported to have been engaging in underwater-demolition experiments in which a live torpedo is strapped to a dolphin and detonated by radio when it nears a prototype enemy submarine. These experiments have been officially denied; but if they're true, I'm afraid we may learn more about man through dolphins than the other way around. The Russians, paradoxically, seem to be one step ahead of us in this area; they recently banned all catching of dolphins in Russian waters on the grounds that "Comrade Dolphin" is a fellow sentient being and killing him would be morally equivalent to murder.

PLAYBOY: *Although flying saucers are frequently an object of public derision, there has been a good deal of serious discussion in the scientific community about the possibility that UFOs could be alien spacecraft. What's your opinion?*
KUBRICK: The most significant analysis of UFOs I've seen recently was written by L.M. Chassin, a French Air Force general who had been a high

ranking NATO officer. He argues that by any legal rules of evidence, there is now sufficient sighting data amassed from reputable sources—astronomers, pilots, radar operators and the like—to initiate a serious and thorough worldwide investigation of UFO phenomena. Actually, if you examine even a fraction of the extant testimony you will find that people have been sent to the gas chamber on far less substantial evidence. Of course, it's possible that all the governments in the world really *do* take UFOs seriously and perhaps are already engaging in secret study projects to determine their origin, nature and intentions. If so, they may not be disclosing their findings for fear that the public would be alarmed—the danger of cultural shock deriving from confrontation with the unknown which we discussed earlier, and which is an element of *2001*, when news of the monolith's discovery on the Moon is suppressed. But I think even the two percent of sightings that the Air Force's Project Blue Book admits is unexplainable by conventional means should dictate a serious, searching probe. From all indications, the current government-authorized investigation at the University of Colorado is neither serious nor searching.

One hopeful sign that this subject may at last be accorded the serious discussion it deserves, however, is the belated but exemplary conversion of Dr. J. Allen Hynek, since 1948 the Air Force's consultant on UFOs and currently chairman of the astronomy department at Northwestern University. Hynek, who in his official capacity pooh-poohed UFO sightings, now believes that UFOs deserve top priority attention—as he wrote in *Playboy* [December 1967]—and even concedes that the existing evidence may indicate a possible connection with extraterrestrial life. He predicts: "I will be surprised if an intensive study yields nothing. To the contrary, I think that mankind may be in for the greatest adventure since dawning human intelligence turned outward to contemplate the universe." I agree with him.

PLAYBOY: *If flying saucers are real, who or what do you think they might be?*
KUBRICK: I don't know. The evidence proves they're up there, but it gives us very little clue as to what they are. Some science-fiction writers theorize half-seriously that they could be time shuttles flicking back and forth between eons to a future age when man has mastered temporal travel; and I understand that biologist Ivan Sanderson has even advanced a theory that they may be some kind of living space animal inhabiting the upper stratosphere—though I can't give much credence to that sugges-

tion. It's also possible that they are perfectly natural phenomena, perhaps chain lightning, as one American science writer has suggested; although this, again, does not explain some of the photographs taken by reputable sources, such as the Argentine navy, which clearly show spherical metallic objects hovering in the sky. As you've probably deduced, I'm really fascinated by UFOs and I only regret that this field of investigation has to a considerable extent been pre-empted by a crackpot fringe that claims to have soared to Mars on flying saucers piloted by three-foot-tall green humanoids with pointy heads. That kind of kook approach makes it very easy to dismiss the whole phenomenon which we do at our risk.

I think another problem here—and one of the reasons that, despite the overwhelming evidence, there has been remarkably little public interest— is that most people don't really *want* to think about extraterrestrial beings patrolling our skies and perhaps observing us like bugs on a slide. The thought is too disturbing; it upsets our tidy, soothing, sanitized suburban *Weltanschauung*; the cosmos is more than light-years away from Scarsdale. This could be a survival mechanism, but it could also blind us to what may be the most dramatic and important moment in man's history— contact with another civilization.

PLAYBOY: *Among the reasons adduced by those who doubt the interstellar origin of UFOs is Einstein's special theory of relativity, which states that the speed of light is absolute and that nothing can exceed it. A journey from even the nearest star to Earth would consequently take thousands of years. They claim this virtually rules out interstellar travel—at least for sentient beings with life spans as short as the longest known to man. Do you find this argument valid?*

KUBRICK: I find it difficult to believe that we have penetrated to the ultimate depths of knowledge about the physical laws of the universe. It seems rather presumptuous to believe that in the space of a few hundred years, we've figured out most of what there is to know. So I don't think it's right to declaim with unshakable certitude that light is the absolute speed limit of the universe. I'm suspicious of dogmatic scientific rules; they tend to have a rather short life span. The most eminent European scientists of the early nineteenth century scoffed at meteorites, on the grounds that "stones can't fall from the sky"; and just a year before Sputnik, one of the world's leading astrophysicists stated flatly that "space flight is bunk." Actually, there are already some extremely interesting theoretical studies underway—one by Dr. Gerald Feinberg at Columbia University—which indicate that short cuts could be found that would enable some things under certain conditions to exceed the speed of light.

In addition, there's always the possibility that the speed-of-light limitation, even if it's rigid, could be circumvented via a spacetime warp, as Arthur Clarke has proposed. But let's take another, slightly more conservative, means of evading the speed of light's restrictions: If radio contact is developed between ourselves and another civilization, within two hundred years we will have reached a stage in genetic engineering where the other race could transmit its genetic code to us by radio and we could then re-create their DNA pattern and artificially duplicate one of their species in our laboratories—and vice versa. This sounds fantastic only to those who haven't followed the tremendous breakthroughs being made in genetic engineering.

But actual interstellar travel wouldn't be impossible even if light speed *can't* be achieved. Whenever we dismiss space flight beyond our solar system on the grounds that it would take thousands of years, we are thinking of beings with life spans similar to ours. Fruit flies, I understand, live out their entire existence—birth, reproduction, and death—within twenty-four hours; well, man may be to other creatures in the universe as the fruit fly is to man. There may be countless races in the universe with life spans of hundreds of thousands or even millions of years, to whom a 10,000-year journey to Earth would be about as intimidating as an afternoon outing in the park. But even in terms of our own time scale, within a few years it should be possible to freeze astronauts or induce a hibernatory suspension of life functions for the duration of an interstellar journey. They could spend 300 or 1000 years in space and be awakened automatically, feeling no different than if they had had a hearty eight hours' sleep.

The speed-of-light theory, too, could work in favor of long journeys; the peculiar "time dilation" factor in Einstein's relativity theory means that as an object accelerates toward the speed of light, time slows down. Everything would appear normal to those on board; but if they had been away from Earth for, say, fifty-six years, upon their return they would be merely twenty years older than when they departed. So, taking all these factors into consideration, I'm not unduly impressed by the claims of some scientists that the speed-of-light limitation renders interstellar travel impossible.

PLAYBOY: *You mentioned freezing astronauts for lengthy space journeys, as in the "hibernacula" of 2001. As you know, physicist Robert Ettinger and others have proposed freezing dead bodies in liquid nitrogen until a future time when they can be revived. What do you think of this proposal?*

KUBRICK: I've been interested in it for many years, and I consider it eminently feasible. Within ten years, in fact, I believe that freezing of the dead will be a major industry in the United States and throughout the world; I would recommend it as a field of investment for imaginative speculators. Dr. Ettinger's thesis is quite simple: If a body is frozen cryogenically in liquid nitrogen at a temperature near absolute zero—minus 459.6 degrees Fahrenheit—and stored in adequate facilities, it may very well be possible at some as-yet-indeterminate date in the future to thaw and revive the corpse and then cure the disease or repair the physical damage that was the original cause of death. This would, of course, entail a considerable gamble; we have no way of knowing that future science will be sufficiently advanced to cure, say, terminal cancer, or even successfully revive a frozen body. In addition, the dead body undergoes damage in the course of the freezing process itself; ice crystallizes within the blood stream. And unless a body is frozen at the precise moment of death, progressive brain-cell deterioration also occurs. But what do we have to lose? Nothing—and we have immortality to gain. Let me read you what Dr. Ettinger has written: "It used to be thought that the distinction between life and death was simple and obvious. A living man breathes, sweats, and makes stupid remarks; a dead one just lies there, pays no attention, and after a while gets putrid. But nowadays nothing is that simple."

Actually, when you really examine the concept of freezing the dead, it's nowhere nearly as fantastic—though every bit as revolutionary—as it appears at first. After all, countless thousands of patients "die" on the operating table and are revived by artificial stimulation of the heart after a few seconds or even a few minutes—and there is really little substantive difference between bringing a patient back to life after three minutes of clinical death or after an "intermezzo" stage of three hundred years. Fortunately, the freezing concept is now gaining an increasing amount of attention within the scientific community. France's Dr. Jean Rostand, an internationally respected biologist, has proposed that every nation begin a freezer program immediately, funded by government money and utilizing the top scientific minds in each country. "For every day that we delay," he says, "untold thousands are going to an unnecessary grave."

PLAYBOY: *Are you interested in being frozen yourself?*

KUBRICK: I would be if there were adequate facilities available at the present time—which, unfortunately, there are not. A number of organizations are attempting to disseminate information and raise funds to implement an effective freezing program—the Life Extension Society of Washington, the Cryonics Society of New York, etc.—but we are still in the infancy of cryobiology. Right now, all existing freezer facilities—and there are only a handful—aren't sufficiently sophisticated to offer any realistic hope. But that could and probably will change far more rapidly than we imagine.

A key point to remember, particularly by those ready to dismiss this whole concept as preposterous, is that science has made fantastic strides in just the past forty years; within this brief period of time, a wide range of killer diseases that once were the scourge of mankind, from smallpox to diphtheria, have been virtually eliminated through vaccines and antibiotics, while others, such as diabetes, have been brought under control—though not yet completely eliminated—by drugs such as insulin. Already, heart transplants are almost a viable proposition and organ banks are being prepared to stock supplies of spleens, kidneys, lungs, and hearts for future transplant surgery.

Dr. Ettinger predicts that a "freezee" who died after a severe accident or massive internal damage would emerge resuscitated from a hospital of the future a "crazy quilt of patchwork." His internal organs—heart, lungs, liver, kidneys, stomach and the rest—may be grafts, implanted after being grown in the laboratory from someone's donor cells. His arms and legs may be "bloodless artifacts of fabric, metal and plastic, directed by tiny motors." His brain cells, writes Ettinger, "may be mostly new, regenerated from the few which would be saved, and some of his memories and personality traits may have had to be imprinted onto the new cells by micro-techniques of chemistry and physics." The main challenge to the scientist of the future will not be revival but eliminating the original cause of death; and in this area, we have every reason for optimism as a result of recent experience. So before anyone dismisses the idea of freezing, he should take a searching look at what we have accomplished in a few decades—and ponder what we're capable of accomplishing over the next few centuries.

PLAYBOY: *If such a program does succeed, the person who is frozen will have no way of knowing, of course, if he will ever be successfully revived. Do you think future scientists will be willing, even if they're able, to bring their ancestors back to life?*

KUBRICK: Well, twentieth-century man may not be quite the cup of tea for a more advanced civilization of even one hundred years in the future; but unless the future culture has achieved immortality—which is scientifically quite possible—they themselves would be frozen at death, and every generation would have a vested interest in the preservation of the preceding frozen generation in order to be, in turn, preserved by its own descendants. Of course, it would be something of a letdown if, three hundred years from now, somebody just pulled the plug on us all, wouldn't it?

Another problem here, quite obviously, is the population explosion; what will be the demographic effect on the Earth of billions of frozen bodies suddenly revived and taking their places in society? But by the time future scientists have mastered the techniques to revive their frozen ancestors, space flight will doubtless be a reality and other planets will be open for colonization. In addition, vast freezer facilities could possibly be constructed on the dark side of the Moon to store millions of bodies. The problems are legion, of course, but so are the potentialities.

PLAYBOY: *Opponents of cryogenic freezing argue that death is the natural and inevitable culmination of life and that we shouldn't tamper with it—even if we're able to do so. How would you answer them?*

KUBRICK: Death is no more natural or inevitable than smallpox or diphtheria. Death is a disease and as susceptible to cure as any other disease. Over the eons, man's powerlessness to prevent death has led him to force it from the forefront of his mind, for his own psychological health, and to accept it unquestioningly as the unavoidable termination. But with the advance of science, this is no longer necessary—or desirable. Freezing is only one possible means of conquering death, and it certainly would not be binding on everyone; those who desire a "natural" death can go ahead and die, just as those in the nineteenth century who desired "God-ordained" suffering resisted anesthesia. As Dr. Ettinger has written, "To each his own, and to those who choose not to be frozen, all I can say is— rot in good health."

PLAYBOY: *Freezing and resuscitation of the dead is just one revolutionary scientific technique that could transform our society. Looking ahead to the year of your film, 2001, what major social and scientific changes do you foresee?*

KUBRICK: Perhaps the greatest breakthrough we may have made by 2001 is the possibility that man may be able to eliminate old age. We've just discussed the steady scientific conquest of disease; even when this is accomplished, however, the scourge of old age will remain. But too many people view senile decay, like death itself, as inevitable. It's nothing of the sort. The highly respected Russian scientist V. F. Kuprevich has written, "I am sure we can find means for switching off the mechanisms which make cells age." Dr. Bernard Strehler, an eminent gerontology expert, contends that there is no inherent contradiction, no inherent property of cells or of Metazoa that precludes their organization into perpetually functioning and self-replenishing individuals.

One encouraging indication that we may already be on this road is the work of Dr. Hans Selye, who in his book *Calciphylaxis* presents an intriguing and well-buttressed argument that old age is caused by the transfer of calcium within the body—a transfer that can be arrested by circulating throughout the system specific iron compounds that flush out the calcium, absorb it and prevent it from permeating the tissue. Dr. Selye predicts that we may soon be able to prevent the man of sixty from progressing to the condition of the man of ninety. This is something of an understatement; Selye could have added that the man of sixty could *stay* sixty for hundreds or even thousands of years if all other diseases have been eradicated. Even accidents would not necessarily impair his relative immortality; even if a man is run over by a steamroller, his mind and body will be completely re-creatable from the tiniest fragment of his tissue, if genetic engineering continues its rapid progress.

PLAYBOY: *What impact do you think such dramatic scientific breakthroughs will have on the life style of society at the turn of the century?*

KUBRICK: That's almost impossible to say. Who could have predicted in 1900 what life in 1968 would be like? Technology is, in many ways, more predictable than human behavior. Politics and world affairs change so quickly that it's difficult to predict the future of social institutions for even ten years with a modicum of accuracy. By 2001, we could be living in a Gandhiesque paradise where all men are brothers, or in a neofascist dictatorship, or just be muddling along about the way we are today. As technology evolves, however, there's little doubt that the whole concept of leisure will be both quantitatively and qualitatively improved.

PLAYBOY: *What about the field of entertainment?*

KUBRICK: I'm sure we'll have sophisticated 3-D holographic television and films, and it's possible that completely new forms of entertainment and education will be devised. You might have a machine that taps the brain and ushers you into a vivid dream experience in which you are the protagonist in a romance or an adventure. On a more serious level, a similar machine could directly program you with knowledge; in this way, you might, for example, easily be able to learn fluent German in twenty minutes. Currently, the learning processes are so laborious and time-consuming that a breakthrough is really needed.

On the other hand, there are some risks in this kind of thing; I understand that at Yale they've been engaging in experiments in which the pleasure center of a mouse's brain has been localized and stimulated by electrodes; the result is that the mouse undergoes an eight-hour orgasm. If pleasure that intense were readily available to all of us, we might well become a race of sensually stultified zombies plugged into pleasure stimulators while machines do our work and our bodies and minds atrophy. We could also have this same problem with psychedelic drugs; they offer great promise of unleashing perceptions, but they also hold commensurate dangers of causing withdrawal and disengagement from life into a totally inner-directed kind of Soma world. At the present time, there are no ideal drugs; but I believe by 2001 we will have devised chemicals with no adverse physical, mental, or genetic results that can give wings to the mind and enlarge perception beyond its present evolutionary capacities.

Actually, up to now, perception on the deepest level has really, from an evolutionary point of view, been detrimental to survival; if primitive man had been content to sit on a ledge by his cave absorbed in a beautiful sunset or a complex cloud configuration, he might never have exterminated his rival species—but neither would he have achieved mastery of the planet. Now, however, man is faced with the unprecedented situation of potentially unlimited material and technological resources at his disposal and a tremendous amount of leisure time. At last, he has the opportunity to look both within and beyond himself with a new perspective—without endangering or impeding the progress of the species. Drugs, intelligently used, can be a valuable guide to this new expansion of our consciousness. But if employed just for kicks, or to dull rather than to expand perception, they can be a highly negative influence. There should be fascinating drugs available by 2001; what *use* we make of them will be the crucial question.

PLAYBOY: *Have you ever used LSD or other so-called consciousness-expanding drugs?*

KUBRICK: No. I believe that drugs are basically of more use to the audience than to the artist. I think that the illusion of oneness with the universe, and absorption with the significance of every object in your environment, and the pervasive aura of peace and contentment is not the ideal state for an artist. It tranquilizes the creative personality, which thrives on conflict and on the clash and ferment of ideas. The artist's transcendence must be within his own work; he should not impose any artificial barriers between himself and the mainspring of his subconscious. One of the things that's turned me against LSD is that all the people I know who use it have a peculiar inability to distinguish between things that are really interesting and stimulating and things that *appear* so in the state of universal bliss the drug induces on a "good" trip. They seem to completely lose their critical faculties and disengage themselves from some of the most stimulating areas of life. Perhaps when *everything* is beautiful, nothing is beautiful.

PLAYBOY: *What stage do you believe today's sexual revolution will have reached by 2001?*

KUBRICK: Here again, it's pure speculation. Perhaps there will have been a reaction against present trends, and the pendulum will swing back to a kind of neo-puritanism. But it's more likely that the so-called sexual revolution, midwifed by the pill, will be extended. Through drugs, or perhaps via the sharpening or even mechanical amplification of latent ESP functions, it may be possible for each partner to simultaneously experience the sensations of the other; or we may eventually emerge into polymorphous sexual beings; with the male and female components blurring, merging and interchanging. The potentialities for exploring new areas of sexual experience are virtually boundless.

PLAYBOY: *In view of these trends, do you think romantic love may have become unfashionable by 2001?*

KUBRICK: Obviously, people are finding it increasingly easy to have intimate and fulfilling relationships outside the concept of romantic love—which, in its present form, is a relatively recent acquisition, developed at the court of Eleanor of Aquitaine in the twelfth century—but the basic love relationship, even at its most obsessional, is too deeply ingrained in man's psyche not to endure in one form or another. It's not going to be easy to circumvent our primitive emotional programming. Man still has essentially the same set of pair-bonding instincts—love, jealousy, possessiveness—imprinted for individual and tribal survival millions of years ago, and these still lie quite close to the surface, even in these allegedly enlightened and liberated times.

PLAYBOY: *Do you think that by 2001 the institution of the family, which some social scientists have characterized as moribund, may have evolved into something quite different from what it is today?*

KUBRICK: One can offer all kinds of impressive intellectual arguments against the family as an institution—its inherent authoritarianism, etc.; but when you get right down to it, the family is the most primitive and visceral and vital unit in society. You may stand outside your wife's hospital room during childbirth muttering, "My God, what a responsibility! Is it right to take on this terrible obligation? What am I really doing here?"; and then you go in and look down at the face of your child and—zap!—that ancient programming takes over and your response is one of wonder and joy and pride. It's a classic case of genetically imprinted social patterns. There are very few things in this world that have an unquestionable importance in and of themselves and are not susceptible to debate or rational argument, but the family is one of them. Perhaps man has been too "liberated" by science and evolutionary social trends. He has been turned loose from religion and has hailed the death of his gods; the imperative loyalties of the old nation-state are dissolving and all the old social and ethical values, however reactionary and narrow they often were, are disappearing. Man in the twentieth century has been cut adrift in a rudderless boat on an uncharted sea; if he is going to stay sane throughout the voyage, he must have someone to care about, something that is more important than himself.

PLAYBOY: *Some critics have detected not only a deep pessimism but also a kind of misanthropy in much of your work. In* Dr. Strangelove, *for example, one reviewer commented that your directorial attitude, despite the film's antiwar message, seemed curiously aloof and detached and unmoved by the annihilation of mankind, almost as if the Earth were being cleansed of an infection. Is there any truth to that?*

KUBRICK: Good God, no. You don't stop being concerned with man because you recognize his essential absurdities and frailties and pretensions. To me, the only real immorality is that which endangers the species; and the only absolute evil, that which threatens its annihilation. In the deepest sense, I believe in man's potential and in his capacity for progress. In *Strangelove*, I was dealing with the inherent irrationality in man that threatens to destroy him; that irrationality is with us as strongly today, and must be conquered. But a recognition of insanity doesn't imply a celebration of it—nor a sense of despair and futility about the possibility of curing it.

PLAYBOY: *In the five years since* Dr. Strangelove *was released, the two major nuclear powers, the U.S. and the U.S.S.R., have reached substantial accommodation with each other. Do you think this has reduced the danger of nuclear war?*

KUBRICK: No. If anything, the overconfident Soviet-American *détente* *increases* the threat of accidental war through carelessness; this has always been the greatest menace and the one most difficult to cope with. The danger that nuclear weapons may be used—perhaps by a secondary power—is as great if not greater than it has ever been, and it is really quite amazing that the world has been able to adjust to it psychologically with so little apparent dislocation.

Particularly acute is the possibility of war breaking out as the result of a sudden unanticipated flare-up in some part of the world, triggering a panic reaction and catapulting confused and frightened men into decisions they are incapable of making rationally. In addition, the serious threat remains that a psychotic figure somewhere in the modern command structure could start a war, or at the very least a limited exchange of nuclear weapons that could devastate wide areas and cause innumerable casualties. This, of course, was the theme of *Dr. Strangelove*; and I'm not entirely assured that somewhere in the Pentagon or the Red army upper echelons there does not exist the real-life prototype of General Jack D. Ripper.

PLAYBOY: *Fail-safe strategists have suggested that one way to obviate the danger that a screwball might spark a war would be to administer psychological-fitness tests to all key personnel in the nuclear command structure. Would that be an effective safeguard?*

KUBRICK: No, because any seriously disturbed individual who rose high within the system would have to possess considerable self-discipline and be able to effectively mask his fixations. Such tests already do exist to a limited degree, but you'd really have to be pretty far gone to betray yourself in them, and the type of individual we're discussing would have to be a highly controlled psychopathic personality not to have given himself away long ago. But beyond those tests, how are you going to objectively assess the sanity of the president, in whom, as commander-in-chief, the ultimate responsibility for the use of nuclear weapons resides? It's improbable but not impossible that we could someday have a psychopathic president, or a president who suffers a nervous breakdown, or an alcoholic president who, in the course of some stupefying binge, starts a war. You could say that such a man would be detected and restrained by his aides—but with the powers of the presidency what they are today, who really knows? Less farfetched and even more terrifying is the possibility that a psychopathic individual could work his way into the lower echelons of the White House staff. Can you imagine what might have happened at the height of the Cuban Missile Crisis if some deranged waiter had slipped LSD into Kennedy's coffee—or, on the other side of the fence, into Khrushchev's vodka? The possibilities are chilling.

PLAYBOY: *Do you share the belief of some psychiatrists that our continued reliance on the balance of nuclear power, with all its attendant risks of global catastrophe, could reflect a kind of collective death wish?*

KUBRICK: No, but I think the *fear* of death helps explain why people accept this Damoclean sword over their heads with such bland equanimity. Man is the only creature aware of his own mortality and is at the same time generally incapable of coming to grips with this awareness and all its implications. Millions of people thus, to a greater or lesser degree, experience emotional anxieties, tensions and unresolved conflicts that frequently express themselves in the form of neuroses and a general joylessness that permeates their lives with frustration and bitterness and increases as they grow older and see the grave yawning before them. As fewer and fewer people find solace in religion as a buffer between themselves and the terminal moment, I actually believe that they unconsciously derive a kind of perverse solace from the idea that in the event of nuclear war, the world dies with them. God is dead, but the bomb endures; thus, they are no longer alone in the terrible vulnerability of their mortality. Sartre once wrote that if there was one thing you could tell a man about to be executed that would make him happy, it was that a comet would strike the earth the next day and destroy every living human being. This is not so much a collective death wish or self-destructive urge as a reflection of the awesome and agonizing loneliness of death. This is extremely pernicious, of course, because it aborts the kind of fury and indignation that should galvanize the world into defusing a situation where a few political leaders on both sides are seriously prepared to incinerate millions of people out of some misguided sense of national interest.

PLAYBOY: *Are you a pacifist?*
KUBRICK: I'm not sure what pacifism really means. Would it have been an act of superior morality to have submitted to Hitler in order to avoid war? I don't think so. But there have also been tragically senseless wars such as World War One and the current mess in Vietnam and the plethora of religious wars that pockmark history. What makes today's situation so radically different from anything that has gone before, however, is that, for the first time in history, man has the means to destroy the entire species—and possibly the planet as well. The problem of dramatizing this to the public is that it all seems so abstract and unreal; it's rather like saying, "The sun is going to die in a billion years." What is required as a minimal first corrective step is a concrete alternative to the present balance of terror—one that people can understand and support.

PLAYBOY: *Do you believe that some form of all-powerful world government, or some radically new social, political, and economic system, could deal intelligently and farsightedly with such problems as nuclear war?*
KUBRICK: Well, none of the present systems has worked very well, but I don't know what we'd replace them with. The idea of a group of philosopher kings running everything with benign and omniscient paternalism is always attractive, but where do we find the philosopher kings? And if we do find them, how do we provide for their successors? No, it has to be con-

ceded that democratic society, with all its inherent strains and contradic-
tions, is unquestionably the best system anyone ever worked out. I believe
it was Churchill who once remarked that democracy is the worst social system in the world, except for all the others.

PLAYBOY: *You've been accused of revealing, in your films, a strong hostility to
the modern industrialized society of the democratic West, and a particular antagonism—ambivalently laced with a kind of morbid fascination—toward
automation. Your critics claim this was especially evident in 2001, where the
archvillain of the film, the computer HAL 9000, was in a sense the only human
being. Do you believe that machines are becoming more like men and men more
like machines—and do you detect an eventual struggle for dominance between
the two?*
KUBRICK: First of all, I'm not hostile toward machines at all; just the
opposite, in fact. There's no doubt that we're entering a mechanarchy,
however, and that our already complex relationship with our machinery
will become even more complex as the machines become more and more
intelligent. Eventually, we will have to share this planet with machines
whose intelligence and abilities far surpass our own. But the interrelation-
ship—if intelligently managed by man—could have an immeasurably
enriching effect on society.

Looking into the distant future, I suppose it's not inconceivable that a
semisentient robot-computer subculture could evolve that might one day
decide it no longer needed man. You've probably heard the story about the
ultimate computer of the future: For months scientists think of the first
question to pose to it, and finally they hit on the right one: "Is there a
God?" After a moment of whirring and flashing lights, a card comes out,
punched with the words: THERE IS NOW. But this problem is a distant one
and I'm not staying up nights worrying about it; I'm convinced that our
toasters and TVs are fully domesticated, though I'm not so sure about integrated telephone circuits, which sometimes strike me as possessing a
malevolent life all their own.

PLAYBOY: *Speaking of futuristic electronics and mechanics, 2001's incredibly
elaborate gadgetry and scenes of space flight have been hailed—even by hostile
critics—as a major cinematic breakthrough. How were you able to achieve such
remarkable special effects?*

KUBRICK: I can't answer that question technically in the time we have available, but I can say that it was necessary to conceive, design and engineer completely new techniques in order to produce the special effects. This took eighteen months and $6,500,000 out of a $10,500,000 budget. I think an extraordinary amount of credit must go to Robert H. O'Brien, the president of MGM, who had sufficient faith to allow me to persevere at what must have at times appeared to be a task without end. But I felt it was necessary to make this film in such a way that every special-effects shot in it would be completely convincing—something that had never before been accomplished in a motion picture.

PLAYBOY: *Thanks to those special effects, 2001 is undoubtedly the most graphic depiction of space flight in the history of films—and yet you have admitted that you yourself refuse to fly, even in a commercial jet liner. Why?*
KUBRICK: I suppose it comes down to a rather awesome awareness of mortality. Our ability, unlike the other animals, to conceptualize our own end creates tremendous psychic strains within us; whether we like to admit it or not, in each man's chest a tiny ferret of fear at this ultimate knowledge gnaws away at his ego and his sense of purpose. We're fortunate, in a way, that our body, and the fulfillment of its needs and functions, plays such an imperative role in our lives; this physical shell creates a buffer between us and the mind-paralyzing realization that only a few years of existence separate birth from death. If man really sat back and thought about his impending termination and his terrifying insignificance and aloneness in the cosmos, he would surely go mad, or succumb to a numbing sense of futility. Why, he might ask himself, should he bother to write a great symphony, or strive to make a living, or even to love another, when he is no more than a momentary microbe on a dust mote whirling through the unimaginable immensity of space?

Those of us who are forced by their own sensibilities to view their lives in this perspective—who recognize that there is no purpose they can comprehend and that amidst a countless myriad of stars their existence goes unknown and unchronicled—can fall prey all too easily to the ultimate *anomie.* I can well understand how life became for Matthew Arnold "a darkling plain . . . where ignorant armies clash by night . . . and there is neither love nor hope nor certitude nor faith nor surcease from pain." But even for those who lack the sensitivity to more than vaguely comprehend their transience and their triviality, this inchoate awareness robs life of meaning and purpose; it's why "the mass of men lead lives of quiet desperation," why so many of us find our lives as absent of meaning as our deaths.

The world's religions, for all their parochialism, did supply a kind of consolation for this great ache; but as clergymen now pronounce the death of God and, to quote Arnold again, "the sea of faith" recedes around the world with a "melancholy, long, withdrawing roar," man has no crutch left on which to lean—and no hope, however irrational, to give purpose to his existence. This shattering recognition of our mortality is at the root of far more mental illness than I suspect even psychiatrists are aware.

PLAYBOY: *If life is so purposeless, do you feel that it's worth living?*
KUBRICK: Yes, for those of us who manage somehow to cope with our mortality. The very meaninglessness of life forces man to create his own meaning. Children, of course, begin life with an untarnished sense of wonder, a capacity to experience total joy at something as simple as the greenness of a leaf; but as they grow older, the awareness of death and decay begins to impinge on their consciousness and subtly erode their *joie de vivre*, their idealism—and their assumption of immortality. As a child matures, he sees death and pain everywhere about him, and begins to lose faith in the ultimate goodness of man. But if he's reasonably strong—and lucky—he can emerge from this twilight of the soul into a rebirth of life's *élan*. Both because of and in spite of his awareness of the meaninglessness of life, he can forge a fresh sense of purpose and affirmation. He may not recapture the same pure sense of wonder he was born with, but he can shape something far more enduring and sustaining. The most terrifying fact about the universe is not that it is hostile but that it is indifferent; but if we can come to terms with this indifference and accept the challenges of life within the boundaries of death—however mutable man may be able to make them—our existence as a species can have genuine meaning and fulfillment. However vast the darkness, we must supply our own light.

PLAYBOY: *Will we be able to find any deep meaning or fulfillment, either as individuals or as a species, as long as we continue to live with the knowledge that all human life could be snuffed out at any moment in a nuclear catastrophe?*

KUBRICK: We *must,* for in the final analysis, there may be no sound way to eliminate the threat of self-extinction without changing human nature; even if you managed to get every country disarmed down to the bow and arrow, you would still be unable to lobotomize either the knowledge of how to build nuclear warheads or the perversity that allows us to rationalize their use. Given these two categorical imperatives in a disarmed world, the first country to amass even a few weapons would have a great incentive to use them quickly. So an argument might be made that there is a greater chance for *some* use of nuclear weapons in a totally disarmed world, though less chance of global extinction; while in a world armed to the teeth you have less chance for *some* use—but a great chance of extinction if they're used.

If you try to remove yourself from an Earthly perspective and look at this tragic paradox with the detachment of an extraterrestrial, the whole thing is totally irrational. Man now has the power in one mad, incandescent moment, as you point out, to exterminate the entire species; our own generation could be the last on Earth. One miscalculation and all the achievements of history could vanish in a mushroom cloud; one misstep and all of man's aspirations and strivings over the millennia could be terminated. One short circuit in a computer, one lunatic in a command structure and we could negate the heritage of the billions who have died since the dawn of man and abort the promise of the billions yet unborn— the ultimate genocide. What an irony that the discovery of nuclear power, with its potential for annihilation, also constitutes the first tottering step into the universe that must be taken by all intelligent worlds. Unhappily, the infant-mortality rate among emerging civilizations in the cosmos may be very high. Not that it will matter except to us; the destruction of this planet would have no significance on a cosmic scale; to an observer in the Andromeda nebulae, the sign of our extinction would be no more than a match flaring for a second in the heavens; and if that match does blaze in the darkness, there will be none to mourn a race that used a power that could have lit a beacon in the stars to light its funeral pyre. The choice is ours.

A Talk with Stanley Kubrick about *2001*

MAURICE RAPF/1969

STANLEY KUBRICK WAS A magazine photographer
before he became a director in 1953 with *Fear and Desire*. He first
drew critical attention with his low-budget *The Killing* in 1956.
Since then his meager but notable output consists of six films:
Paths of Glory, Spartacus, Lolita, Dr. Strangelove, and *2001: A Space
Odyssey*. Of these, probably none received so inauspicious a critical reception as *2001* and, perversely, none has equalled its huge
grosses at the box office.

Why this gap between critical and commercial reaction? Kubrick
conceded that the all-important first preview in New York was a
disaster. He also admitted that it was the first time he himself had
seen the film in the presence of an audience. Aware of the unfa-
vorable reaction, he made thirty cuts in the composite print,
shortening the film by nineteen minutes within a week after its
opening.

Could a few excisions (actually a twelve percent cut in total
length) turn what the critics had called "a monumental bore" or,
at best, "a glorious failure" into what many, seeing the film after
the cut, were to regard as one of the most visually stimulating
movies of all time? As one who admired the shortened version,
Maurice Rapf, then a critic for *Life* magazine, sought out Kubrick

From *Action*, January/February 1969. Reprinted by permission of the Directors Guild of
America.

for an explanation of the changes. What follows are excerpts
from Kubrick's comments on this and other questions of film
technique. — Bob Thomas

From the day it opened *2001: A Space Odyssey* got great reaction from the
paying audience. All the theater managers say the only adjective they can
use is "phenomenal," because of the numbers of people who buy tickets a
second, third, and fourth time to see the film. The managers report that
after each show people come up and want to know where they can buy
tickets again. So this poor reaction on that first [preview] screening I
attribute to the audience and to the originality of the film. The film
departs about as much from the convention of the theater and the three-
act play as is possible; not many films have departed further than that,
certainly not big films. I don't know why there was this concentration of
nonreceptive people, but there was.

First of all, the audience that is seeing the film now is reported as being
eighty percent thirty-five or under, down to five years old. I would say the
audience must have been ninety percent from thirty-five to sixty at that
screening. So the preview audience and the paying audience have been
two ends of the moviegoing scale.

Secondly, the lukewarm New York reaction has not been the case anywhere else, for some strange reason. I haven't had time to look through
this, but in Chicago we got three rave reviews out of four. In Boston we got
all rave reviews, including critics whom you wouldn't expect to like it,
such as Marjorie Adams, who said the film is like adding a new dimension
to life. It's gotten virtually unanimous rave reviews out of New York. I
don't know the reason for the New York reaction. The audience, with the
exception of a few mumblers that go out, has reacted more intensely, more
favorably than to any other picture that the managers can remember.

I myself usually get ten or twelve letters about a picture over a period of
the whole life of the film. I've been getting about two letters a day since
the film opened. Two or three have been cranky letters, asking for their
money back; the rest are from people saying, "This film has changed my
life," and "I've seen the film six times," and things like that. So all indices
of the film would indicate that for some strange reason chemistry that
night was bad and also very unrepresentative of anything that's happened
since then.

I tightened the picture all the way through. I had started thinking about doing it right from the first screening because even though the total reaction of that screening was not representative or good, I could still see places that, as I watched it with an audience, I thought were just going on a bit. It's probably the hardest thing to determine, as to how much weight to give. I just felt as I looked at it and looked at it that I could see places all the way through the film where I would tighten up, and I took out nineteen minutes. The picture had been originally two hours and forty-one minutes long.

A number of very perceptive people, and a lot of just ordinary people, saw the long version and flipped over that. I don't believe that the change made a crucial difference. I think it just tightened up, and some marginal people who might have gotten restless won't get restless. But the people that dug the film dug it in its original length, and the people that hated it hate it at the present length.

Special effects were the reason the film was late, the reason that it was so close to the wire. I spent a year and a half, June 1966 practically up to the beginning of March 1967, running through the 205 special-effects shots. The last ones were arriving in California as they were doing the negative printing. You can't finish this picture without the special effects; they're integrated in almost every sequence so the thing never really got put together except a sequence at a time to look at it, or a reel at a time.

All of the money spent on the film shows on the screen. In most films you have a bunch of guys talking to each other and you make use of about three or four sets and that's about it. There really isn't a lot to look at, and everybody is waiting for the big action sequence. I remember as a child being frustrated by one war picture after another where John Payne and Randolph Scott would talk and talk and you'd be waiting for the big attack. It would finally come at the end of the film for two minutes with some process shots and a lot of cheated action. Forgetting all the other things that a film is, there is always—to me anyway—a disappointment in not really seeing anything up on the screen that is beautiful or interesting to look at. Largely it's just a matter of photographing a lot of people talking to each other on sets that are more or less interesting with actors that are better or worse. Essentially films are confined to being elaborated three-act stage plays. They have had a great problem breaking out of that form.

In *Space Odyssey* the mood hitting you is the visual imagery. The people who didn't respond, I now, for want of coming up with a better explanation, categorize as "verbally oriented people." Every child that sees the film—and I've spoken to twenty or thirty kids—knows that Doctor Floyd goes to the moon. You say, "Well, how do you know?" and they say, "Well, we saw the moon." Whereas a number of people, including critics, thought he went to the planet Clavius. Why they think there's a planet Clavius I'll never know. But they hear him asked, "Where are you going?" and he says, "I'm going to Clavius." Now, I knew at that time that most people wouldn't realize that Clavius was a crater on the moon, but it seemed to me a realistic way of talking about the moon. He wouldn't say, "I'm going to the moon to the crater Clavius." With many people— BOOM—that one word registers in their head and they don't look at fifteen shots of the moon; they don't see that he's going to the moon.

Communicating visually and through music gets past the verbal pigeon-hole concepts that people are stuck with. You know, words have a highly subjective and very limited meaning, and they immediately limit the possible emotional and subconscious designating effect of a work of art. Movies have tied themselves into that because the crucial things that generally come out of a film are still word-delivered. There's emotion backing them up, you've got the actors generating feeling, etc. It's basically word communication.

The Blue Danube is a magnificent piece of music for the beautiful, graceful motion of the space station. To me it just seemed like a perfect representation of what was going on. Also it helped to get away from the idea that space would be eerie and strange. Space travel will become very ordinary very soon, and it will be particularly significant for its beauty. It seemed to me *The Blue Danube* was a magnificent piece of music to use, particularly since I had decided to use existing music and not original music.

The screenplay is the most uncommunicative form of writing ever devised. It's hard to convey mood and it's hard to convey imagery. You can convey dialogue, but if you stick to the conventions of a screenplay, the description has to be very brief and telegraphic. You can't create a mood or anything like that, so the screenplay that was written was about a 40,000-word prose piece by Arthur B. Clarke and me. That was the basis of the deal and the budget, etc. Then a screenplay was made from that by me and Arthur, and then Arthur afterwards wrote the novel based on the screenplay.

I've always said the two people who are worthy of film study are Charlie Chaplin and Orson Welles as representing the two most diverse approaches to filmmaking. Charlie Chaplin must have had the crudest, simplest lack of interest in cinematics. Just get the image on the screen; it's the content of the shot that matters. Welles is probably, at his best, the most baroque kind of stylist in the conventional film-telling style. I think perhaps Eisenstein might be a better example because where Chaplin had all content and no style, to me Eisenstein has all style and no content. *Alexander Nevsky* stylistically is possibly one of the most beautiful movies ever made; its content to me is a moronic story, moronically told, full of lies. It's the most dishonest kind of a film. And I would have thought that perhaps a study of Chaplin's greatest films and *Alexander Nevsky* would be worthwhile, because somewhere within that you'd see how two completely diverse approaches can make a fascinating film.

People now realize how easy it is to make a film. Everybody knows that you use a camera and everybody knows that you use a tape recorder, and it's now getting to the point where a filmmaker almost has the same freedom a novelist has when he buys himself some paper. I haven't seen all the underground films; I've been away for three years. If they haven't already, there's no doubt that at some point someone's going to do something on a level that's going to be shattering. First of all, they all need a little more experience. It's getting to the point now for a few thousand dollars you can make a film, and a hell of a lot of people can lay their hands on a few thousand dollars if they want it badly enough.

The Film Director as Superstar:
Stanley Kubrick

JOSEPH GELMIS/1970

THE MOST CONTROVERSIAL FILM of 1968 was Stanley Kubrick's *2001: A Space Odyssey*. It started out as a $6,000,000 science fiction movie and escalated into a $10,500,000 underground film. It polarized critical and public opinion. Most of its young admirers considered it a prophetic masterpiece. Its detractors praised the special effects but found it confusing and pretentious as drama.

Despite Kubrick's own ready interpretation of the action, the ending of *2001* was confusing to some people. The final scenes in the alien "zoo" or heaven and the metamorphosis of the astronaut into a star baby remained for many an enigmatic, purely emotional, nonverbal experience. Understanding became a function of the emotions, rather than one's reasoning powers.

Less than half the film had dialogue. It was a reorganization of the traditional dramatic structure. Process became more important than plot. The tedium was the message. It was a film not about space travel; it was space travel. "The truth of a thing is in the feel of it, not the think of it," Kubrick asserted.

Kubrick traces some of his fascination with the fluid camera back to Max Ophuls. His oeuvre, with the single exception of the optimistic transfiguration in *2001*, is a bleak skepticism and fatalism.

2001 was Kubrick's first experiment with restructuring the conventions of the three-act drama. It's quite possible it started out to be something entirely different. The book based on the original screenplay by Arthur C. Clarke and Kubrick is literal, verbal, explicit. The film, in its early stages, had a narrator's voice. It was cut bit by bit and then eliminated completely, by virtue of which *2001* evolved as a nonverbal experience.

In his next film, *Napoleon,* Kubrick says he plans to return to the use of a narrator and perhaps even animation or charts to illustrate and explain the battle tactics and campaigns. Kubrick's personal interest in the aesthetics of a well-staged campaign goes back to his days as a young chess hustler in Greenwich Village.

Born July 1928 in the Bronx, Kubrick was introduced to still photography as a hobby by his father, who was a physician. He achieved a certain youthful prominence as his class photographer at Taft High School. Later, with a sixty-eight average, he was unable to compete with returning GIs for a place in college. So, "out of pity," he recalls, *Look* magazine hired him as a photographer.

Kubrick's early training in movies was with two documentaries. At twenty-five, he made his first feature film, the 35-mm *Fear and Desire,* for $9000—plus another $30,000 because he didn't know what he was doing with the soundtrack. He didn't make any money on his first four feature films. He has never earned a penny on *The Killing* and *Paths of Glory,* which some of his early fans still consider his best films.

The only film he disclaims is *Spartacus.* He says he worked on it as just a hired hand. Every other film he's directed he has made to suit himself, within prescribed bounds of existing community standards. He wishes *Lolita* had been more erotic. The lag time between conception and completion of his films is now up to an average of three years. In part, this is the result of his wish to handle every artistic and business function himself.

To concentrate all control in his own hands, Kubrick produces as well as directs his films. He originates, writes, researches, directs, edits, and even guides the publicity campaigns for his films. Though he gets his financing from the major studios, he is as independent as he was when he was raising his money from his father and uncle.

The following interview is the outcome of meetings that took place in 1968 in New York and London and of correspondence that continued through 1969. Kubrick lives near London. His third wife is Suzanne Christiane Harlan, a German actress who appeared briefly at the end of *Paths of Glory.*

GELMIS: *2001 took about three years to make—six months of preparation, four and a half months of working with the actors, and a year and a half of shooting special effects. How much time will* Napoleon *take out of your life?*
KUBRICK: Considerably less. We hope to begin the actual production work by the winter of 1969, and the exterior shooting—battles, location shots, etc.—should be completed within two or three months. After that, the studio work shouldn't take more than another three or four months.

G: *Where would the exteriors be shot? Actual sites?*
K: I still haven't made a final decision, although there are several promising possibilities. Unfortunately, there are very, very few actual Napoleonic battlefields where we could still shoot; the land itself has either been taken over by industrial and urban development, preempted by historical trusts, or is so ringed by modern buildings that all kinds of anachronisms would present themselves—like a Hussars's charge with a Fiat plant in the background. We're now in the process of deciding the best places to shoot, and where it would be most feasible to obtain the troops we need for battle scenes. We intend to use a maximum of forty thousand infantry and ten thousand cavalry for the big battles, which means that we have to find a country which will hire out its own armed forces to us—you can just imagine the cost of fifty thousand extras over an extended period of time. Once we find a receptive environment, there are still great logistic problems—for example, a battle site would have to be contiguous to a city or town or barracks area where the troops we'd use are already bivouacked. Let's say we're working with forty thousand infantry—if we could get forty men into a truck, it would still require a thousand trucks to move them around. So in addition to finding the proper terrain, it has to be within marching distance of military barracks.

G: *Aside from the Russian* War and Peace, *where they reportedly used sixty thousand of their own troops, has there ever been a film that used forty thousand men from somebody else's army?*
K: I would doubt it.

G : *Then how do you expect to persuade another government to give you as many as forty thousand soldiers?*

K : One has to be an optimist about these things. If it turned out to be impossible I'd obviously have no other choice than to make do with a lesser number of men, but this would only be as a last resort. I wouldn't want to fake it with fewer troops because Napoleonic battles were out in the open, a vast tableau where the formations moved in an almost choreographic fashion. I want to capture this reality on film, and to do so it's necessary to re-create all the conditions of the battle with painstaking accuracy.

G : *How many men did you use in the trench battle of* Paths of Glory?

K : That was another story entirely. We employed approximately eight hundred men, all German police—at that time the German police received three years of military training, and were as good as regular soldiers for our purposes. We shot the film at Geiselgesteig Studios in Munich, and both the battle site and the château were within thirty-five to forty minutes of the studio.

G : *If you can't use the actual battle sites, how will you approximate the terrain on the sites you do choose?*

K : There are a number of ways this can be done and it's quite important to the accuracy of the film, since terrain is the decisive factor in the flow and outcome of a Napoleonic battle. We've researched all the battle sites exhaustively from paintings and sketches, and we're now in a position to approximate the terrain. And from a purely schematic point of view, Napoleonic battles are so beautiful, like vast lethal ballets, that it's worth making every effort to explain the configuration of forces to the audience. And it's not really as difficult as it at first appears.

G : *How do you mean "explain"? With a narrator, or charts?*

K : With a narrative voice-over at times, with animated maps and, most importantly, through the actual photography of the battles themselves. Let's say you want to explain that at the battle of Austerlitz the Austro-Russian forces attempted to cut Napoleon off from Vienna, and then extended the idea to a double envelopment and Napoleon countered by striking at their center and cutting their forces in half—well, this is not difficult to show by photography, maps and narration. I think it's extremely important to communicate the essence of these battles to the viewer, because they all have an aesthetic brilliance that doesn't require a military mind to appreciate. There's an aesthetic involved; it's almost like a great piece of music, or the purity of a mathematical formula. It's this quality I want to bring across, as well as the sordid reality of battle. You know, there's a weird disparity between the sheer visual and organizational beauty of the historical battles sufficiently far in the past, and their human conse-quences. It's rather like watching two golden eagles soaring through the sky from a distance; they may be tearing a dove to pieces, but if you are far enough away the scene is still beautiful.

G : *Why are you making a movie about Napoleon?*
K : That's a question it would really take this entire interview to answer. To begin with, he fascinates me. His life has been described as an epic poem of action. His sex life was worthy of Arthur Schnitzler. He was one of those rare men who move history and mold the destiny of their own times and of generations to come — in a very concrete sense, our own world is the result of Napoleon, just as the political and geographic map of postwar Europe is the result of World War Two. And, of course, there has never been a good or accurate movie about him. Also, I find that all the issues with which it concerns itself are oddly contemporary — the responsibilities and abuses of power, the dynamics of social revolution, the relationship of the individual to the state, war, militarism, etc., so this will not be just a dusty historic pageant but a film about the basic questions of our own times, as well as Napoleon's. But even apart from those aspects of the story, the sheer drama and force of Napoleon's life is a fantastic subject for a film biography. Forgetting everything else and just taking Napoleon's romantic involvement with Josephine, for example, here you have one of the great obsessional passions of all time.

G : *How long a film biography are you contemplating?*
K : It's obviously a huge story to film, since we're not just taking one segment of Napoleon's life, military or personal, but are attempting to encompass all the major events of his career. I haven't set down any rigid guidelines on length; I believe that if you have a truly interesting film it doesn't matter how long it is — providing, of course, you don't run on to

such extremes that you numb the attention span of your audience. The longest film that has given consistent enjoyment to generations of viewers is *Gone With the Wind,* which would indicate that if a film is sufficiently interesting people will watch it for three hours and forty minutes. But in actual fact, the Napoleon film will probably be shorter.

G : *What kind of research do you have going on right now?*
K : The first step has been to read everything I could get my hands on about Napoleon, and totally immerse myself in his life. I guess I must have gone through several hundred books on the subject, from contemporary nineteenth-century English and French accounts to modern biographies. I've ransacked all these books for research material and broken it down into categories on everything from his food tastes to the weather on the day of a specific battle, and cross-indexed all the data in a comprehensive research file. In addition to my own reading, I've worked out a consultant arrangement with Professor Felix Markham of Oxford, a history don who has spent the past thirty-five years of his life studying Napoleon and is considered one of the world's leading Napoleonic experts. He's available to answer any questions that derive from my own reading or outside of it. We're also in the process of creating prototypes of vehicles, weapons, and costumes of the period which will subsequently be mass-produced, all copied from paintings and written descriptions of the time and accurate in every detail. We already have twenty people working full time on the preparatory stage of the film.

G : *What movies on Napoleon have you gone back to see?*
K : I've tried to see every film that was ever made on the subject, and I've got to say that I don't find any of them particularly impressive. I recently saw Abel Gance's movie, which has built up a reputation among film buffs over the years, and I found it really terrible. Technically he was ahead of his time and he introduced inventive new film techniques — in fact Eisenstein credited him with stimulating his initial interest in montage — but as far as story and performance goes it's a very crude picture.

G : *What did you think about the Russian* War and Peace?
K : It was a cut above the others and did have some very good scenes, but I can't say I was overly impressed. There's one in particular I admired,

where the Tsar entered a ballroom and everyone scurried in his wake to see what he was doing and then rushed out of his way when he returned. That seemed to me to capture the reality of such a situation. Of course, Tolstoy's view of Napoleon is so far removed from that of any objective historian's that I really can't fault the director for the way he was portrayed. It was a disappointing film, and doubly so because it had the potential to be otherwise.

G : *Can you imagine yourself going down with just a cameraman and sound man and half a dozen people and shooting a film?*
K : Sure I can. In fact, any contemporary story is best done just that way. The only time you need vast amounts of money and a huge crew is when you require complex special effects, as in *2001,* or big battle or crowd scenes, as in the Napoleon film. But if you're just dealing with a story set in modern times, then you could do it very easily with both limited funds and a limited crew. [Kubrick never made *Napoleon—Ed.*]

G : *In your own case,* Lolita *was set in America, and yet you shot it on an English sound stage. Couldn't that film have been shot in this way, with just a handful of people on location?*
K : Yes, it could certainly have been shot on location, although you'd still have needed more than a handful of people to do it.

G : *Would you have done it that way if you were making the film now?*
K : I would have done it at the time if the money to film had been available in America. But as it turned out the only funds I could raise for the film had to be spent in England. There's been such a revolution in Hollywood's treatment of sex over just the past few years that it's easy to forget that when I became interested in *Lolita* a lot of people felt that such a film couldn't be made—or at least couldn't be shown. As it turned out, we didn't have any problems, but there was a lot of fear and trembling. And filming in England we obviously had no choice but to rely mainly on studio shooting.

G : *Obviously* Napoleon *wouldn't permit you to shoot with a small crew and flexible conditions on location. But in the foreseeable future do you see yourself shedding the shell of the studio superstructure and working simply again?*

Paul Mazursky in *Fear and Desire*, Kubrick's first feature, 1953.
(Museum of Modern Art Film Stills Archive)

Elisha Cook Jr., Sterling Hayden, and Jay C. Flippen in *The Killing*, 1956. (National Film Archive, London)

Kirk Douglas in *Paths of Glory*, 1957. (Editor's collection)

Kirk Douglas (foreground) in the title role of *Spartacus*, 1960. (Larry Edmunds Bookshop)

Sue Lyon and James Mason in *Lolita*, 1962. (Museum of Modern Art Film Stills Archive)

Stanley Kubrick (right) directs Sterling Hayden and Peter Sellers in *Dr. Strangelove*, 1964. (Cinemabilia)

An astronaut floats through space in Kubrick's
science-fiction film, *2001: A Space Odyssey*, 1968.
(Musuem of Modern Art Film Stills Archive)

Warren Clarke, Malcolm McDowell, and James Marcus in *A Clockwork Orange*, 1972. (Museum of Modern Art Film Stills Archive)

Ryan O'Neal in *Barry Lyndon*, 1975. (Collectors Book Store)

Jack Nicholson plays a deranged husband threatening his wife (Shelley Duvall) in Kubrick's horror film, *The Shining*, 1980. (Museum of Modern Art Film Stills Archive)

Matthew Modine (right) in *Full Metal Jacket*, 1987. (Collectors Book Store)

Tom Cruise (right) as a physician discussing his recent brush with evil with an associate (Sydney Pollack) in Kubrick's psychological drama, *Eyes Wide Shut*, 1999. (The Kubrick Collection)

K : Yes, if I could find a contemporary story susceptible to such an approach which I liked enough to do. But I would certainly enjoy filming primarily on location. If you have the right story, it's a waste of time and energy to re-create conditions in a studio which exist outside. And if you make sensible arrangements, there are no technical difficulties about location shooting. Sound, which once presented problems, really doesn't anymore, since with skirt mikes you get a favorable voice-to-noise ratio. And in any case, background noise just adds to the verisimilitude of the scene. It's only when you're doing a period film that causes difficulties; in *Napoleon,* for example, I'd hardly want a jet to fly overhead in the middle of the battle of Jena.

G : *Your last film was about the twenty-first century. Your next film is about the nineteenth century. Do you think it's significant that you aren't very interested or satisfied with contemporary stories or themes of twentieth-century life?*
K : It's not a question of my own satisfaction or lack of it, but of the basic purpose of a film, which I believe is one of illumination, of showing the viewer something he can't see any other way. And I think at times this can be best accomplished by staying away from his own immediate environment. This is particularly true when you're dealing in a primarily visual experience, and telling a story through the eyes. You don't find reality only in your own backyard, you know—in fact, sometimes that's the last place you find it. Another asset about dealing with themes that are either futuristic or historic is that it enables you to make a statement with which you're not personally blinded; it removes the environmental blinkers, in a sense, and gives you a deeper and more objective perspective.

G : *In your last genuinely contemporary film,* Lolita, *you were frustrated in your efforts to make the movie as erotic as the novel, and there was some criticism that the girl was too old to play the nymphet of the novel.*
K : She was actually just the right age. Lolita was twelve and a half in the book; Sue Lyon was thirteen. I think some people had a mental picture of a nine-year-old. I would fault myself in one area of the film, however; because of all the pressure over the Production Code and the Catholic Legion of Decency at the time, I believe I didn't sufficiently dramatize the erotic aspect of Humbert's relationship with Lolita, and because his sexual obsession was only barely hinted at, many people guessed too quickly that

Humbert was in love with Lolita. Whereas in the novel this comes as a discovery at the end, when she is no longer a nymphet but a dowdy, pregnant suburban housewife; and it's this encounter, and his sudden realization of his love, that is one of the most poignant elements of the story. If I could do the film over again, I would have stressed the erotic component of their relationship with the same weight Nabokov did. But that is the only major area where I believe the film is susceptible to valid criticism.

G : *At what point did you decide to structure the film so that Humbert is telling the story to the man he's going to shoot?*

K : I discussed this approach with Nabokov at the very outset, and he liked it. One of the basic problems with the book, and with the film even in its modified form, is that the main narrative interest boils down to the question, "Will Humbert get Lolita into bed?" And you find in the book that, despite the brilliant writing, the second half has a drop in narrative interest after he does. We wanted to avoid this problem in the film, and Nabokov and I agreed that if we had Humbert shoot Quilty without explanation at the beginning, then throughout the film the audience would wonder what Quilty was up to. Of course, you obviously sacrifice a great ending by opening with Quilty's murder, but I felt it served a worthwhile purpose.

G : *Starting with* Lolita, *you've been making all your films abroad. Why?*

K : Circumstances have just dictated it that way. As I explained earlier, it was necessary to make *Lolita* in England for financial reasons and to mitigate censorship problems, and in the case of *Dr. Strangelove,* Peter Sellers was in the process of getting a divorce and could not leave England for an extended period, so it was necessary to film there. By the time I decided to do *2001,* I had gotten so acclimated to working in England that it would have been pointless to tear up roots and move everything to America. And with *Napoleon* we'll be doing a great deal of the shooting on the continent, so London is a convenient base of operations.

G : *Are there any specific advantages to working in London?*

K : Next to Hollywood, London is probably the second best place to make a film, because of the degree of technical expertise and facilities you find in England, and that isn't really a backhanded compliment.

G : *Do you have any reluctance to work in Hollywood while the studio chiefs stand over the director's shoulder?*

K : No, because I'm in the fortunate position where I can make a film without that kind of control. Ten years ago, of course, it would have been an entirely different story.

G : *You don't consider yourself an expatriate then?*
K : Not at all.

G : *Why not? You've lived in England seven years and made your last three films there—even those which were set in America.*
K : Yes, but there's nothing permanent about my working and living in England. Circumstances have kept me there until now, but it's quite possible I'll be making a film in America in the future. And in any case, I commute back and forth several times a year.

G : *But always by ocean liner. You have a pilot's license but you don't like flying anymore. Why?*
K : Call it enlightened cowardice, if you like. Actually, over the years I discovered that I just didn't enjoy flying, and I became aware of compromised safety margins in commercial aviation that are never mentioned in airline advertising. So I decided I'd rather travel by sea, and take my chances with the icebergs.

G : *In your profession isn't it a problem not to fly?*
K : It would be if I had to hop about all the time from spot to spot like many people do. But when I'm working on a film I'm tied down to one geographic area for long periods of time and I travel very little. And when I do, I find boats or railroads adequate and more relaxing.

G : Dr. Strangelove *was a particularly word-oriented film, whereas* 2001 *seemed to be a total breakaway from what you'd done before.*
K : Yes, I feel it was. *Strangelove* was a film where much of its impact hinged on the dialogue, the mode of expression, the euphemisms employed. As a result, it's a picture that is largely destroyed in translation or dubbing. *2001*, on the other hand, is basically a visual, nonverbal experience. It avoids intellectual verbalization and reaches the viewer's subconscious in

a way that is essentially poetic and philosophic. The film thus becomes a subjective experience which hits the viewer at an inner level of consciousness, just as music does, or painting.

Actually, film operates on a level much closer to music and to painting than to the printed word, and, of course, movies present the opportunity to convey complex concepts and abstractions without the traditional reliance on words. I think that *2001*, like music, succeeds in short-circuiting the rigid surface cultural blocks that shackle our consciousness to narrowly limited areas of experience and is able to cut directly through to areas of emotional comprehension. In two hours and twenty minutes of film there are only forty minutes of dialogue.

I think one of the areas where *2001* succeeds is in stimulating thoughts about man's destiny and role in the universe in the minds of people who in the normal course of their lives would never have considered such matters. Here again, you've got the resemblance to music; an Alabama truck driver, whose views in every other respect would be extremely narrow, is able to listen to a Beatles record on the same level of appreciation and perception as a young Cambridge intellectual, because their emotions and subconscious are far more similar than their intellects. The common bond is their subconscious emotional reaction; and I think that a film which can communicate on this level can have a more profound spectrum of impact than any form of traditional verbal communication.

The problem with movies is that since the talkies the film industry has historically been conservative and word-oriented. The three-act play has been the model. It's time to abandon the conventional view of the movie as an extension of the three-act play. Too many people over thirty are still word-oriented rather than picture-oriented.

For example, at one point in *2001* Dr. Floyd is asked where he's going and he replies, "I'm going to Clavius," which is a lunar crater. Following that statement you have more than fifteen shots of Floyd's spacecraft approaching and landing on the moon, but one critic expressed confusion because she thought Floyd's destination was a planet named Clavius. Young people, on the other hand, who are more visually oriented due to their new television environment, had no such problems. Kids all know he went to the moon. When you ask how they know they say, "Because we *saw* it."

So you have the problem that some people are only listening and not really paying attention with their eyes. Film is *not* theater—and until that basic lesson is learned I'm afraid we're going to be shackled to the past and miss some of the greatest potentialities of the medium.

G : *Did you deliberately try for ambiguity as opposed to a specific meaning for any scene or image?*
K : No, I didn't have to try for ambiguity; it was inevitable. And I think in a film like *2001,* where each viewer brings his own emotions and perceptions to bear on the subject matter, a certain degree of ambiguity is valuable, because it allows the audience to "fill in" the visual experience themselves. In any case, once you're dealing on a nonverbal level, ambiguity is unavoidable. But it's the ambiguity of all art, of a fine piece of music or a painting—you don't need written instructions by the composer or painter accompanying such works to "explain" them. "Explaining" them contributes nothing but a superficial "cultural" value which has no value except for critics and teachers who have to earn a living. Reactions to art are always different because they are always deeply personal.

G : *The final scenes of the film seemed more metaphorical than realistic. Will you discuss them—or would that be part of the "road map" you're trying to avoid?*
K : No, I don't mind discussing it, on the *lowest* level, that is, straightforward explanation of the plot. You begin with an artifact left on earth four million years ago by extraterrestrial explorers who observed the behavior of the man-apes of the time and decided to influence their evolutionary progression. Then you have a second artifact buried on the lunar surface and programmed to signal word of man's first baby steps into the universe—a kind of cosmic burglar alarm. And finally there's a third artifact placed in orbit around Jupiter and waiting for the time when man has reached the outer rim of his own solar system.

When the surviving astronaut, Bowman, ultimately reaches Jupiter, this artifact sweeps him into a force field or star gate that hurls him on a journey through inner and outer space and finally transports him to another part of the galaxy, where he's placed in a human zoo approximating a hospital terrestrial environment drawn out of his own dreams and imagination. In a timeless state, his life passes from middle age to senescence to death. He is reborn, an enhanced being, a star child, an angel, a superman, if you like, and returns to earth prepared for the next leap forward of man's evolutionary destiny.

That is what happens on the film's simplest level. Since an encounter with an advanced interstellar intelligence would be incomprehensible within our present earthbound frames of reference, reactions to it will have elements of philosophy and metaphysics that have nothing to do with the bare plot outline itself.

G : *What are those areas of meaning?*

K : They are the areas I prefer not to discuss because they are highly subjective and will differ from viewer to viewer. In this sense, the film becomes anything the viewer sees in it. If the film stirs the emotions and penetrates the subconscious of the viewer, if it stimulates, however inchoately, his mythological and religious yearnings and impulses, then it has succeeded.

G : *Why does 2001 seem so affirmative and religious a film? What has happened to the tough, disillusioned, cynical director of* The Killing, Spartacus, Paths of Glory, *and* Lolita, *and the sardonic black humorist of* Dr. Strangelove?

K : The God concept is at the heart of this film. It's unavoidable that it would be, once you believe that the universe is seething with advanced forms of intelligent life. Just think about it for a moment. There are a hundred billion stars in the galaxy and a hundred billion galaxies in the visible universe. Each star is a sun, like our own, probably with planets around them. The evolution of life, it is widely believed, comes as an inevitable consequence of a certain amount of time on a planet in a stable orbit which is not too hot or too cold. First comes chemical evolution — chance rearrangements of basic matter, then biological evolution.

Think of the kind of life that may have evolved on those planets over the millennia, and think, too, what relatively giant technological strides man has made on earth in the six thousand years of his recorded civilization — a period that is less than a single grain of sand in the cosmic hourglass. At a time when man's distant evolutionary ancestors were just crawling out of the primordial ooze, there must have been civilizations in the universe sending out their starships to explore the farthest reaches of the cosmos and conquering all the secrets of nature. Such cosmic intelligences, growing in knowledge over the aeons, would be as far removed from man as we are from the ants. They could be in instantaneous telepathic communication throughout the universe; they might have achieved total mastery over matter so that they can telekinetically transport themselves instantly across billions of light years of space; in their ultimate form they might shed the corporeal shell entirely and exist as a disembodied immortal consciousness throughout the universe.

Once you begin discussing such possibilities, you realize that the religious implications are inevitable, because all the essential attributes of such extraterrestrial intelligences are the attributes we give to God. What we're really dealing with here is, in fact, a scientific definition of God. And if these beings of pure intelligence ever did intervene in the affairs of man, we could only understand it in terms of God or magic, so far removed would their powers be from our own understanding. How would a sentient ant view the foot that crushes his anthill—as the action of another being on a higher evolutionary scale than itself? Or as the divinely terrible intercession of God?

G : *Although 2001 dealt with the first human contact with an alien civilization, we never did actually see an alien, though you communicated through the monoliths an experience of alien beings.*
K : From the very outset of work on the film we all discussed means of photographically depicting an extraterrestrial creature in a manner that would be as mind-boggling as the being itself. And it soon became apparent that you cannot imagine the unimaginable. All you can do is try to represent it in an artistic manner that will convey something of its quality. That's why we settled on the black monolith—which is, of course, in itself something of a Jungian archetype, and also a pretty fair example of "minimal art."

G : *Isn't a basic problem with science fiction films that alien life always looks like some creature from the Black Lagoon, a plastic rubber monster?*
K : Yes, and that's one of the reasons we stayed away from the depiction of biological entities, aside from the fact that truly advanced beings would probably have shed the chrysalis of a biological form at one stage of their evolution. You cannot design a biological entity that doesn't look either overly humanoid or like the traditional bug-eyed monster of pulp science fiction.

G : *The man-ape costumes in 2001 were impressive.*

K : We spent an entire year trying to figure out how to make the ape-heads look convincing, and not just like a conventional makeup job. We finally constructed an entire sub-skull of extremely light and flexible plastic, to which we attached the equivalent of face muscles which pulled the lips back in a normal manner whenever the mouth was opened. The mouth itself took a great deal of work—it had artificial teeth and an artificial tongue which the actors could manipulate with tiny toggles to make the lips snarl in a lifelike fashion. Some of the masks even had built-in devices whereby the artificial muscles in the cheeks and beneath the eyes could be moved. All the apes except for two baby chimps were men, and most of them were dancers or mimes, which enabled them to move a little better than most movie apes.

G : *Was the little girl Dr. Floyd telephoned from the orbital satellite one of your daughters?*

K : Yes, my youngest girl, Vivian. She was six then. We didn't give her any billing, a fact I hope she won't decide to take up with me when she's older.

G : *Why was Martin Balsam's voice as HAL, the computer, redubbed by Douglas Rain the Canadian actor?*

K : Well, we had some difficulty deciding exactly what HAL should sound like, and Marty just sounded a little bit too colloquially American, whereas Rain had the kind of bland mid-Atlantic accent we felt was right for the part.

G : *Some critics have detected in HAL's wheedling voice an undertone of homosexuality. Was that intended?*

K : No. I think it's become something of a parlor game for some people to read that kind of thing into everything they encounter. HAL was a "straight" computer.

G : *Why was the computer more emotional than the human beings?*

K : This was a point that seemed to fascinate some negative critics, who felt that it was a failing of this section of the film that there was more interest in HAL than in the astronauts. In fact, of course, the computer is the central character of this segment of the story. If HAL had been a human being, it would have been obvious to everyone that he had the best part, and was the most interesting character; he took all the initiatives, and all the problems related to and were caused by him.

Some critics seemed to feel that because we were successful in making a voice, a camera lens, and a light come alive as a character this necessarily meant that the human characters failed dramatically. In fact, I believe that Keir Dullea and Gary Lockwood, the astronauts, reacted appropriately and realistically to their circumstances. One of the things we were trying to convey in this part of the film is the reality of a world populated—as ours soon will be—by machine entities who have as much, or more, intelligence as human beings, and who have the same emotional potentialities in their personalities as human beings. We wanted to stimulate people to think what it would be like to share a planet with such creatures.

In the specific case of HAL, he had an acute emotional crisis because he could not accept evidence of his own fallibility. The idea of neurotic computers is not uncommon—most advanced computer theorists believe that once you have a computer which is more intelligent than man and capable of learning by experience, it's inevitable that it will develop an equivalent range of emotional reactions—fear, love, hate, envy, etc. Such a machine could eventually become as incomprehensible as a human being, and could, of course, have a nervous breakdown—as HAL did in the film.

G : *Since* 2001 *is a visual experience, what happened when your collaborator, Arthur C. Clarke, finally put the screenplay down in black and white in the novelization of the film?*
K : It's a totally different kind of experience, of course, and there are a number of differences between the book and the movie. The novel, for example, attempts to explain things much more explicitly than the film does, which is inevitable in a verbal medium. The novel came about after we did a 130-page prose treatment of the film at the very outset. This initial treatment was subsequently changed in the screenplay, and the screenplay in turn was altered during the making of the film. But Arthur took all the existing material, plus an impression of some of the rushes, and wrote the novel. As a result, there's a difference between the novel and the film.

G : *To take one specific, in the novel the black monolith found by curious man-apes three million years ago does explicit things which it doesn't do in the film. In the movie, it has an apparent catalytic effect which enables the ape to discover how to use a bone as a weapon-tool. In the novel, the slab becomes milky and luminous and we're told it's a testing and teaching device used by higher intelligences to determine if the apes are worth helping. Was that in the original screenplay? When was it cut out of the film?*

K : Yes, it was in the original treatment but I eventually decided that to depict the monolith in such an explicit manner would be to run the risk of making it appear no more than an advanced television teaching machine. You can get away with something so literal in print, but I felt that we could create a far more powerful and magical effect by representing it as we did in the film.

G : *Do you feel that the novel, written so explicitly, in some way diminishes the mysterious aspect of the film?*

K : I think it gives you the opportunity of seeing two attempts in two different mediums, print and film, to express the same basic concept and story. In both cases, of course, the treatment must accommodate to the necessities of the medium. I think that the divergencies between the two works are interesting. Actually, it was an unprecedented situation for someone to do an essentially original literary work based on glimpses and segments of a film he had not yet seen in its entirety. In fact, *nobody* saw the film in its final form until eight days before we held the first press screening in April 1968, and the first time I saw the film completed with a proper soundtrack was one week before it opened. I completed the portion of the film in which we used actors in June 1966 and from then until the first week of March 1968 I spent most of my time working on the 205 special effects shots. The final shot was actually cut into the negative at MGM's Hollywood studios only days before the film was ready to open. There was nothing intentional about the fact that the film wasn't shown until the last minute. It just wasn't finished.

G : *Why did you cut scenes from the film after it opened?*

K : I always try to look at a completed film as if I had never seen it before. I usually have several weeks to run the film, alone and with audiences. Only in this way can you judge length. I've always done precisely that with my previous films; for example, after a screening of *Dr. Strangelove* I cut out a final scene in which the Russians and Americans in the War Room engage in a free-for-all fight with custard pies. I decided it was farce and not consistent with the satiric tone of the rest of the film. So there was nothing unusual about the cutting I did on *2001*, except for the eleventh-hour way in which I had to do it.

G : Strangelove *was based on a serious book,* Red Alert. *At what point did you decide to make it a comedy?*

K : I started work on the screenplay with every intention of making the film a serious treatment of the problem of accidental nuclear war. As I kept trying to imagine the way in which things would really happen, ideas kept coming to me which I would discard because they were so ludicrous. I kept saying to myself: "I can't do this. People will laugh." But after a month or so I began to realize that all the things I was throwing out were the things which were most truthful. After all, what could be more absurd than the very idea of two mega-powers willing to wipe out all human life because of an accident, spiced up by political differences that will seem as meaningless to people a hundred years from now as the theological conflicts of the Middle Ages appear to us today?

So it occurred to me that I was approaching the project in the wrong way. The only way to tell the story was as a black comedy or, better, a nightmare comedy, where the things you laugh at most are really the heart of the paradoxical postures that make a nuclear war possible.

Most of the humor in *Strangelove* arises from the depiction of everyday human behavior in a nightmarish situation, like the Russian premier on the hot line who forgets the telephone number of his general staff headquarters and suggests the American President try Omsk information, or the reluctance of a U.S. officer to let a British officer smash open a Coca-Cola machine for change to phone the President about a crisis on the SAC base because of his conditioning about the sanctity of private property.

G : *When you read a book like* Red Alert *which you're interested in turning into a film, do you right away say to yourself, this character should be played by such and such an actor?*

K : Not usually. I first try to define the character fully as he will appear in the film and then try to think of the proper actor to play the role. When

I'm in the process of casting a part I sit down with a list of actors I know. Of course, once you've narrowed the list down to several possibilities for each part then it becomes a question of who's currently available, and how the actor you choose to play one part will affect the people you're considering for other parts.

G : *How do you get a good performance from your actors?*

K : The director's job is to know what emotional statement he wants a character to convey in his scene or his line, and to exercise taste and judgment in helping the actor give his best possible performance. By knowing the actor's personality and gauging his strengths and weaknesses a director can help him to overcome specific problems and realize his potential. But I think this aspect of directing is generally overemphasized. The director's taste and imagination play a much more crucial role in the making of a film. Is it meaningful? Is it believable? Is it interesting? Those are the questions that have to be answered several hundred times a day.

It's rare for a bad performance to result from an actor ignoring everything a director tells him. In fact it's very often just the opposite. After all, the director is the actor's sole audience for the months it takes to shoot a film, and an actor would have to possess supreme self-confidence and supreme contempt for the director to consistently defy his wishes. I think you'll find that most disappointing performances are the mutual fault of both the actor and the director.

G : *Some directors don't let their actors see the daily rushes. Do you?*

K : Yes. I've encountered very few actors who are so insecure or self-destructive that they're upset by the rushes or find their self-confidence undermined. Actually, most actors profit by seeing their rushes and examining them self-critically. In any case, a professional actor who's bothered by his own rushes just won't turn up to see them — particularly in my films, since we run the rushes at lunch time and unless an actor is really interested, he won't cut his lunch to half an hour.

G : *On the first day of shooting on the set, how do you establish that rapport or fear or whatever relationship you want with your actors to keep them in the right frame of mind for the three months you'll be working with them?*

K : Certainly not through fear. To establish a good working relationship I think all the actor has to know is that you respect his talent enough to want him in your film. He's obviously aware of that as long as *you've* hired him and he hasn't been foisted on you by the studio or the producer.

G : *Do you rehearse at all?*
K : There's really a limit to what you can do with rehearsals. They're very useful, of course, but I find that you can't rehearse effectively unless you have the physical reality of the set to work with. Unfortunately, sets are practically never ready until the last moment before you start shooting, and this significantly cuts down on your rehearsal time. Some actors, of course, need rehearsals more than others. Actors are essentially emotion-producing instruments, and some are always tuned and ready while others will reach a fantastic pitch on one take and never equal it again, no matter how hard they try. In *Strangelove,* for example, George Scott could do his scenes equally well take after take, whereas Peter Sellers was always incredibly good on one take, which was never equaled.

G : *At what point do you know what take you're going to use?*
K : On some occasions the take is so obviously superior you can tell immediately. But particularly when you're dealing with dialogue scenes, you have to look them over again and again and select portions of different takes and make the best use of them. The greatest amount of time in editing is this process of studying the takes and making notes and struggling to decide which segments you want to use; this takes ten times more time and effort than the actual cutting, which is a very quick process. Purely visual action scenes, of course, present far less of a problem; it's generally the dialogue scenes, where you've got several long takes printed on each angle on different actors, that are the most time-consuming to cut.

G : *How much cutting are you responsible for, and how much is done by somebody you trust as an editor?*
K : Nothing is cut without me. I'm in there every second, and for all practical purposes I cut my own film; I mark every frame, select each segment, and have everything done exactly the way I want it. Writing, shooting, *and* editing are what you have to do to make a film.

G : *Where did you learn film editing? You started out as a still photographer.*
K : Yes, but after I quit *Look* in 1950—where I had been a staff photographer for five years, ever since I left high school—I took a crack at films

and made two documentaries, *Day of the Fight,* about prize fighter Walter Cartier, and *The Flying Padre,* a silly thing about a priest in the Southwest who flew to his isolated parishes in a small airplane. I did all the work on those two films, and all the work on my first two feature films, *Fear and Desire* and *Killer's Kiss.* I was cameraman, director, editor, assistant editor, sound effects man — you name it, I did it. And it was invaluable experience, because being forced to do everything myself I gained a sound and comprehensive grasp of all the technical aspects of filmmaking.

G : *How old were you when you decided to make movies?*

K : I was around twenty-one. I'd had my job with *Look* since I was seventeen, and I'd always been interested in films, but it never actually occurred to me to make a film on my own until I had a talk with a friend from high school, Alex Singer, who wanted to be a director himself (and has subsequently become one) and had plans for a film version of the *Iliad.* Alex was working as an office boy for The March of Time in those days, and he told me they spent forty thousand dollars making a one-reel documentary. A bit of simple calculation indicated that I could make a one-reel documentary for about fifteen hundred. That's what gave me the financial confidence to make *Day of the Fight.*

I was rather optimistic about expenses; the film cost me thirty-nine hundred. I sold it to RKO-Pathé for four thousand dollars, a hundred-dollar profit. They told me that was the most they'd ever paid for a short. I then discovered that The March of Time itself was going out of business. I made one more short for RKO, *The Flying Padre,* on which I just barely broke even. It was at this point that I formally quit my job at *Look* to work full time on filmmaking. I then managed to raise ten thousand dollars, and shot my first feature film, *Fear and Desire.*

G : *What was your own experience making your first feature film?*

K : *Fear and Desire* was made in the San Gabriel Mountains outside Los Angeles. I was the camera operator and director and just about everything else. Our "crew" consisted of three Mexican laborers who carried all the equipment. The film was shot in 35-mm without a soundtrack and then dubbed by a post-synchronized technique. The dubbing was a big mistake on my part; the actual shooting cost of the film was nine thousand dollars but because I didn't know what I was doing with the soundtrack it cost me another thirty thousand. There were other things I did expensively and foolishly, because I just didn't have enough experience to know the proper and economical approach. *Fear and Desire* played the art house circuits and some of the reviews were amazingly good, but it's not a film I remember with any pride, except for the fact it was finished.

G : *After* Fear and Desire *failed to pay back the investors, how did you get the money to make your next film,* Killer's Kiss?

K : *Fear and Desire* was financed mainly by my friends and relatives, whom I've since paid back, needless to say. Different people gave me backing for *Killer's Kiss,* which also lost half of its forty-thousand-dollar budget. I've subsequently repaid those backers also. After *Killer's Kiss* I met Jim Harris, who was interested in getting into films, and we formed a production company together. Our first property was *The Killing,* based on Lionel White's story "The Clean Break." This time we could afford good actors, such as Sterling Hayden, and a professional crew. The budget was larger than the earlier films—$320,000—but still very low for a Hollywood production. Our next film was *Paths of Glory,* which nobody in Hollywood wanted to do at all, even though we had a very low budget. Finally Kirk Douglas saw the script and liked it. Once he agreed to appear in the film United Artists was willing to make it.

G : *How'd you get that great performance out of Douglas?*

K : A director can't get anything out of an actor that he doesn't already have. You can't start an acting school in the middle of making a film. Kirk is a good actor.

G : *What did you do after* Paths of Glory?

K : I did two scripts that no one wanted. A year went by and my finances were rather rocky. I received no salary for *The Killing* or *Paths of Glory* but had worked on one hundred percent deferred salary—and since the films didn't make any money, I had received nothing from either of them. I subsisted on loans from my partner, Jim Harris. Next I spent six months working on a screenplay for a Western, *One-Eyed Jacks,* with Marlon Brando and Calder Willingham. Our relationship ended amicably a few weeks before Marlon began directing the film himself. By the time I had left Brando I had spent two years doing nothing. At this point, I was hired to direct *Spartacus* with Kirk Douglas. It was the only one of my films over which I did not have complete control; although I was the director, mine was only one of many voices to which Kirk listened. I am disappointed in the film. It had everything but a good story.

G : *What do you consider the director's role?*
K : A director is a kind of idea and taste machine; a movie is a series of creative and technical decisions, and it's the director's job to make the right decisions as frequently as possible. Shooting a movie is the worst milieu for creative work ever devised by man. It is a noisy, physical apparatus; it is difficult to concentrate—and you have to do it from eight-thirty to six-thirty, five days a week. It's not an environment an artist would ever choose to work in. The only advantage it has is that you must do it, and you can't procrastinate.

G : *How did you learn to actually* make *the films, since you'd had no experience?*
K : Well, my experience in photography was very helpful. For my two documentaries I'd used a small 35-mm hand camera called an Eyemo, a daylight loading camera which was very simple to operate. The first time I used a Mitchell camera was on *Fear and Desire*. I went to the Camera Equipment Company, at 1600 Broadway, and the owner, Bert Zucker, spent a Saturday morning showing me how to load and operate it. So that was the extent of my formal training in movie camera technique.

G : *As a beginner, you mean you just walked cold into a rental outfit and had them give you a cram course in using movie equipment?*
K : Bert Zucker, who has subsequently been killed in an airline crash, was a young man, in his early thirties, and he was very sympathetic. Anyway, it was a sensible thing for them to do. I was paying for the equipment. At that time I also learned how to do cutting. Once somebody showed me how to use a Movieola and synchronizer and how to make a splice I had no trouble at all. The technical fundamentals of moviemaking are not difficult.

G : *What kind of movies did you go to in those days?*
K : I used to want to see almost anything. In fact, the bad films were what really encouraged me to start out on my own. I'd keep seeing lousy films

and saying to myself, "I don't know anything about moviemaking but I *couldn't* do anything worse than this."

G : *You had technical skills and audacity, but what made you think you could get a good performance out of an actor?*
K : Well, in the beginning I really didn't get especially good performances, either in *Fear and Desire* or *Killer's Kiss*. They were both amateurish films. But I did learn a great deal from making them, experience which helped me greatly in my subsequent films. The best way to learn is to do—and this is something few people manage to get the opportunity to try. I was also helped a great deal by studying Stanislavski's books, as well as an excellent book about him, *Stanislavski Directs*, which contains a great deal of highly illustrative material on how he worked with actors. Between those books and the painful lessons I learned from my own mistakes I accumulated the basic experience needed to start to do good work.

G : *Did you also read film theory books?*
K : I read Eisenstein's books at the time, and to this day I still don't really understand them. The most instructive book on film aesthetics I came across was Pudovkin's *Film Technique,* which simply explained that editing was the aspect of the film art form which was completely unique, and which separated it from all other art forms. The ability to show a simple action like a man cutting wheat from a number of angles in a brief moment, to be able to see it in a special way not possible except through film—that this is what it was all about. This is obvious, of course, but it's so important it cannot be too strongly stressed. Pudovkin gives many clear examples of how good film editing enhances a scene, and I would recommend his book to anyone seriously interested in film technique.

G : *But you weren't impressed by Eisenstein's books. What do you think of his films?*
K : Well, I have a mixed opinion. Eisenstein's greatest achievement is the beautiful visual composition of his shots, and his editing. But as far as content is concerned, his films are silly, his actors are wooden and operatic. I sometimes suspect that Eisenstein's acting style derives from his desire to keep the actors framed within his compositions for as long as possible; they move very slowly, as if under water. Interesting to note, a lot of his

work was being done concurrently with Stanislavski's work. Actually, anyone seriously interested in comparative film techniques should study the differences in approach of two directors, Eisenstein and Chaplin. Eisenstein is all form and no content, whereas Chaplin is content and no form. Of course, a director's style is partly the result of the manner in which he imposes his mind on the semicontrollable conditions that exist on any given day — the responsiveness and talent of actors, the realism of the set, time factors, even weather.

G : *You've been quoted as saying that Max Ophuls's films fascinated you when you were starting out as a director.*
K : Yes, he did some brilliant work. I particularly admired his fluid camera techniques. I saw a great many films at that time at the Museum of Modern Art and in movie theaters, and I learned far more by seeing films than from reading heavy tomes on film aesthetics.

G : *If you were nineteen and starting out again, would you go to film school?*
K : The best education in film is to make one. I would advise any neophyte director to try to make a film by himself. A three-minute short will teach him a lot. I know that all the things I did at the beginning were, in microcosm, the things I'm doing now as a director and producer. There are a lot of noncreative aspects to filmmaking which have to be overcome, and you will experience them all when you make even the simplest film: business, organization, taxes, etc., etc. It is rare to be able to have uncluttered, artistic environment when you make a film, and being able to accept this is essential.

The point to stress is that anyone seriously interested in making a film should find as much money as he can as quickly as he can and go out and do it. And this is no longer as difficult as it once was. When I began making movies as an independent in the early 1950s I received a fair amount of publicity because I was something of a freak in an industry dominated by a handful of huge studios. Everyone was amazed that it could be done at all. But anyone can make a movie who has a little knowledge of cameras and tape recorders, a lot of ambition and — hopefully — talent. It's gotten down to the pencil and paper level. We're really on the threshold of a revolutionary new era in film.

Mind's Eye: *A Clockwork Orange*

JOHN HOFSESS/1971

SHORTLY BEFORE THE OPENING engagements of *A Clockwork Orange*, I travelled to Borehamwood, outside London, to have lunch with Stanley Kubrick. The man I met—soft-spoken, wide ranging in his reading and interests, immediately accessible and friendly—was just the outer edges of the man who directed *Lolita, Dr. Strangelove* and *2001: A Space Odyssey.* It takes years of close acquaintance before one can write authoritatively about an artist. I had only six hours of conversation.

Kubrick takes a dim view of the current craze that would make opiates the religion of the masses. Yet he knows that a good part of *2001*'s popularity stems from an advertising campaign that heralded the film as "the ultimate trip" and which encouraged people to see it stoned. He knows that he has become a cult figure—irrationally liked and promoted as a "mind-blower," and irrationally disliked and denigrated by those sceptical of any mass media cult. The controversies surrounding his films are noisy and mindless but they serve a purpose: they publicize his films. It is my guess that the career of Orson Welles is not lost on Kubrick: who wants to be known as an unemployed genius—making *Citizen Kane* when you're twenty-six, and narrating Eastern Airlines "Wings of Man" commercials when you're fifty-seven? Welles is generally revered by critics, while Kubrick is treated as a Goliath that must be slain.

"Have you ever read a critic who taught you anything new about your films?" I asked him.

From *Take One*, May/June 1971. Reprinted by permission.

"No," came the quick reply. "Very few critics work carefully, thoughtfully enough. To see a film once and write a review is an absurdity."

"Are there no critics who work at their jobs as diligently as a film director does?" I asked.

"I don't think any of them could possibly take as much trouble to write a review as we take to make a film," he replied, "but maybe it doesn't take *that* much trouble. Unfortunately the reviews that distinguish most critics are bad reviews, which are easy to write and fun to write but are absolutely useless."

"Do critics have any measurable influence at the box office?"

"The only way a picture sustains itself—because advertising only affects a week or so of a film's initial receipts—is by people saying with enough emphasis to their friends, you *must* see it. There is no movie-going habit of any size any more, and a film has to overcome a lot of inertia to make people interested in going out to see it. Critics only appear to have importance when their views coincide with those of the audience."

Kubrick's films require large budgets. Ten million for *2001*. Two and a half million for *A Clockwork Orange*. His next projects—a film about Napoleon and an adaptation of Arthur Schnitzler's *A Dream Novel*—require substantial sums. Most directors never successfully resolve the dilemma of wanting to be artists and needing to be popular. A distressing aspect of intellectual and artistic growth is that it principally means *outgrowing* other people: there are progressively fewer people to share one's ideas, and who understand, without over-simplification, what one is trying to communicate.

Kubrick's solution is "ambiguity." A film-goer is obliged to understand a great deal more of Ingmar Bergman's *Persona* or *The Passion of Anna* before realizing their worth than he does of *Dr. Strangelove* or *2001*. Kubrick makes his films so that they can be enjoyed superficially *or* in depth. In so doing he greatly broadens the spectrum of viewers who like *something* in his work. Bergman's films don't offer the public this option. Either you respond with a full, complex understanding or else you become baffled and bored. In Kubrick's view: "The emotions of people are far more similar than their intellects. The common bond is their subconscious emotional reaction. Watching a film is like having a daydream. It operates on portions of your mind that are only reached by dreams or dramas, and there you can explore things without any responsibility of conscious ego or conscience."

"*A Clockwork Orange* asks provocative questions to which there are no easy answers," I remarked. "Do you anticipate that violent behaviour will be a growing problem in the future?"

"Yes, especially by those who fail to appreciate the realities of a complex society," he replied. "There is an accelerating erosion of any kind of mystique which authority may have once had, and an over-awareness of the romantic concept of rebellion. Mind you I don't regard *A Clockwork Orange* as being primarily or even significantly, a topical, social story. I use Alex to explore an aspect of the human personality. He does things which one knows are wrong, and yet you find yourself being taken in by him and accepting his frame of reference. As in a dream, the film demands a suspension of moral judgment.".

"Are you as dark visioned about man as your films appear to indicate?" I asked. "Is hope only possible in the world of *2001* with its white, clean, aesthetically perfect environment in which virtually all human problems have been removed?"

"A satirist is someone who has a very skeptical, pessimistic view of human nature," he replied, "but who still has the optimism to make some sort of joke out of it. However brutal the joke might be."

Kubrick's films are filled with tension. He knows that life is a constant struggle between creative and destructive impulses, between people who build and those who destroy. "We are such rapacious creatures," he remarked. "How many trees have to be chopped down to give one individual all the newspapers he uses in a lifetime? How many animals have to be killed to feed him? How much of the earth's precious and limited mineral resources are consumed to give him his technological comforts? And for what? What does man ever give back?" The answer, in most cases, is "Nothing." With Kubrick, the answer is the triumph of art.

Kubrick Country

PENELOPE HOUSTON/1971

STANLEY KUBRICK LIVES JUST north of London, in filmmaking territory; the Elstree Studios and the old MGM Studios at Borehamwood are both just around the corner, not much farther away than a Jack Nicklaus drive. Kubrick has made all his films in Britain since *Lolita* (1961); but in a remarkable way he has kept himself apart from all worlds, appearing neither as an expatriate American filmmaker nor as a resident British director. From *Lolita* on, his films have been set in Kubrick country.

After *2001: A Space Odyssey* (1968), Kubrick had intended to make a film about Napoleon and had advanced some considerable way toward the project when it was postponed in the wake of studio retrenchments and nervousness about big-budget commitments. He turned instead to *A Clockwork Orange,* Anthony Burgess's tour de force of identification with Alex, the ultimate teenager. Part of the attraction of the novel for Kubrick was obviously its language, the Russian-based argot that Burgess's called Nadsat. But, interestingly, it also strikes one as in a sense his first English film. *Lolita* almost consciously played down the American landscape aspects of Nabokov's novel; *Dr. Strangelove* and *2001* were both international movies that could have been made in any country with the filmmaking resources. The satire of *A Clockwork Orange,* however, seems specifically English in its lines of attack. Stanley Kubrick himself hardly reacts to questions along these lines, preferring to suggest that he has simply filmed an English novel on London locations, and that equivalents for most of the

From *Saturday Review,* 25 December 1971. Reprinted by permission of the Kubrick Estate.

characters could be found in America or anywhere else. Perhaps—but the impression persists that Kubrick country has acquired an English province.

HOUSTON: *Did you read Anthony Burgess's book when it first came out in 1962?*

KUBRICK: I first read the book about two-and-a-half years ago. It was given to me by Terry Southern while I was making *2001*, and due to the time pressure I was in, it joined that certain number of books that one has sitting on the shelf waiting to be read. Then one evening I passed the bookshelf, glanced at the paperback still patiently waiting on the shelf, and picked it up. I started to read the book and finished it in one sitting. By the end of Part One, it seemed pretty obvious that it might make a great film. By the end of Part Two, I was *very* excited about it. As soon as I finished it, I immediately reread it. For the next two or three days, I reread it in whole and in part, and did little else but think about it. It seemed to me to be a unique and marvelous work of imagination and perhaps even genius. The narrative invention was magical, the characters were bizarre and exciting, the ideas were brilliantly developed, and, equally important, the story was of a size and density that could be adapted to film without oversimplifying it or stripping it to the bones. In fact, it proved possible to retain most of the narrative in the film. Many people have praised the special language of the book, which is itself a stunning conception; but I don't think sufficient praise has been given for what might be called, for want of a better phrase, the ordinary language, which is, of course, quite extraordinary. For example, when the Minister says at the end of his speech to the press, "But enough of words. Actions speak louder than. Action now. Observe all," Burgess is doing something with language that is really marvelous.

HOUSTON: *Both your last two films involved you in a great deal of research and background reading. It looks here as though you had filmed the novel fairly straight, but did you in fact do research around the edges of the film—the brain-washing technique, for instance?*

KUBRICK: Some of my films have started with the accumulating of facts, and from the facts narrative ideas seemed to develop, but of course *A Clockwork Orange* started with a finished story, and I was quite happy to skip the birth pangs of developing an original narrative. As far as technical research is concerned, there obviously wasn't a great deal required. I had certainly read about behavioral psychology and conditioned-reflex therapy, and that was about all that was required in terms of any serious technical background for the story.

HOUSTON: *The shock in the book is when Alex gets to prison, and he says something like, "I'd done all this, and I was fifteen." I don't imagine it could ever work on the screen, but did you even think of casting someone as young as that in the part?*

KUBRICK: No. I had Malcolm McDowell in mind right from the third or fourth chapter of my first reading of the book. One doesn't find actors of his genius in all shapes, sizes, and ages. Nor does an actor find many characters like Alex, who is certainly one of the most surprising and enjoyable inventions of fiction. I can think of only one other literary or dramatic comparison, and that is with Richard III. Alex, like Richard, is a character whom you should dislike and fear, and yet you find yourself drawn very quickly into his world and find yourself seeing things through his eyes. It's not easy to say how this is achieved, but it certainly has something to do with his candor and wit and intelligence, and the fact that all the other characters are lesser people, and in some way worse people.

HOUSTON: *The Richard III comparison is superb, but of course with Richard you are safely in the past. There aren't all the immediate associations your audience is going to have with contemporary violence.*

KUBRICK: I don't think there's anything to be concerned about here. There is a very wide gulf between reality and fiction, and when one is looking at a film the experience is much closer to a dream than anything else. In this daydream, if you like, one can explore ideas and situations which one is not able to do in reality. One could obviously not enjoy the activities of Richard III if one were actually involved with them, but we *do* enjoy Richard III—and so with Alex.

Alex's adventures are a kind of psychological myth. Our subconscious finds release in Alex, just as it finds release in dreams. It resents Alex being stifled and repressed by authority, however much our conscious mind recognizes the necessity of doing this. The structure of the story is very much like a fairy tale inasmuch as it depends for much of its charm and many of its strong effects on coincidence, and in the symmetry of its plot wherein each of Alex's victims appears again in the final section to deliver retribution. Of course, the story functions on another level, as a social satire dealing with the question of whether behavioral psychology and psychological conditioning are dangerous new weapons for a totalitarian government to use to impose vast controls on its citizens and turn them into little more than robots.

HOUSTON: *How about the stylization of the violence? A lot of it is very funny, and what actually happens to Alex, in the brainwashing sequence, is much more unpleasant to watch than what he does to anyone else.*
KUBRICK: Well, of course, the violence in the film is stylized, just as it is in the book. My problem, of course, was to find a way of presenting it in the film without benefit of the writing style. The first section of the film that incorporates most of the violent action is principally organized around the Overture to Rossini's *Thieving Magpie,* and, in a very broad sense, you could say that the violence is turned into dance, although, of course, it is in no way any kind of formal dance. But in cinematic terms, I should say that movement and music must inevitably be related to dance, just as the rotating space station and the docking Orion space ship in *2001* moved to *The Blue Danube.* From the rape on the stage of the derelict casino, to the superfrenzied fight, through the Christ figures cut, to Beethoven's Ninth, the slow-motion fight on the water's edge, and the encounter with the cat lady where the giant white phallus is pitted against the bust of Beethoven, movement, cutting, and music are the principal considerations—dance?

HOUSTON: *And the use of speeded-up motion, in the scene with the two girls Alex picks up at the drugstore?*
KUBRICK: Yes, of course, I forgot to mention the high-speed orgy. This scene lasts about forty seconds on the screen and, at two frames per second, took twenty-eight minutes to shoot. I had the idea one night while listening to *Eine kleine Nachtmusik.* The vision of an orgy suggested itself, shot at two frames per second. As it worked out in the film, though, the fast movement of *William Tell* was more suitable to the purpose of the scene.

HOUSTON: *In the book, every impression comes to you through Alex's language, through the language Burgess invented. In the film, of course, one's mind*

switches off the language except when Alex and his droogs are actually talking.
What did you feel about the words?

KUBRICK: Well, I think that the special language in the book is certainly
one of Burgess's most novel inventions. The words have the advantage of
being real words, mostly Russian-based, which are spelled out in phonetic
English, specially enhanced by Burgess's wit. Because they are real words,
they have an onomatopoetic connection with their meanings. Tolchock
sounds like a blow, devotchka evokes a female image, etc.

HOUSTON: *How much of the film was shot on location, and how did you find*
the places?

KUBRICK: The only sets in the film were the Korova Milkbar, the prison
reception area, a mirrored bathroom, and a mirrored hall at the writer's
house. These were built because we couldn't find any suitable locations.
All the remaining scenes were done on location. I tried to be systematic
about the location search. We wanted to find interesting modern architecture; and it seemed that the best way to do this was to buy ten years of
back issues of two or three architectural magazines. I spent two weeks
going through them with John Barry, the production designer, and we
carefully filed and cross-referenced all of the interesting photographs that
we found. This proved to be a much more effective approach than just
having a couple of location scouts driving around London. As it worked
out, most of the interesting locations we finally chose originated from this
sifting through of the architectural magazines.

The exteriors of Alex's flat block were filmed at Thamesmead, the largest
and most interesting architectural project in London. The striking audito-
rium, at which the press conference is held, is in a library in South
Norwood. The author's house is actually two houses: The exterior was
filmed in Oxfordshire and the interior at Radlett. A certain amount of
filming was done at Brunel University. The record boutique was filmed at
the Chelsea Drugstore. It's very simple now filming in even the most confined interiors. One has a very wide choice of fast, wide-angle lenses to
choose from. For example, in the record boutique we shot with a 9.8 mm
lens, which has a ninety-degree viewing angle. Another lens, the very fast
10.95, made it possible to shoot with natural light in room interiors, late
into the afternoon. It allows you to shoot in two hundred percent less
light than the normal 1.2 movie lenses.

HOUSTON: *Still on the shooting, is it true that there is practically no post-synchronized dialogue in the film?*

KUBRICK: There was no post-synchronizing of dialogue at all. Unusable sync-dialogue used to be one of the problems of shooting on location, but it is no longer a problem with the equipment now available. There is a tremendous range of special microphones to choose from, including one the size of a paper clip which can be hidden in the shot or on the actor, and which results in a very favorable voice-to-noise ratio. With FM transmitters, also hidden on the actor, it's no longer necessary to use cumbersome microphone booms. Each actor can have his own concealed microphone transmitting its signal via a pocket-sized FM transmitter to a receiver, which feeds it into a portable sound mixer. We filmed the scene where Alex is recognized by the tramp under the Albert Bridge. The traffic noise was so loud that you had to shout in order to be heard. But we recorded a dialogue track where the voices were so above the traffic that it was necessary to add quite a lot of traffic noise on the final sound mix.

The special mikes also made it possible to shoot sound takes under certain conditions without even blimping the camera. I did quite a few handheld shots with the Arriflex merely wrapped in an Anorak, sometimes as close as six feet away from the actors, but you don't hear the camera noise, and the dialogue is fine. On interiors, I had a lightweight blimp for the Arriflex which weighed only thirty-seven pounds with the camera in it. One has to compare this to a Mitchell camera, which weighs about one hundred twenty-five pounds. As far as lighting is concerned, the secret of location lighting is to make sure that the practical lamps that you see in the scene are actually lighting the scene. The convention of film lighting in the past was such that the practical lamps were just props, and although the bulb was on it did nothing actually to light the shot. In this case, I went to a great deal of trouble in selecting useful and interesting-looking lamps into which we could put photofloods or small quartz lights.

The lights that you see in the scene are almost always the only source of lighting that's being used. This also makes it possible to shoot 360-degree pans without worrying about photographing any of the normal studio lights. I might add, it's also very fast to work this way.

HOUSTON: *How much do you preplan scenes? You don't do the Hitchcockian kind of detailed advance planning?*

KUBRICK: I do a tremendous amount of planning and try to anticipate everything that is humanly possible to imagine prior to shooting the scene, but when the moment actually comes, it is always different. Either you discover new ideas in the scene, or one of the actors by some aspect of his personality has changed something—or any one of a thousand things that fail to coincide with one's preconceived notions of the scene. This is, of course, the most crucial time of a film. The actual shooting of a scene, once you know what you are going to do, is relatively simple. But it is here that the picture always hangs in the balance. The problem, expressed perhaps a bit too simply, is to make sure that something happens worth putting on film. It is always tempting to think of *how* you're going to film something before you know what it is you're going to film, but it's almost always a waste of time.

HOUSTON: *Alex is the only great character—almost the only developed character—in* A Clockwork Orange. *In* 2001 *the most human character is of course HAL, the computer, and in* Dr. Strangelove *you are dealing with degrees of caricature. I suppose one could go back in your work to* Paths of Glory, *or even* The Killing, *to find a film where you were working in what might be called a realistic convention.*

KUBRICK: I have always enjoyed dealing with a slightly surrealistic situation and presenting it in a realistic manner. I've always liked fairy tales and myths, magical stories, supernatural stories, ghost stories, surrealistic and allegorical stories. I think they are somehow closer to the sense of reality one feels today than the equally stylized "realistic" story in which a great deal of selectivity and omission has to occur in order to preserve its "realistic" style. In *Lolita,* for example, the character of Quilty is straight out of a nightmare, as are many of the characters in *Dr. Strangelove.* In this sense *A Clockwork Orange* bears strong resemblance to several of my previous films.

HOUSTON: *What about your Napoleon film? Is that still going to be made, and on what sort of a scale are you planning to deal with his life?*

KUBRICK: I plan to do *Napoleon* next. It will be a big film but certainly not on the scale that big films had grown to just before the lights went out in Hollywood. Most of the palatial interiors can be shot in real locations in France where the furniture and set dressing are already there, and one has only to move in with a small documentary-size crew, actors, wardrobe, and some hand props. The large crowd and battle scenes would be done in Yugoslavia, Hungary, or Rumania, where undertakings of this sort can be accomplished by using regular army formations.

HOUSTON: *What motivates your choice of subjects?*

KUBRICK: Well, of course, this is obviously the most important decision ever made with respect to a film. Actually, the only sensible thing I can say is that I'm very, very careful about this. And so far, at least, I've never found myself wondering halfway through why I had decided to do the film. A great narrative is a kind of miracle. It's not something that can be forced. At the same time, I trust that I shall never be tempted to become an alchemist and believe that I can turn lead into gold. I might try to make something of an imperfect story with my efforts as a writer, but I would never attempt a film story that I was not finally in love with.

Kubrick's Creative Concern

GENE SISKEL/1972

THE STORIES ABOUT STANLEY Kubrick's fierce, some say compulsive, attention to detail are legion.

At a party here last week I met actor Clive Francis who has one scene of perhaps five minutes in Kubrick's ninth and latest feature film, *A Clockwork Orange.*

In the scene, Alex, the happy-go-violent hero of the movie, has been released from prison and, through a scientific aversion therapy program, rid of his preference for rape and plunder. Returning home to his mum and dad after a four-year absence, Alex finds an interloper. His parents have taken in a lodger [the part played by Francis] and put him up in Alex's room. Alex wants him out, but the lodger is not easily moved.

"He's amazing," said Francis of Kubrick. "We rehearsed that scene for two weeks. Kubrick searched all over London for the right apartment. He finally found one in Elstree [a northern suburb]. After he paid off and kicked out the couple that were living in it, he brought in his designer and together they completely redecorated it with tacky, futuristic furnishings at a cost of about 5,000 pounds [$13,000].

"After we had completed shooting, and the apartment had been restored to its original condition and returned to the couple, I got a call from Kubrick. He wanted to re-shoot two close-ups.

"We went back to the apartment in Elstree. The couple was again paid off and kicked out and Kubrick again had the apartment completely redecorated.

"That couple must be relieved to see the film finally released," someone else said.

But stories such as this don't really prepare one for the experience of meeting Kubrick. He has had a string of enormously successful films — *Paths of Glory, Lolita, Dr. Strangelove,* and *2001: A Space Odyssey* — and one reasonably expects him to be an impatient tyrant.

Not so.

Kubrick enters a restaurant near his home in suburban Borehamwood without fanfare. There is no press agent with him. His dress is a study in contrast. He is wearing a blazer with an ascot, topped by cheap, olive drab parka, the kind that was popular here about fifteen years ago. A scruffy beard rings his chin. Bronx-born, his accent is decidedly American. He is forty-three years old, yet his voice is surprisingly young and soft, sounding very much like Warren Beatty's, and it lacks authority. That is to say, Kubrick's authority comes from what he says, not how he says it.

Before I could start my tape recorder, he began saying how he hopes the article I will write will turn out. Once a director...

He says he doesn't want it to contain only or primarily his words. If that is the case, he explains, it will turn out to be like an article *he* had neglected to write and now had hastily conceived.

He stresses he does not want two or more of his answers strung together for the sake of reading simplicity. If that is done, he explains, it will leave the reader with the impression that Kubrick has logorrhea.

Furthermore, he asks if I had been informed [I had] that he wants to edit any quotes of his I plan to use. It's not so much that he doesn't want to be caught making an untoward remark, he explains, it is that he cares about what he says. [The changes he made bear that out.]

All of this is being said to me in the most pleasant of voices, and yet it has impact. He is informed. He knows the interviewing process. And this prologue, as I later learned, is an example of what he calls "problem avoidance techniques."

Because Kubrick has speculated about threats to man's existence in each of his last three films [a fail-safe system that fails in *Dr. Strangelove*; a computer that lies in *2001: A Space Odyssey*; and scientists tinkering with the human personality in *A Clockwork Orange*], and because it is well-known that Kubrick is interested in things scientific, one is inclined to ask him "big questions," the answers to which may or may not relate to his films.

More to the point, if Kubrick was afraid of something new, I wanted to know about it.

And so, the first question.

What are you concerned about in the way the world is? What troubles you? It would grow out of your choosing Anthony Burgess's novel, A Clockwork Orange, *that you are concerned about experimentation with the human mind.*
"First of all, I don't choose stories as political tracts. The fact that Burgess's novel happens to be about something that now happens to be particularly topical—behavioral psychology and the conditioning of antisocial behavior, with its particular relevance to [psychologist B. F.] Skinner's book, *Beyond Freedom and Dignity*—is really just a part of what my interest was in *A Clockwork Orange*.

"What attracted me to the book was its qualities as a work of art. Essentially, that's what attracts me to stories for films. I don't start by saying, 'What am I concerned about, and where can I find a story that relates to that?'"

Well, I do get the feeling from your films that you are concerned about where the world is going, so I'll ask the question directly: What worries you now?
"That's such a vast question. . . . Certainly one thing which relates to the story [*A Clockwork Orange*] is the question of how authority can cope with problems of law and order without becoming too oppressive, and, more particularly, in relation to the ever-increasing view that politics are irrelevant to the solution of social problems, that there's no time for political and legal solutions, that social issues have to be solved immediately even if this means going outside law and politics.

"What solutions authority may evolve certainly concerns me, and is one of the great unanswered social problems."

It has been suggested a principal cause of our society's impatience in solving complex social problems is that on television and in the movies we see complex social problems solved in thirty, sixty, or one hundred minutes. Do you agree?

"I would say it's probably more due to pie-in-the-sky political promises about ushering in new eras that have created this mood. That and the intense over-communication of ideas which contributes to this feeling that if a problem can't be solved in a very short time one shouldn't attempt political or legal solutions but more radical or antisocial or extralegal solutions."

But every politician seems to be compelled to make campaign promises, and the media is similarly compelled to report them. Isn't this trend, then, irreversible?
"No, I don't think it's irreversible, but it needs a great politician who has enough charm and intelligence and character to get elected and still talk realistically to the people."

But is the electorate intelligent enough to elect someone like that?
"I would say it would depend to a great extent on the individual because most elections are decided on the personalities of the candidates rather than on issues. It's rare where there's a clear major issue which decides the election. I don't think it's impossible, but I don't see that person on the [United States] political horizon."

Maybe what I'm really after is how you see the world ending, how you see social order dissolving into chaos?
"I think the danger is not that authority will collapse, but that, finally, in order to preserve itself, it [established authority] will become very repressive. Law and order is not a phony issue, not just an excuse for the Right to go further right.

"Obviously it is a problem in a city like New York where people feel very unsafe. One of the things you expect from society when you surrender your rights as an individual is safety and a comfortable material life. As soon as society cannot guarantee safety, people eventually will become very disturbed and they may make some extremely irrational choices, leaning toward more authority of a much tougher kind.

"I don't think people can indefinitely tolerate the kind of emotional uncertainty that being unsafe creates."

Along these lines, I've been thinking that we may be moving toward an eerie point in social progress where all disease is preventable or curable and the only

way in which people will die is by crime or accident. Do you see something like that coming up?
"Biological immortality is something that we'll probably have in one hundred years, maybe one hundred-fifty years. There will be rejuvenation of cells and no aging. You'll probably have cell banks where even if you are totally destroyed you can be reconstituted from a patch of skin from your big toe.

[It is for information such as this that one asks Kubrick "big questions." One other thing. He added "from a patch of skin from your big toe" in his editing. Constantly revising is the way he works in the movies too, and this example shows, I think, its salutory effect].
"This will add to the problem of population control, but this is just another social problem for which we can find solutions.

    "On the other hand, I think a lot of the problems of the human condition derive from an awareness of our own mortality. This is the curse of intelligence and language.

    "No other creature except man has to deal with it. It results in the view: 'Okay, I may be happy right now, but am I really doing what will make me the happiest? And, even if I am, will I still be happy tomorrow? And I better make the most of it because it's all going, and so forth.'

    "This produces a lot of despair and manic solutions and at least will be gone when we're all immortal."

Have you made any preparations for preserving your own body?
"No. . . . Only because they haven't developed anything which seems realistic—but I have hopes."

    This was the ending of the first section of our conversation. Upon re-reading it, I find two points of interest.
    In his response to the question about what worries him, he selects an answer which he says "relates to the story."
    Because for the last year he has been dealing with the movie and not the book—indeed, that morning, and many previous mornings and many mornings to come, he was and would be checking each of the key release prints of the film for the sound and color quality—I would have thought he would have said, "which relates to the *movie*."

The explanation is obvious. Movies, for Kubrick, are principally picture stories. His exceptional films are conventional in that they build toward climaxes and make use of editing techniques.

But what about *2001*, you say? Wasn't that something completely different? Kubrick got into that when I began asking him what changes he would like to see in the mentality of the moviegoing audience.

"I always revert back to E. M. Forster's *Aspects of the Novel* where he tells about the first caveman telling his friends a story as they sit around a fire. They either fell asleep, threw a rock at him, or listened.

"The problem obviously is you've got to make people pay attention long enough to get across what you've got to say.

"Most films don't have any purpose other than to mechanically figure out what people want and to construct some artificial form of entertainment for them. Even when this is the sole purpose it rarely succeeds."

So it really comes back to the craft of the filmmaker rather than the intelligence of the audience?
"Well, it comes back to somehow, by narrative or surprise or whatever it is that you've got to keep their interest for more than fifteen or twenty minutes, which is about as long as you can keep it if no narrative or major character interest develops."

Did that affect your construction of 2001, *specifically the opening passages?*
"It affects everything I do. I mean *2001* is really four short stories, all told with short story narratives.

"I was surprised when people said they thought *2001* didn't have a story. Each episode is a great short story."

There is another theme that runs through Kubrick's answers to the questioning about man's fate. Twice he indicates his concern about mankind making "irrational choices" and "manic solutions." Kubrick says this may happen when people feel unsafe and when they consider their own mortality.

Here, I think, is an excellent distillation of the problems of contemporary man. The '40s and '50s brought us The Bomb and the '60s brought us Law and Order. Maybe, in fact, the only reason people seem less concerned about inhaling fallout from an atomic blast is that they are too busy thinking about getting hit over the head with a blackjack when they leave their homes?

Dr. Strangelove was Kubrick's superb movie about The Bomb, and I think, *A Clockwork Orange* is his equally superb movie about Law and Order.

Violence in movies is "hot copy" in Great Britain. Film critics are writing about it; politicians are investigating it.

Two movies—both parables, set in England, and directed by Americans—have sparked the controversy: Sam Peckinpah's *Straw Dogs* and Stanley Kubrick's *A Clockwork Orange*.

But Kubrick's picture, because of his reputation and the film's commercial and critical success, was in the spotlight.

Home Secretary Reginald Maulding asked the local office of Warner Bros. for a special screening to determine if British censors were correct in letting the film be shown intact. Maulding said he does not object to total nudity on the screen but is worried by "anything which could contribute to violence in Britain."

In *A Clockwork Orange*, set in England in the very near future, teenage gangs run amok, raping, stealing, and plundering at will. The central figure is a young gang leader named Alex who lands in jail and is set free to participate in a scientific aversion therapy program, the Ludovico Technique, designed to rid him of his desire to do evil.

Continuing my conversation with Stanley Kubrick, we discussed his movie and the controversy it has stimulated.

Who in your mind are the heroes and villains in A Clockwork Orange?
"Well, you can't really put it that way. It's a satire, which is to say that you hold up current vices and folly to ridicule. You pretend to say the opposite of the truth in order to destroy it. The only exception to this is the chaplain [who befriends Alex in prison]. He states the moral of the story even though he is trotted out looking a bit of the buffoon.

"The essential moral of the story hinges on the question of choice, and the question of whether man can be good without having the choice to be evil, and whether a creature who no longer has this choice is still a man.

"The fact that Alex is the very personification of evil and is still in some strange way attractive is due to several things: his honesty, his lack of hypocrisy, his energy, and his intelligence. I've always compared him to

Richard III, and I think it's a very good comparison. Why do you find yourself liking Richard III? But you do, in a very stylized way.

"Eventually, you begin to sympathize with Alex because you begin to identify with him as a victim of a much greater evil.

"Perhaps, more importantly, we recognize our own unconscious. This may also account for some of the antagonism the film has created. The unconscious has no conscience—and the perception of this makes some people very anxious and angry."

Some persons have criticized you for celebrating evil by making Alex attractive. Would your answer be that you are making evil attractive so as to make your point with even the most extreme example?
"Yes, of course. If Alex were a lesser villain, then you would dilute the point of the film. It would then be like one of those westerns where they purport to be doing a film which is against lynching and so they lynch innocent people.

"The point of the film seems to be: You shouldn't lynch people because you might lynch innocent people; rather than: You shouldn't lynch anybody.

"Obviously, if Alex were a lesser villain, it would be very easy to reject his 'treatment.' But when you reject the treatment of even a character as wicked as Alex the moral point is clear."

You left out some of his more nasty habits that are in Burgess's novel. Alex rapes ten-year-old girls and squashes small animals for thrills.
"In the book Alex is fifteen. We really don't want to see fifteen-year-olds abusing ten-year-old girls, but that is still a very different matter from a twenty-five-year-old man abusing ten-year-old girls."

Your film contains a number of rapes, brutal beatings, and slashings. Do you think violence in movies has a cumulative effect of desensitizing people to the evil of violence?
"No, I don't. I think man's capacity for violence is an evolutionary hangover which no longer serves a useful purpose but it's there, all the same."

Do you think your film should be "X" rated? In Illinois that means persons under eighteen years of age are not to be admitted to the theater.

"No, of course not. I don't think any serious film should be banned for people of sixteen and seventeen. If their parents want them to see it, they should not be legally prevented from doing so."

Have you shown your film to your daughters?
"My eighteen-year-old daughter saw it, but I wouldn't show it to my twelve-year-old."

Why not?
"Because I think there are obviously films which young children could find upsetting. I don't think there can be any confusion about that."

Do you think people seeing a violent act on the screen are impelled to commit a similar act in society?
"No, I don't, but I think there's an even more important point. It has been demonstrated that even after deep hypnosis, in the post hypnotic state, people will not do what is contrary to their nature, so that the idea that people can be corrupted by a film is, I think, completely wrong.

"But I would go even further. I would say, even hypothetically, granting that it did, which I'm sure it does not, I should think that realistic violence is far less likely to cause violence than the fun violence of James Bond, or the *Tom and Jerry* cartoons where the eight-foot lump on their head shrinks and they're off to the next caper.

"That's the kind of violence, if any kind, that might cause emulation. It's like when young boys were fed nonsense about the glory of war. They might have gone off to war with expectations that didn't turn out to be true, whereas if they had been exposed to brutal, violent war films, they might have realized what was in store for them.

"So I don't think that realistic violence, which at the moment seems to be the kind that is causing all of the commotion, could conceivably make someone wish to copy it, even if they were influenceable by films which is contrary to all evidence."

I must admit it does strike me as a little odd that motion pictures are getting the rap for causing today's lawlessness. There would seem to be other more significant factors.

"Exactly. By directing a lot of media attention to whether films and television contribute to violence, politicians conveniently escape looking at the real causes of violence in society which could be listed as:

1. Original sin: the theological view
2. Unjust economic exploitation: the Marxist view
3. Emotional frustrations and pressures: the psychological view
4. Genetic factors based on the 'Y' chromosome theory: the biological view."

Is it the media or the politicians that are directing attention to violence in films and television?
"Well, the media is doing it, but the politicians are chiming in. They see the way it's going. It's convenient for them."

Modern Times:
An Interview with Stanley Kubrick

PHILIP STRICK AND

PENELOPE HOUSTON/1972

WE MET KUBRICK LAST November at his home near Boreham-
wood, a casual labyrinth of studios, offices, and seemingly dual-purpose
rooms in which family life and filmmaking overlap as though the one
were unthinkable without the other. Despite his reputed aversion to the
ordeals of interrogation, Kubrick proved an immensely articulate conversa-
tionalist, willing to talk out in detail any aspect, technical or theoretical,
of his devotion to the cinema. When we came to transcribe our tapes,
what indeed emerged was perhaps rather more of a conversation, covering
a lot of ground, than a formal interview.

When *A Clockwork Orange* opened in London a few weeks later, Kubrick
found himself in the front line of somebody else's war. The critics were up
in arms about *Straw Dogs,* in particular, and *A Clockwork Orange* became
caught in the crossfire, especially after the Home Secretary's much publi-
cized visit to the film. It was an extraordinary fuss (the novel was, after all,
first published ten years ago), the more so for seeming to be about a
Clockwork Orange that sounded like it had nothing much to do with the
film Kubrick made. But it also meant that some of his replies to our original questions would have to be revised, to make due allowance for the
arguments the film had caused. So what follows is to some extent a
Kubrick rewrite of a Kubrick interview—in the interests, as always with
Kubrick, of precision.

From *Sight and Sound,* Spring, 1972. Reprinted by permission.

How closely did you work with Anthony Burgess in adapting A Clockwork
Orange *for the screen?*
STANLEY KUBRICK: I had virtually no opportunity of discussing the
novel with Anthony Burgess. He phoned me one evening when he was
passing through London and we had a brief conversation on the telephone. It was mostly an exchange of pleasantries. On the other hand, I
wasn't particularly concerned about this because in a book as brilliantly
written as *A Clockwork Orange* one would have to be lazy not to be able to
find the answers to any questions which might arise within the text of the
novel itself. I think it is reasonable to say that, whatever Burgess had to say
about the story was said in the book.

*How about your own contributions to the story? You seem to have preserved the
style and structure of the original far more closely than with most of your previous films, and the dialogues are often exactly the same as in the novel.*
My contribution to the story consisted of writing the screenplay. This was
principally a matter of selection and editing, though I did invent a few
useful narrative ideas and reshape some of the scenes. However, in general,
these contributions merely clarified what was already in the novel—such
as the Cat Lady telephoning the police, which explains why the police
appear at the end of that scene. In the novel, it occurs to Alex that she
may have called them, but this is the sort of thing that you can do in a
novel and not in the screenplay. I was also rather pleased with the idea of
"Singin' in the Rain" as a means of Alexander identifying Alex again
towards the end of the film.

How did you come to use "Singin' in the Rain" in the first place?
This was one of the more important ideas which arose during rehearsal.
This scene, in fact, was rehearsed longer than any other scene in the film
and appeared to be going nowhere. We spent three days trying to work out
just what was going to happen and somehow it all seemed a bit inadequate. Then suddenly the idea popped into my head—I don't know where
it came from or what triggered it off.

*The main addition you seem to have made to the original story is the scene of
Alex's introduction to the prison. Why did you feel this was important?*

It may be the longest scene but I would not think it is the most important. It was a necessary addition because the prison sequence is compressed, in comparison with the novel, and one had to have something in it which gave sufficient weight to the idea that Alex was actually imprisoned. The routine of checking into prison which, in fact, is quite accurately presented in the film, seemed to provide this necessary weight.

In the book there is another killing by Alex while he is in prison. By omitting this, don't you run the risk of seeming to share Alex's own opinion of himself as a high-spirited innocent?
I shouldn't think so, and Alex doesn't see himself as a high-spirited innocent. He is totally aware of his own evil and accepts it with complete openness.

Alex seems a far pleasanter person in the film than in the book . . .
Alex makes no attempt to deceive himself or the audience as to his total corruption and wickedness. He is the very personification of evil. On the other hand, he has winning qualities: his total candor, his wit, his intelligence and his energy; these are attractive qualities and ones, I might add, which he shares with Richard III.

The violence done to Alex in the brainwashing sequence is in fact more horrifying than anything he does himself . . .
It was absolutely necessary to give weight to Alex's brutality, otherwise I think there would be moral confusion with respect to what the government does to him. If he were a lesser villain, then one could say: "Oh, yes, of course, he should not be given this psychological conditioning; it's all too horrible and he really wasn't that bad after all." On the other hand, when you have shown him committing such atrocious acts, and you still realize the immense evil on the part of the government in turning him into something less than human in order to make him good, then I think the essential moral idea of the book is clear. It is necessary for man to have choice to be good or evil, even if he chooses evil. To deprive him of this choice is to make him something less than human—a clockwork orange.

But aren't you inviting a sort of identification with Alex?
I think, in addition to the personal qualities I mentioned, there is the basic psychological, unconscious identification with Alex. If you look at the

story not on the social and moral level, but on the psychological dream content level, you can regard Alex as a creature of the id. He is within all of us. In most cases, this recognition seems to bring a kind of empathy from the audience, but it makes some people very angry and uncomfortable. They are unable to accept this view of themselves and, therefore, they become angry at the film. It's a bit like the king who kills the messenger who brings him bad news and rewards the one who brings him good news.

The comparison with Richard III makes a striking defense against accusations that the film encourages violence, delinquency and so on. But as Richard is a safely distant historical figure, does it meet them completely?
There is no positive evidence that violence in films or television causes social violence. To focus one's interest on this aspect of violence is to ignore the principal causes, which I would list as:

    1. Original sin: the religious view.

    2. Unjust economic exploitation: the Marxist view.

    3. Emotional and psychological frustration: the psychological view.

    4. Genetic factors based on the "Y" chromosome theory: the biological view.

    5. Man—the killer ape: the evolutionary view.

    To try to fasten any responsibility on art as the cause of life seems to me to have the case put the wrong way around. Art consists of reshaping life but it does not create life, or cause life. Furthermore to attribute powerful suggestive qualities to a film is at odds with the scientifically accepted view that, even after deep hypnosis, in a post-hypnotic state, people cannot be made to do things which are at odds with their natures.

Is there any kind of violence in films which you might regard as socially dangerous?
Well, I don't accept that there is a connection, but let us hypothetically say that there might be one. If there were one, I should say that the kind of violence that might cause some impulse to emulate it is the "fun" kind of violence: the kind of violence we see in the Bond films or the *Tom and Jerry* cartoons. Unrealistic violence, sanitized violence, violence presented as a joke. This is the only kind of violence that could conceivably cause anyone to wish to copy it, but I am quite convinced that not even this has any effect.

There may even be an argument in support of saying that any kind of violence in films, in fact, serves a useful social purpose by allowing people a means of vicariously freeing themselves from the pent up, aggressive emotions which are better expressed in dreams, or in the dreamlike state of watching a film, than in any form of reality of sublimation.

Isn't the assumption of your audience in the case of Clockwork Orange *likely to be that you support Alex's point of view and in some way assume responsibility for it?*
I don't think that any work of art has a responsibility to be anything but a work of art. There obviously is a considerable controversy, just as there always has been, about what is a work of art, and I should be the last to try to define that. I was amused by Cocteau's *Orphée* when the poet is given the advice: "Astonish me." The Johnsonian definition of a work of art is also meaningful to me, and that is that a work of art must either make life more enjoyable or more endurable. Another quality, which I think forms part of the definition, is that a work of art is always exhilarating and never depressing, whatever its subject matter may be.

In view of the particular exhilaration of Alex's religious fantasies, has the film run into trouble with clerical critics?
The reaction of the religious press has been mixed, although a number of superb reviews have been written. One of the most perceptive reviews by the religious press, or any other press, appeared in the *Catholic News* written by John E. Fitzgerald, and I would like to quote one portion of it:
"In print we've been told (in B. F. Skinner's *Beyond Freedom and Dignity*) that man is but a grab-bag of conditioned reflexes. On screen with images rather than words, Stanley Kubrick shows that man is more than a mere product of heredity and/or environment. For as Alex's clergyman friend (a character who starts out as a fire-and-brimstone-spouting buffoon but ends up the spokesman for the film's thesis) says: 'When a man cannot choose, he ceases to be a man.'
"The film seems to say that to take away a man's choice is not to redeem but merely restrain him: otherwise we have a society of oranges, organic but operating like clockwork. Such brainwashing, organic and psychological, is a weapon that totalitarians in state, church, or society

might wish for an easier good even at the cost of individual rights and dignity. Redemption is a complicated thing and change must be motivated from within rather than imposed from without if moral values are to be upheld. But Kubrick is an artist rather than a moralist and he leaves it to us to figure what's wrong and why, what should be done and how it should be accomplished."

Your choice of lenses for the shooting of the film often gives it a subtly distorted visual quality. Why did you want that particular look?
It may sound like an extremely obvious thing to say, but I think it is worth saying nevertheless that when you are making a film, in addition to any higher purpose you may have in mind, you must be interesting; visually interesting, narratively interesting, interesting from an acting point of view. All ideas for creating interest must be held up against the yardstick of the theme of the story, the narrative requirements and the purpose of the scene; but, within that, you must make a work of art interesting. I recall a comment recorded in a book called *Stanislavski Directs,* in which Stanislavski told an actor that he had the right understanding of the character, the right understanding of the text of the play, that what he was doing was completely believable, but that it was still no good because it wasn't interesting.

Were you looking after the hand-held camera for the fight with the Cat Lady?
Yes, all of the hand-held camerawork is mine. In addition to the fun of doing the shooting myself, I find it is virtually impossible to explain what you want in a hand-held shot to even the most talented and sensitive camera operator.

To what extent do you rationalize a shot before setting it up?
There are certain aspects of a film which can meaningfully be talked about, but photography and editing do not lend themselves to verbal analysis. It's very much the same as the problem one has talking about painting, or music. The questions of taste involved and the decision-making criteria are essentially nonverbal, and whatever you say about them tends to read like the back of a record album. These are decisions that have to be made every few minutes during the shooting, and they are just down to the director's taste and imagination.

How did you come to choose the Purcell piece—the "Music for the Funeral of Queen Mary"?
Well, this answer is going to sound a lot like the last one. You're in an area where words are not particularly relevant. In thinking about the music for the scene, the Purcell piece occurred to me and, after I listened to it several times in conjunction with the film, there was simply no question about using it.

The arrangements by Walter Carlos are extraordinarily effective...
I think that Walter Carlos has done something completely unique in the field of electronic realization of music—that's the phrase that they use. I think that I've heard most of the electronic and *musique concrète* LPs there are for sale in Britain, Germany, France, Italy, and the United States; not because I particularly like this kind of music, but out of my researches for *2001* and *Clockwork Orange*. I think Walter Carlos is the only electronic composer and realizer who has managed to create a sound which is not an attempt at copying the instruments of the orchestra and yet which, at the same time, achieves a beauty of its own employing electronic tonalities. I think that his version of the fourth movement of Beethoven's Ninth Symphony rivals hearing a full orchestra playing it, and that is saying an awful lot.

There is very little post-synchronization for the dialogue...
There is no post-synchronization. I'm quite pleased about this because every scene was shot on location; even the so-called sets that we built which were, in fact, built in a factory about forty feet off the noisy High Street in Borehamwood, a few hundred yards from the old MGM Studio. Despite this, we were able to get quite acceptably clean soundtracks.

   With the modern equipment that's available today in the form of microphones, radio transmitters and so forth, it should be possible to get a usable soundtrack almost anywhere. In the scene where the tramp recognizes Alex who is standing looking at the Thames, next to the Albert Bridge, there was so much traffic noise on the location that you had to shout in order to be heard, but we were able to get such a quiet soundtrack that it was necessary to add street noise in the final mix to make it realistic. We used a microphone the size of a paper clip, and it was secured with black tape on the tramp's scarf. In several shots you can see the microphone, but you don't know what you are looking at.

In concentrating on the action of the film, as you do, isn't there a danger that the lesser characters may appear rather one-dimensional?
The danger of everything that you do in a film is that it may not work, it may be boring, or bland, or stupid . . .

When you think of the greatest moments of film, I think you are almost always involved with images rather than scenes, and certainly never dialogue. The thing a film does best is to use pictures with music, and I think these are the moments you remember. Another thing is the way an actor did something: the way Emil Jannings took out his handkerchief and blew his nose in *The Blue Angel,* or those marvellous slow turns that Nikolai Cherkassov did in *Ivan the Terrible.*

How did you manage the subjective shot of Alex's suicide attempt?
We bought an old Newman Sinclair clockwork mechanism camera (no pun intended) for £50. It's a beautiful camera and it's built like a battleship. We made a number of polystyrene boxes which gave about eighteen inches of protection around the camera, and cut out a slice for the lens. We then threw the camera off a roof. In order to get it to land lens first, we had to do this six times and the camera survived all six drops. On the final one, it landed right on the lens and smashed it but it didn't do a bit of harm to the camera. This, despite the fact that the polystyrene was literally blasted away from it each time by the impact. The next day we shot a steady test on the camera and found there wasn't a thing wrong with it. On this basis, I would say that the Newman Sinclair must be the most indestructible camera ever made.

How much planning do you do before you start to shoot a scene?
As much as there are hours in the day, and days in the weeks. I think about a film almost continuously. I try to visualize it and I try to work out every conceivable variation of ideas which might exist with respect to the various scenes, but I have found that when you finally come down to the day the scene is going to be shot and you arrive on the location with the actors, having had the experience of already seeing some scenes shot, somehow

it's always different. You find out that you have not really explored the scene to its fullest extent. You may have been thinking about it incorrectly, or you may simply not have discovered one of the variations which now in context with everything else that you have shot is simply better than anything you had previously thought of. The reality of the final moment, just before shooting, is so powerful that all previous analysis must yield before the impressions you receive under these circumstances, and unless you use this feedback to your positive advantage, unless you adjust to it, adapt to it and accept the sometimes terrifying weaknesses it can expose, you can never realize the most out of your film.

How do you usually work when you get to the reality of the final moment? Whenever I start a new scene, the most important thing in my mind is, within the needs of the theme and the scene, to make something happen worth putting on film. The most crucial part of this comes when you start rehearsals on a new scene. You arrive on the location, the crew is standing around eating buns and drinking tea, waiting to be told what to do. You've got to keep them outside the room you're rehearsing in and take whatever time is necessary to get everything right, and have it make sense. There's no way to define what this process consists of. It obviously has to do with taste and imagination and it is in this crucial period of time that a film is really created. Once you know you've got something worthwhile, the shooting becomes a matter of recording (improving if you can) what you have already done in rehearsal. Whatever problems exist during the actual shooting are not the kind of problems that worry me. If the actor isn't getting it right, well, he'll get it right eventually. If the camera operator spoils a shot, it can be done again. The thing that can never be changed, and the thing that is the make or break of a picture, are those few hours you spend alone in the actual place with the actors, with the crew outside drinking their tea.

Sometimes you find that the scene is absolutely no good at all. It doesn't make sense when you see it acted. It doesn't provide the necessary emotional or factual information in an interesting way, or in a way which has the right weight to it. Any number of things can suddenly put you in a position where you've got nothing to shoot. The only thing you can say about a moment like this is that it's better to realize it while you still have a chance to change it and to create something new, than it is to record forever something that is wrong. This is the best and the worst time: it is the time you have your most imaginative ideas, things that have not occurred to you before, regardless of how much you've thought about the scene. It's also the time when you can stand there and feel very dumb and unhappy with what you're seeing, and not have the faintest idea of what to do about it.

Do you very consciously favour a particular style of shooting?
If something is really happening on the screen, it isn't crucial how it's shot. Chaplin had such a simple cinematic style that it was almost like *I Love Lucy,* but you were always hypnotized by what was going on, unaware of the essentially non-cinematic style. He frequently used cheap sets, routine lighting and so forth, but he made great films. His films will probably last longer than anyone else's. You could say that Chaplin was no style and all content. On the other hand, the opposite can be seen in Eisenstein's films, who is all style and no content or, depending on how generous you want to be, little content. Many of Eisenstein's films are really quite silly; but they are so beautifully made, so brilliantly cinematic, that, despite their heavily propagandistic simplemindedness, they become important. Obviously, if you can combine style and content, you have the best of all possible films.

Do you have a preference for any one aspect of the whole filmmaking process?
I think I enjoy editing the most. It's the nearest thing to some reasonable environment in which to do creative work. Writing, of course, is very satisfying, but, of course, you're not working with film. The actual shooting of a film is probably the worst circumstances you could try to imagine for creating a work of art. There is, first of all, the problem of getting up very early every morning and going to bed very late every night. Then there is the chaos, confusion and frequently physical discomfort. It would be, I suppose, like a writer trying to write a book while working at a factory lathe in temperatures which range from ninety-five to negative ten degrees Fahrenheit. In addition to this, of course, editing is the only aspect of the cinematic art that is unique. It shares no connection with any other art form: writing, acting, photography, things that are major aspects of the cinema, are still not unique to it, but editing is.

How long did the editing take on Clockwork Orange*?*
The editing up to the point of dubbing took about six months, working seven days a week.

Do you ever have problems cutting out your own material?
When I'm editing, I'm only concerned with the questions of "Is it good or bad?" "Is it necessary?" "Can I get rid of it?" "Does it work?" My identity changes to that of an editor. I am never concerned with how much difficulty there was to shoot something, how much it cost and so forth. I look at the material with completely different eyes. I'm never troubled losing material. I cut everything to the bone. When you're shooting, you want to make sure that you don't miss anything and you cover it as fully as time and budget allow. When you're editing, you want to get rid of everything that isn't essential.

How much support coverage do you shoot?
There's always a conflict between time, money, and quality. If you shoot a lot of coverage, then you must either spend a lot of money, or settle for less quality of performance. I find that when I'm shooting a scene where the acting is primarily important, I shoot a lot of takes but I don't try to get a lot of coverage from other angles. I try to shoot the scene as simply as possible to get the maximum performance from the actors without presenting them with the problem of repeating the performance too many times from different angles. On the other hand, in an action scene, where it's relatively easy to shoot, you want lots and lots of angles so that you can do something interesting with it in the cutting room.

Do you direct actors in every detail, or do you expect them to some extent to come up with their own ideas?
I come up with the ideas. That is essentially the director's job. There is a misconception, I think, about what directing actors means: it generally goes along the lines of the director imposing his will over difficult actors, or teaching people who don't know how to act. I try to hire the best actors in the world. The problem is comparable to one a conductor might face. There's little joy in trying to get a magnificent performance from a student orchestra. It's difficult enough to get one with all the subtleties and nuances you might want out of the greatest orchestra in the world. You

want to have great virtuoso soloists, and so with actors. Then it's not necessary to teach them how to act or to discipline them or to impose your will upon them because there is usually no problem along those lines. An actor will almost always do what you want him to do if he is *able* to do it; and, therefore, since great actors are able to do almost anything, you find you have few problems. You can then concentrate on what you want them to do, what is the psychology of the character, what is the purpose of the scene, what is the story about? These are things that are often muddled up and require simplicity and exactitude. The director's job is to provide the actor with ideas, not to teach him how to act or to trick him into acting. There's no way to give an actor what he hasn't got in the form of talent. You can give him ideas, thoughts, attitudes. The actor's job is to create emotion. Obviously, the actor may have some ideas too, but this is not what his primary responsibility is. You can make a mediocre actor less mediocre, you can make a terrible actor mediocre, but you cannot go very far without the magic. Great performances come from the magical talent of the actor, plus the ideas of the director.

The other part of the director's job is to exercise taste: he must decide whether what he is seeing is interesting, whether it's appropriate, whether it is of sufficient weight, whether it's credible. These are decisions that no one else can make.

You made what might seem some unusual casting choices for your last two films—how do you find the actors you want?
Well, that really comes down to a question of taste, doesn't it? A lot of pictures are cast by producers and their decisions are frequently based on proven success rather than unproven hints at talent. Many producers aren't willing to decide whether an actor who is unknown and who has done very little work is really good. I have nothing against people of proven talent, but sometimes there may be no one in that category who is right for the part.

Do you enjoy working with different actors? With a few exceptions—Peter Sellers, for instance—you haven't often used the same actor twice, unlike a lot of directors who obviously prefer to build up a sort of stock company of people who know their work.
I don't really think in those terms. I try to choose the best actors for the parts, whether I know them or not. I would avoid actors who have reputa-

tions for being destructive and neurotic but, other than that, there is no one whom I would not consider using for a part.

The only thing that is really important in your relationship with actors is that they must know that you admire them, that you admire their work, and there's no way to fake that. You must really admire them or you shouldn't use them. If they know that you admire their work, which they can sense in a thousand different ways, it doesn't really matter what you think of each other or what you say to them, or whether you are terribly friendly or not. The thing they care about is their work. Some actors are very amusing and pleasant and always cheerful. They are, of course, more pleasant to have around than those who are morose, vacant, or enigmatic. But how they behave when you're not shooting has very little to do with what happens when the camera turns over.

You made Clockwork Orange *initially because you had to postpone your Napoleon project. How do you see the Napoleon film developing?*
First of all, I start from the premise that there has never been a great historical film, and I say that with all apologies and respect to those who have made historical films, including myself. I don't think anyone has ever successfully solved the problem of dealing in an interesting way with the historical information that has to be conveyed, and at the same time getting a sense of reality about the daily life of the characters. You have to get a feeling of what it was like to be with Napoleon. At the same time, you have to convey enough historical information in an intelligent, interesting, and concise way so that the audience understands what happened.

Would you include Abel Gance's Napoleon *in this verdict?*
I think I would have to. I know that the film is a masterpiece of cinematic invention and it brought cinematic innovations to the screen which are still being called innovations whenever someone is bold enough to try them again. But on the other hand, as a film about Napoleon, I have to say I've always been disappointed in it.

Did you think of Clockwork Orange *as being in any way a form of relaxation between two very big films?*

I don't think in terms of big movies, or small movies. Each movie presents problems of its own and has advantages of its own. Each movie requires everything that you have to give it, in order to overcome the artistic and logistic problems that it poses. There are advantages in an epic film, just as there are disadvantages. It is much easier to do a huge crowd scene and make it interesting than it is to film a man sitting at a table thinking.

Stop the World: Stanley Kubrick

GENE D. PHILLIPS/1973

As a director Stanley Kubrick is virtually in a class by himself because he taught himself the various aspects of the film making process and became a director without serving the usual apprenticeship in a film studio, where he would have had to work his way up to the status of director by way of lesser jobs. By the time he began directing films for the major studios, he was able to do so with a degree of independence that few other directors have been able to match. Kubrick oversees every aspect of production when he makes a film: script writing, casting, shooting (often operating the camera himself), editing, and choosing the musical score.

The following interview is the outcome of a meeting with Stanley Kubrick which took place at his home near London.

When asked why he thought the major film companies had decided to extend wide artistic freedom to directors like himself, Kubrick replied, "The invulnerability of the majors was based on their consistent success with virtually anything they made. When they stopped making money, they began to appreciate the importance of people who could make good films." Kubrick was one of the directors they turned to; and when they did, it was after he had learned the business of film making from the ground up and was ready to answer the call.

Kubrick was born in the Bronx section of New York City in July, 1928, and took his first step toward film making when he began selling pictures to *Look* magazine while he was still a student at Taft High School. He

From *The Movie Makers: Artists in an Industry,* 1973. Reprinted by permission of the author.

joined the staff after graduation and, while working there, decided to expand a picture story he had done on boxer Walter Cartier into a documentary short called *Day of the Fight* (1950). "I did everything from keeping an accounting book to dubbing in the punches on the soundtrack," Kubrick remembers. "I had no idea what I was doing, but I knew I could do better than most of the films that I was seeing at the time." Kubrick had spent his savings, $3,900, to make the film; and the RKO circuit bought it for $4,000. At the age of twenty Kubrick had made a film on his own that had shown a profit, however small. From that moment on he was a confirmed film maker.

RKO advanced him $1,500 for a second short, *Flying Padre* (1951), about a priest in New Mexico who flies to see his isolated parishioners in a Piper Cub. When he broke even on that one, Kubrick borrowed $10,000 from his father and his uncle and decided to take the plunge into feature film making. He went on location to the San Gabriel Mountains near Los Angeles to make *Fear and Desire* (1953), a movie dealing with a futile military patrol trapped behind enemy lines in an unnamed war.

Kubrick made the film almost singlehandedly, serving as his own cameraman, sound man and editor, as well as director. The film was shot silent, and he added the soundtrack afterward. The young director was pleasantly surprised when *Fear and Desire* received some rather good reviews and played the arthouse circuit. As a consequence he borrowed money, chiefly from another relative, a Bronx druggist, and made *Killer's Kiss* (1955), again handling most of the production chores himself. He moved another step closer to the big time when United Artists agreed to distribute it.

Kubrick shot the film on location in the shabbier sections of New York, which gave it a visual realism unmatched by the postsynchronized soundtrack. Money began running out during the post production work, and Kubrick was unable to afford an editing assistant. "I had to spend four months just laying in the sound effects, footstep by footstep," Kubrick says. Nevertheless he was able to inject some life into the routine story with the inclusion of two key fight sequences, one in the ring and one in a mannequin factory at the climax of the movie.

The hero of the story is a fighter named Davy (Jamie Smith), who is a loser in the ring but who is able to save his girl from being kidnapped by slugging it out with her abductor. In this scene Davy and Rapallo, the kidnapper (Frank Silvera), fight to the death amid the mannequins, using whatever blunt instruments they can lay their hands on. When Davy delivers the death blow, Rapallo falls backward with dummies crashing all around him. Kubrick ends the scene with a closeup of the smashed head of a mannequin, a metaphor for the dead Rapallo.

Later Davy and the girl meet in the congestion of Grand Central Station to leave New York for good, in favor of making a home on Davy's family's farm. In their departure from the brutal big city, which had proved a harsh and unpleasant place for both of them, we see the first indication of Kubrick's dark vision of contemporary society. In this and even more in his subsequent films, Kubrick shows us modern man gradually being dehumanized by living in a materialistic, mechanized world, in which one man exploits another in the mass effort to survive. Moreover, in his later motion pictures Kubrick extends his vision into the future to suggest that man's failure to cooperate with his fellow man in mastering the world of the present can only lead to man's being mastered by the world of tomorrow.

In 1955 Kubrick met James B. Harris, an aspiring producer, who put up more than a third of the $320,000 budget needed to finance *The Killing* (1956), with United Artists providing the rest. This was the first of the three-film partnership between Kubrick and Harris.

Based on Lionel White's novel *Clean Break,* Kubrick's tightly constructed script follows the preparations of a group of smalltime crooks bent on making a big killing by robbing a race track. They have planned the robbery to coincide with the actual running time of the seventh race; and Kubrick photographs the robbery in great detail, with all of its split-second timing. He builds suspense with great intensity by quickly cutting from one member of the gang to another, in a series of flashbacks that show how each has simultaneously carried out his part of the plan—all leading up to the climactic moment when they get away with the money.

Kubrick was confident that his method of telling the story by means of fragmented flashbacks would work as well on the screen as it did in the novel. "It was the handling of time that may have made this more than just a good crime film," he says. Another thing that attracted him to White's book, Alexander Walker points out very perceptively in *Stanley Kubrick Directs,* is that the novel touches on a theme that is a frequent preoccupation of Kubrick's films: the presumably perfect plan of action that goes wrong through human fallibility and/or chance: "It is characteristic of Kubrick what while one part of him pays intellectual tribute to the rationally constructed master plan, another part reserves the skeptic's right to anticipate human imperfections or the laws of chance that militate against its success."

We shall see reverberations of this theme most notably in films like *Dr. Strangelove,* in which a mad general (played by Sterling Hayden) upsets the carefully planned U.S. nuclear fail-safe system, and in *2001,* in which Hal the "infallible" computer goes lethally awry.

Since Kubrick's films reflect the extreme precariousness of everything, it is not surprising that he is meticulous in planning his films. He wants, he says, to keep the disorder and confusion that dog human existence away from his set as much as possible.

Because of union regulations Kubrick could no longer act as his own cameraman for *The Killing,* and so veteran cinematographer Lucien Ballard was engaged to shoot the film. Occasionally friction developed between director and cameraman when they disagreed on how a shot should be lit. Eventually, however, a mutual respect developed between the two men. Kubrick, after all, is one of the few movie directors who has belonged to the cinematographers' union and who still operates his own camera from time to time when making a film. In fact, Jeremy Bernstein noticed while *2001* was in production a decade later that Kubrick often took Polaroid shots of a camera setup in order to check lighting effects with his cinematographer, Geoffrey Unsworth. "I asked Kubrick if it was customary for movie directors to participate so actively in photographing a film," Bernstein records in *The New Yorker,* "and he said succinctly that he never watched any other directors work."

The movie's real merit lies in the ensemble acting Kubrick elicited from a group of capable Hollywood supporting players, who rarely got a chance to give performances of any substance. Sterling Hayden plays Johnny Clay, the tough organizer of the caper; Jay C. Flippen is the cynical older member of the group; Elisha Cook, Jr., is the timid husband who hopes to impress his voluptuous wife (Marie Windsor) with stolen money, since presumably he cannot otherwise give her satisfaction. In the end the milk-toast shoots his wife dead—the impotent husband finally penetrating his wife with bullets. Together this first-rate cast help Kubrick create the grim atmosphere of the film, which builds to an ironic conclusion when Clay's suitcase blows open just as he and his girl friend Fay are about to board a plane for the tropics; and the stolen money flutters all over the windy airfield. Like Davy and his girl in *Killer's Kiss*, Johnny and Fay hoped to escape the corrosive atmosphere of the big city by flight to a cleaner environment. But for Johnny, brutalized by a life of crime, it is already too late.

The Killing is the kind of crime melodrama that Pauline Kael had in mind when she wrote of the sort of film that has a "sordid, semi-documentary authenticity about criminal activities" and exudes "the nervous excitement of what it might be like to rob and tangle with the law." *Time* applauded Kubrick for having shown "more imagination with dialogue and camera than Hollywood has seen since the obstreperous Orson Welles went riding out of town." "It was a profitable picture for UA," says Kubrick, "and this is the only measure of success in financial terms."

Kubrick next acquired the rights to Humphrey Cobb's 1935 novel *Paths of Glory*, which he had read in high school, and set about writing a script. But no major studio was interested in financing the film until Kirk Douglas agreed to star. Then United Artists backed the project with $935,000. Despite the flood of antiwar films over the years, *Paths of Glory* (1957) ranks with Joseph Losey's *King and Country* as one of the most uncompromising examples of the genre.

The ghastly irresponsibility of officers toward their men is climaxed by the behavior of General Mireau (George Macready), who hopes to gain a promotion by ordering his men to carry out a suicidal charge. When they falter, he madly orders other troops to fire into the trenches on their own comrades. Afterwards, Colonel Dax (Kirk Douglas) must stand by while three soldiers are picked almost at random from the ranks to be court-martialed and executed for desertion of duty, as an "example" to the rest of the men, for failing to attack the enemy stronghold as Mireau had commanded.

The title of the story is a reference to Thomas Gray's "Elegy in a Country Churchyard," in which the poet warns that the "paths of glory lead but to the grave." It becomes increasingly clear as the film progresses that the paths of glory the generals are following lead, not to their graves, but to the graves of the enlisted men, who are ordered to die in battles fought according to a strategy manipulated by the generals for their own self-advancement.

Peter Cowie has written that Kubrick uses his camera in the film "unflinchingly, like a weapon": darting into close-up to capture the indignation on Dax's face, sweeping across the slopes to record the wholesale slaughter of a division, or advancing relentlessly at eye level toward the stakes against which the condemned men will be shot.

The film is filled with both visual and verbal ironies that reinforce its theme. Toward the end of the central battle scene, Dax must attempt to lead yet another hopeless charge on the impregnable German lines. As he climbs the ladder out of the trench, exhorting his men all the while to renew their courage, he is thrown backwards into the trench by the body of a French soldier rolling in on top of him. In the scene in which the condemned await execution, one of them complains that the cockroach which he sees on the wall of their cell will be alive after he is dead. One of his comrades smashes the cockroach with his fist, saying, "Now you've got the edge on *him*."

The epilogue to the film ends on a note of hope for humanity. Dax watches his men join in the singing of a song about love in wartime, led by a timid German girl prisoner (played by German actress Suzanne Christian, who is now Mrs. Stanley Kubrick). Dax walks away, convinced by the good-natured singing that his men have not lost their basic humanity, despite the inhuman conditions in which they live and die. The thematic implications of Kubrick's later films will not be quite so optimistic.

In *Paths of Glory* Kirk Douglas gave one of his best performances, and he therefore wanted to work with Kubrick again. He did so when Kubrick took over the direction of *Spartacus* (1960), a spectacle about slavery in pre-Christian Rome. But this time their association was less satisfactory than it had been on *Paths of Glory*. Douglas was not only the star of the film but its producer as well, and friction developed between producer and director.

"*Spartacus* is the only film over which I did not have absolute control," says Kubrick. "Anthony Mann began the picture and filmed the first sequence, but his disagreements with Kirk made him decide to leave after the first week of shooting. The film came after two years in which I had not directed a picture. When Kirk offered me the job of directing *Spartacus*, I thought that I might be able to make something of it if the script could be changed. But my experience proved that if it is not explicitly stipulated in the contract that your decisions will be respected, there's a very good chance that they won't be. The script could have been improved in the course of shooting, but it wasn't. Kirk was the producer. He and Dalton Trumbo, the scriptwriter, and Edward Lewis, the executive producer, had everything their way." Kubrick's experience with the making of *Spartacus* served to strengthen his resolve to safeguard his artistic independence on future films, a resolution that he has kept.

To ensure total control on his next film, he joined forces with his former producer, James Harris, with whom he acquired the rights to Vladimir Nabokov's *Lolita*. Kubrick is not happy that critics tend to place *Lolita* only ahead of *Spartacus* in terms of quality; *Lolita* is perhaps his most underrated film.

With the collapse in the 1950s of Hollywood as the center of world filmmaking, many of America's independent filmmakers moved to Europe, where they could make films more economically, and therefore more easily obtain financial backing. Kubrick settled in England to make *Lolita* (1962) because M-G-M had funds frozen there. He has remained in England and made all of his subsequent films there.

Nonetheless he still considers himself an American director, for it was not until the fourth film he directed in England, *A Clockwork Orange,* that he used a British setting and a predominantly British cast. In this respect Kubrick can be sharply contrasted with Joseph Losey, another American-born director who migrated to England. Losey's films, such as *The Servant* and *The Go-Between,* have become so thoroughly British in concept and character that one can easily forget that they were made by a director who hails from Wisconsin.

Kubrick engaged Nabokov to write the screenplay of *Lolita.* Kubrick vividly recalls his consternation when he received Nabokov's first draft and discovered that it would run for several hours if all of its four hundred pages were filmed as they stood. The novelist then prepared a shorter version, of which he speculates that Kubrick finally used about twenty per cent.

When Nabokov finally saw *Lolita* at a private screening, he later declared that he found that Kubrick was "a great director, and that his *Lolita* was a first-rate film with magnificent actors," even though much of his version of the script had gone unused. Alfred Appel of Northwestern University, who has had several interviews with Nabokov, told me that the novelist has never had anything but good comments to make about Kubrick's film of his book, largely because after the writer had spent six months working on the scenario himself he came to realize vividly how difficult adapting a novel to the screen really is. Indeed, the novelist has said that "infinite fidelity may be the author's ideal but can prove a producer's ruin."

In *Lolita* Peter Sellers plays Clare Quilty, a television personality who is the rival of middle-aged Humbert Humbert (James Mason) for the affections of twelve-year-old Dolores Haze (Sue Lyon), known to her friends as Lolita. Because, at the time that Kubrick made *Lolita,* the freedom of the screen had not advanced to the point it has reached now, he had to be more subtle and indirect than Vladimir Nabokov had been in his novel about suggesting the sexual obsession of an older man for a nymphet.

"I wasn't able to give any weight at all to the erotic aspect of Humbert's relationship with Lolita in the film," says Kubrick, "and because I could only hint at the true nature of his attraction to Lolita, it was assumed too quickly by filmgoers that Humbert was in love with her," as opposed to being merely attracted to her sexually. "In the novel this comes as a discovery at the end, when Lolita is no longer a nymphet but a pregnant housewife; and it's this encounter, and the sudden realization of his love for her, that is one of the most poignant elements of the story."

Even in the film as it stands, Kubrick has managed to suggest something of the erotic quality of Humbert's relationship with Lolita from the very beginning. The first image of the film, seen behind the credits, is Humbert's hand reaching across the wide screen to caress Lolita's foot as he begins to paint her toenails, thus indicating the subservient nature of his infatuation for Lolita.

In order to avoid giving the plot too serious a treatment, Kubrick decided to emphasize the black comedy inherent in the story. Pauline Kael writes, "The surprise of *Lolita* is how enjoyable it is; it's the first new American comedy since those great days in the forties when Preston Sturges recreated comedy with verbal slapstick. *Lolita* is black slapstick and at times it's so far out that you gasp as you laugh." Kubrick strikes this note of black comedy at the outset in the prologue that follows the credits.

Humbert Humbert threatens Clare Quilty with a gun as the latter stumbles about among the cluttered rooms of his grotesque mansion, not taking too seriously Humbert's threats to kill him, until it is too late. Quilty seeks refuge behind a painting that is propped up against a piece of furniture, and we watch the painting become filled with bullet holes as Humbert empties his gun into it. As the plot unfolds in flashback, we discover that Humbert shot Quilty, not just because Quilty had lured Lolita away from him, but because, after he had done so, Quilty merely used her for a while and then coldly discarded her.

In the difficult role of Humbert, James Mason gives a perfect portrayal of a man who has been victimized by his own obsession, but who strives nevertheless to maintain an air of surface propriety in his relationship with Lolita. There is, for example, the look of consternation that steals across his face when Lolita's dowdy mother (Shelley Winters), whom Humbert only married to be near Lolita, tells him that she has packed her daughter off to summer camp so that *they* can be alone. Peter Sellers is equally good as Clare Quilty, especially in the scenes in which Quilty dons a variety of disguises in his efforts to badger Humbert by a succession of ruses into giving up Lolita. Because of Seller's brilliant flair for impersonation, these scenes are among the best in the film.

For those who appreciate the black comedy of *Lolita*, it is not hard to see that it was just a short step from that film to Kubrick's masterpiece in that genre, *Dr. Strangelove, or: How I Learned to Stop Worrying and Love the Bomb* (1964), the first of Kubrick's science-fiction trilogy. He had originally planned the film as a serious adaptation of Peter George's *Red Alert*, which is concerned with the insane General Jack D. Ripper (Sterling Hayden) and his decision to order a troup of B-52 bombers to launch an attack inside Russia. But gradually Kubrick's attitude toward his material changed: "My idea of doing it as a nightmare comedy came in the early weeks of working on the screenplay. I found that in trying to put meat on the bones and to imagine the scenes fully, one had to keep leaving things out of it which were either absurd or paradoxical in order to keep it from being funny; and these things seems to be close to the heart of the scenes in question."

Kubrick kept revising the script right through the production period, he says. "During shooting many substantial changes were made in the script, sometimes together with the cast during improvisations. Some of the best dialogue was created by Peter Sellers himself." Sellers played, not only the title role of the eccentric scientist, but also Merken Muffley, the president of the United States, as well as Captain Mandrake, a British officer who fails to dissuade General Ripper from his set purpose.

In making a film Kubrick's abiding respect for his actors is always evident, especially in his encouraging them to make suggestions during rehearsals. Sterling Hayden recalls experiencing just this sense that Kubrick respected him when he was making *Dr. Strangelove* for the director. On the first day of shooting Hayden found that he could not handle the technical jargon in his lines. "I was utterly humiliated and Stanley told me, 'The terror on your face may yield just the quality we want and if it doesn't, the hell with it. We'll shoot the thing over.' He was beautiful."

General Ripper's mad motivation for initiating a nuclear attack is his paranoid conviction that his diminishing sexual potency can be traced to an international Communist conspiracy to poison the drinking water. Kubrick subtly reminds us of the General's obsession by a series of sexual metaphors that occur in the course of the film. The very opening image of the film shows a nuclear bomber being refueled in mid-flight by another aircraft, with "Try a Little Tenderness" on the sound track to accompany their symbolic coupling. As Ripper describes to Mandrake his concern about preserving his potency, which he refers to as his "precious bodily essence," Kubrick photographs him in close-up from below, with a huge phallic cigar jutting from between his lips all the time he is talking.

One of the film's key sets, Kubrick notes, is the War Room, a murky, cavernous place, where President Muffley sits at a vast circular table with his advisors, reminiscent of King Arthur and his Knights of the Round Table. Overhead is a bank of lights which bathes the men below it in an eerie glow similar to that in which Ripper sits.

Ironies abound throughout the picture. During an emergency conference called by President Muffley, a disagreement between General Buck Turgidson (George C. Scott) and the Russian ambassador (Peter Bull) threatens to turn into a brawl, and the president intervenes by reminding them, "Please, gentlemen, you can't fight here; this is the War Room."

Later, when Mandrake tries to reach the president in order to warn him about the imminent attack on Russia, he finds that he lacks the correct change for the coin telephone—and that the White House will not accept a collect call! He demands that Colonel Guano (Keenan Wynn) fire into a Coca-Cola machine in order to obtain the necessary money. Guano reluctantly agrees, ruefully reminding Mandrake that it is he who will have to answer to the Coca-Cola Company. Guano blasts the machine, bends down to scoop up the cascading coins, and is squirted full in the face with Coke by the vindictive machine.

Kubrick had originally included a scene in the film in which the War Room personnel engage in a free-for-all with pastry from a buffet table.

But he deleted it from the final print of the film when he decided that "it was too farcical and not consistent with the satiric tone of the rest of the film." Very much in keeping with the satiric mood of the picture is the figure of Dr. Strangelove himself, who is Kubrick's vision of man's final capitulation to the machine. He is more a robot than a human being: his mechanical arm spontaneously salutes Hitler, his former employer; his mechanical hand, gloved in black, at one point even tries to strangle the flesh and blood that still remain in him.

In the end a single U.S. plane reaches its Russian target. Major "King" Kong (Slim Pickens), the skipper of the bomber, manages to dislodge a bomb that has been stuck in its chamber as he sits astride it and to unleash it on its target. As the bomb hurtles toward the earth, it looks like a mighty symbol of potency clamped between his flanks, thus rounding out the sexual metaphors that permeate the film. The bomb hits its target, setting off the Russians' retaliatory Doomsday machine. There follows a series of blinding explosions, while on the sound track we hear a popular ditty Kubrick resurrected from the Second World War: "We'll meet again, don't know where, don't know when." Kubrick used the original World War II recording by Vera Lynn, which served to bring back to popularity not only the song but Miss Lynn as well.

Alexander Walker has noted that *Dr. Strangelove* is basically about a crisis of communication. The film takes place in three locations, each of which is totally shut off from the others: the air base where the crazed Ripper sits in a locked room; the B-52 (aptly named *The Leper Colony*) which is presided over by a pilot obsessed with carrying out what he thinks is his duty; and the War Room, where the film ends, which is ultimately dominated by the mad nuclear scientist of the film's title.

One critic summed up the film by saying that the humor Kubrick had originally thought to exclude from *Dr. Strangelove* provides some of its most meaningful moments. These are made up of the incongruities and misunderstandings we are constantly aware of in our lives. But on the brink of annihilation they become irresistibly absurd.

Critic Pauline Kael, however, who adored the black comedy of *Lolita*, was not happy with *Strangelove*'s further foray into the same territory. "*Dr. Strangelove* opened a new movie era. It ridiculed everything and everybody it showed," she wrote in *Kiss Kiss Bang Bang*. "*Dr. Strangelove* was clearly intended as a cautionary movie; it meant to jolt us awake to the dangers of the bomb by showing us the insanity of the course we were pursuing. But artists' warnings about war and the dangers of total annihilation never tell us how we are supposed to regain control, and *Dr. Strangelove*, chortling over madness, did not indicate any possibilities for sanity."

Kubrick's own response to this kind of criticism would be to point out, as he often did, that "in the deepest sense I believe in man's potential and in his capacity for progress. In *Dr. Strangelove* I was dealing with the inherent irrationality in man that threatens to destroy him; that irrationality is with us as strongly today, and must be conquered. But a recognition of insanity doesn't imply celebration of it; nor a sense of despair and futility about the possibility of curing it."

Asked if the film suggested that he was a misanthrope with contempt for the human race, Kubrick shot back, "Oh God, no. One doesn't give up being concerned for mankind because one acknowledges their fundamental absurdities and weaknesses. I still have hope that the human race can continue to progress."

In essence, *Dr. Strangelove* depicts the plight of fallible man putting himself at the mercy of his infallible machines and bringing about by this abdication of moral responsibility his own destruction. These sentiments are very close to those which Chaplin expressed in his closing speech in *The Great Dictator*: "We think too much and feel too little. More than machinery we need humanity. More than cleverness we need kindness and gentleness. Without these qualities, life will be violent and all will be lost."

Kubrick further explored his dark vision of man in a mechanistic age in *2001: A Space Odyssey* (1968). In explaining how the original idea for the film came to him, he says, "Most astronomers, and other scientists interested in the whole question, are strongly convinced that the universe is crawling with life; much of it, since the numbers are so staggering, equal to us in intelligence, or superior, simply because human intelligence has existed for so relatively short a period." He got in touch with Arthur C. Clarke, whose science-fiction short story "The Sentinel" Kubrick thought could be made the basis of a screenplay; and the rest is motion picture history. They first turned the short story into a novel, in order to develop completely its potentialities, and then turned that into a screenplay. MGM bought their package and financed the film for six million dollars, a budget that, after four years of work on the film, eventually rose to ten million. *2001* opened to indifferent and even hostile reviews, which subsequent critical opinion has completely overwhelmed, and went on to win a large audience.

The film begins at the dawn of civilization, with an ape-man who learns to employ a bone as a weapon in order to destroy a rival. In learning to extend his own physical powers through the use of a tool-weapon to kill one of his own kind, the ape-man has ironically taken a step toward humanity. As the victorious ape-man throws his weapon spiralling into the air, there is a dissolve to a spaceship soaring through space in the year *2001*. "It's simply an observable fact," Kubrick has commented, "that all of man's technology grew out of his discovery of the tool-weapon. There's no doubt that there is a deep emotional relationship between man and his machine-weapons, which are his children. The machine is beginning to assert itself in a very profound way, even attracting affection and obsession."

This concept is dramatized in the film when astronauts Dave Bowman (Keir Dullea) and Frank Poole (Gary Lockwood) find themselves at the mercy of computer HAL 9000 (voiced by Douglas Rain), which controls their spaceship. There are repeated juxtapositions in the film of man, with his human failings and fallibility, alongside machinery—beautiful, functional, but heartless. When Hal the computer makes an error, he refuses to admit the evidence of his own fallibility and proceeds to destroy the occupants of the spaceship to cover it up. Kubrick, as always, is on the side of man, and he indicates here as in *Strangelove* that human fallibility is less likely to destroy man than the abdication of his moral responsibilities to supposedly infallible machines.

Kubrick believes man must also strive to gain mastery over himself and not just over his machines. "Somebody said that man is the missing link between primitive apes and civilized human beings. You might say that the idea is inherent in the story of *2001* too. We are semicivilized, capable of cooperation and affection, but needing some sort of transfiguration into a higher form of life. Since the means to obliterate life on earth exist, it will take more than just careful planning and reasonable cooperation to avoid some eventual catastrophe. The problem exists as long as the potential exists, and the problem is essentially a moral and spiritual one."

Hence the film ends with Bowman, the only survivor of the mission, being reborn as "an enhanced human being, a star child, a superhuman, if you like," says Kubrick, "returning to earth prepared for the next leap forward of man's evolutionary destiny." Kubrick feels that "the God concept

is at the heart of the film" since, if any of the superior beings that inhabit
the universe beyond earth were to manifest itself to a man, the latter
would immediately assume that it was God or an emissary of God. When
an artifact of these extraterrestrial intelligences does appear in the film, it
is represented as a black monolithic slab. Kubrick thought it better not to
try to be too specific in depicting these beings. "You have to leave something to the audience's imagination," he explains.

In summary, the final version of *2001*, which neither shows nor explains
too much, enables the moviegoer to participate more fully in creating for
himself the experience which constitutes the film. As Kubrick himself
comments, "The feel of the experience is the important thing, not the
ability to verbalize it. I tried to create a visual experience which directly
penetrates the subconscious content of the material." The movie consequently becomes for the viewer an intensely subjective experience which
reaches his inner consciousness in the same way that music does, leaving
him free to speculate about its philosophical and allegorical content.

It is significant that Kubrick set the film in the year *2001*, because Fritz
Lang's groundbreaking silent film *Metropolis* (1927) takes place in the year
2000. This reference to Lang's film is a homage to the earlier master's
accomplishment in science fiction, an achievement that Kubrick's film
has built on and surpassed.

The overall implications of *2001* seem to suggest a more optimistic tinge
to Kubrick's view of life than had been previously detected in his work. For
in *2001* he presents man's creative encounters with the universe and his
unfathomed potential for the future. In the third film of the trilogy, *A
Clockwork Orange* (1972), the future appears to be less promising than it was
in *2001*. If in *2001* Kubrick showed the machine becoming human, in *A
Clockwork Orange* he shows man becoming a machine. Ultimately, however, the latter film only reiterates in somewhat darker terms the theme of
all of Kubrick's previous work, namely, that man must retain his humanity
if he is to survive in a dehumanized, materialistic world. Moreover, *A
Clockwork Orange* echoes the warning of *Strangelove* and *2001* that man
must strive to gain mastery over himself if he is to master his machines.

Stanley Kubrick gave me a copy of Anthony Burgess's 1962 novel *A
Clockwork Orange* at the time that he was working on the screenplay.
Reading it, I could see why the book, set up as it is in a series of dramatic
encounters, seemed to Kubrick to be eminently filmable. He said that he

had had a copy of the novel lying on a shelf of books that he wanted to read for a long time and finally got around to reading it in the summer of 1969. Before he had even read through it once the director realized that it would make a fine film: "The story was of a size and density that could be adapted to the screen without oversimplifying it." Burgess's book amounted to a blueprint for the script.

Hence there was no need to collaborate with the novelist on the screen version as there had been with Arthur C. Clarke in the case of *2001* or with Peter George on *Dr. Strangelove*. Kubrick remembers Burgess phoning him one evening for a friendly chat when the latter was passing through London. That was the only discussion that the two men had about the film while Kubrick was working on the script.

A Clockwork Orange is a nightmarish fantasy of England in the not too distant future (policemen in the film wear an emblem of Elizabeth II on their lapels). The story concerns a young hoodlum named Alex (Malcolm McDowell) whose only salutary characteristic seems to be his predilection for Beethoven, to whom he refers affectionately as Ludwig Van. In order to keep Alex from committing any more crimes the State deprives him of his free will and he therefore becomes "a clockwork orange," something that appears to be fully human but is basically mechanical in all of his responses. Burgess borrowed the term from an old Cockney phrase, "as queer as a clockwork orange."

Kubrick spent a minimum of ten hours a day for six months editing *Clockwork Orange*, but he did not mind this large expenditure of time and effort, since editing is his favorite part of the moviemaking process. With Sergei Eisenstein, the great Russian director, Kubrick believes that the way a movie is edited can make or break it. "When I'm editing," Kubrick says, "my identity changes from that of a writer or a director to that of an editor. I am no longer concerned with how much time or money it cost to shoot a given scene. I cut everything to the bone and get rid of anything that doesn't contribute to the total effect of the film." He sees editing as the only unique phase of filmmaking, for it does not resemble any other art form.

As always, Kubrick was putting the finishing touches on *Clockwork Orange* right up to the release date. Just before the premiere on December 20, 1971, he chose the shade of orange for the plain background against which the opening credits would be projected. The plain background indicates that Kubrick has not gone along with the recent trend toward clever title sequences, preferring to spend the money that such expensive techniques entail on the film itself. He believes that the first shot of the picture should be what engages the audience's attention, not eye-catching credits.

Just as *2001* ended with a close-up of the star child staring into the camera as it journeys back to earth in anticipation of the next step in man's evolution, so *A Clockwork Orange* begins with a close-up of Alex staring into the camera with a smirk on his face, as he looks forward to the coming night of sexual escapades and "ultra-violence" with his gang. Since the brutal Alex is a long way from the evolutionary progress that the star child represents, one might infer that Kubrick is saying in this film that the world will get worse before it gets better.

Alex's world as it is projected in the picture has a basis in reality, in that it reflects in an exaggerated form tendencies which already exist in contemporary society. Antiutopian novels like Waugh's *Love Among the Ruins,* Orwell's *1984,* and Burgess's *A Clockwork Orange* are not so much predictions of the future as parodies of the materialism, sexual indulgence, and mindless violence of the present. That is why Mr. Alexander, the writer in *A Clockwork Orange,* whose wife eventually dies of a vicious assault by Alex and his henchmen, remarks late in the film that his wife was really a victim of the Modern Age.

In essence, the ugly and erratic behavior of Alex and his clan is their way of asserting themselves against the depersonalized regimentation of the socialized state in which they live. Alex, for example, lives with his family in Municipal Flat Block 18A, a sterile and characterless apartment building. Later on, when his crimes catch up with him and he is sent to prison, he is referred to as 655321. But one wonders if he can be any more anonymous in jail than he was when he was a member of the regimented society that lies beyond the prison walls.

In an effort to get his jail term shortened, Alex volunteers to undergo "the Ludovico treatment." This is a brainwashing technique that renders him nauseous when confronted with opportunities for indulging in sex and violence, the very experiences that once gave him delight. Only the prison chaplain speaks up against the treatment. "Goodness comes from within," he insists. "Goodness must be chosen; when a man can no longer choose he ceases to be a man."

Upon his release Alex is totally unprepared to cope with the calloused and corrupt society that awaits him. He is beaten senseless by two of his old gang members, now policemen of a state that is becoming more and more fascist in its efforts to impose law and order on the populace. After he attempts suicide, however, Alex realizes with great joy during his convalescence in the hospital that the effects of the brainwashing are wearing off; indeed, he is returning to his old self, complete with all of his former proclivities. In brief Alex has regained his free will.

Because Kubrick has been unsparing in detailing Alex's depraved behavior in *A Clockwork Orange,* the film was a source of great controversy when first released. In defending his film and the philosophy that underlies it, Kubrick countered, "The fact that Alex is evil personified is important, to clarify the moral point that the film is making about human freedom." He explained that the chaplain really expresses the theme of the movie when he asserts, "The question is whether or not the Ludovico treatment really makes a man good." It is true, the chaplain concedes, that, because of the treatment, Alex ceases to be a wrongdoer. But he ceases also to be a creature capable of choice.

Kubrick continued, "The essential moral question is whether or not a man can be good without having the option to be evil and whether such a creature is still human." In short, he concluded, "To restrain man is not to redeem him." Redemption, as the prison chaplain says more than once in the movie, must come from within.

"The film and the book are about the danger of reclaiming sinners through sapping their capacity to choose between good and evil," Anthony Burgess adds. "Most of all, I wanted to show in my story that God made man free to choose either good or evil; and that this is an astounding gift." Malcolm McDowell's own feelings about Alex at the end of the film bear out Burgess's remarks, as well as Kubrick's: "Alex is free at the end; that's hopeful. Maybe in his freedom, he'll be able to find someone to help him without brainwashing. If his 'Ludwig van' can speak to him, perhaps others can."

In analyzing *A Clockwork Orange,* one cannot overlook the musical score. Kubrick has always taken an interest in the choice of music in his films, stemming from the early days when he performed every job in the film-making process by himself. He often likes to employ recordings of familiar melodies on the sound track as an ironic counterpoint to the action, as when "We'll Meet Again" served as the accompaniment to the nuclear holocaust in *Dr. Strangelove*.

His use of "Singing in the Rain" in *A Clockwork Orange* is another stroke of genius. Early in the film Alex sings this song while beating a writer and raping his wife with the help of his gang. Then, during the closing credits of the movie, as a final irony, Kubrick has Gene Kelly's original rendition of the song from the 1951 film *Singin' in the Rain* played on the soundtrack, just after Alex has jubilantly declared that he is cured—which means that he is fully able to go back to his previous vicious behavior. The words of the song in this context take on an ironic quality, as Kelly exults that it is "a glorious feeling" to be "happy again." As Kelly proclaims that "there's a smile on my face for the whole human race" and that he's "ready for love," one remembers the circumstances in which Alex sang the song earlier in the film and realizes that to Alex they would mean that he is ready to resume his "ultra-violence" and lustful behavior. One might go a step further in tying the song in with the film and say that anyone who is not concerned for mankind's future as depicted in *A Clockwork Orange* is indeed singing in the rain.

"It takes about a year to let an idea reach an obsessional state, so I know what I really want to do with it," Kubrick says of the way that he initiates a new project. After spending some time looking for a project to follow *A Clockwork Orange*, he finally decided to step back into the past and dramatize *Barry Lyndon*, a tale of an eighteenth-century rogue written by Victorian novelist William Makepeace Thackeray.

Kubrick believes that location shooting is just as viable for a period picture like *Barry Lyndon* as for a contemporary story like *The Killing*, or for one set in the near future like *Clockwork Orange*. "Most of the interiors of a period film can be shot in mansions and castles that are still preserved in Europe, where the furniture and decor are already there," he has pointed out. "You only have to move in your cast and crew and get to work."

Kubrick states that he was determined not to turn out an elaborate period picture like those made especially in England in the forties—stodgy pageants filled with empty spectacle. After a steady diet of historical epics of this sort, one small-town American exhibitor wrote to his distributor back in the forties, "Don't send me no more pictures about people who write with feathers!" In *Barry Lyndon* Kubrick was determined that, although his characters might write with feathers, they would inhabit a historical era, not as part of a dead past but of a living present.

In *Barry Lyndon* one finds resonances of a theme that has reasserted itself in much of Kubrick's best work, that the best laid plans often go awry. He has frequently shown in his films how human error and chance can thwart an individual's best efforts to achieve his goals, as in *The Killing* and his science-fiction trilogy. In this list of movies about human failures, the story of Barry Lyndon easily finds a place, for Barry's lifelong schemes to become a wealthy nobleman in the end come to nothing.

Summing up his personal vision as it appears in his films, Kubrick has said, "The destruction of this planet would have no significance on a cosmic scale. Our extinction would be little more than a match flaring for a second in the heavens. And if that match does blaze in the darkness, there will be none to mourn a race that used a power that could have lit a beacon to the stars to light its own funeral pyre."

Kubrick's Grandest Gamble: *Barry Lyndon*

MARTHA DUFFY AND
RICHARD SCHICKEL/1975

FIRST PARADOX: *Barry Lyndon,* a story of an eighteenth century Irish gen-
tleman-rogue, is the first novel of a great nineteenth century writer,
William Makepeace Thackeray. It shows early signs of a genius that would
flourish only after creative struggle and personal adversity. In time, this
forgotten book becomes the basis for the tenth feature film by a well-estab-
lished, well-rewarded twentieth century artist—director Stanley Kubrick.
In it, he demonstrates the qualities that eluded Thackeray: singularity of
vision, mature mastery of his medium, near-reckless courage in asserting
through this work a claim not just to the distinction critics have already
granted him but to greatness that time alone can—and probably will—
confirm.

SECOND PARADOX: As he did in *2001: A Space Odyssey,* Kubrick relies not
on words—he is as sparing of them as Thackeray is profligate—but images
to tell his story. Yet *Barry Lyndon* lacks the experimental, hallucinatory
visual quality that made *2001* a cultural touchstone of the tripped-out '6os.
Kubrick has shot and edited *Barry Lyndon* with the classic economy and
elegance associated with the best works of the silent cinema. The frantic
trompe l'oeil manner—all quick cuts and crazy angles—recently favored
by ambitious filmmakers (and audiences) has been rigorously rejected.
    This drive for cinematic purity has consumed three years of Kubrick's
life and $11 million of Warner Bros. money. The film is three hr., four min.

From *Time,* 15 December 1975. © 1975 Time Inc. Reprinted by permission.

and four sec. long, and it does not easily yield up its themes. "The essence of dramatic form," says Kubrick, "is to let an idea come over people without its being plainly stated. When you say something directly, it is simply not as potent as it is when you allow people to discover it for themselves."

THIRD PARADOX: *Barry Lyndon* is obviously a costume drama but in a much more literal sense than any movie easily dismissed by that contemptuous phrase. Many of the clothes are not costumes at all but authentic antiques. The equally real interiors and landscapes—every foot of the film was shot on location—are intended to function as something more than exotic delights for the eye. Close scrutiny of the settings reveals not only the character of the people who inhabit them but the spirit of the entire age as Kubrick understands it.

Though *Barry Lyndon* includes the duels, battles, and romantic intrigues that we are conditioned to expect in movies about the past, it more often than not cuts away from this easy-to-savor material. This cool distancing suggests that the melodramatic passions normally sustaining our interest in films are petty matters. This vision of the past, like Kubrick's vision of the future in *2001*, invites us to experience an alien world not through its characters but with them—sensorially, viscerally. Stanley Kubrick's idea of what constitutes historical spectacle does not coincide with many people's—least of all, those in Warner's sales department. Which brings us to the...

FOURTH PARADOX: Having made what amounts to an art-film spectacle—something few directors since Griffith and Eisenstein have brought off—Kubrick now requires that his backers go out and sell the damned thing. Because of distribution and promotion costs, the film must gross at least $30 million to make a profit. Kubrick has his own ideas about how to proceed: a tasteful ad campaign, a limited-release pattern permitting good word of mouth to build, saturation bookings timed to coincide with the Academy Award nominations that the director and studio believe are inevitable. Warner salesmen wish they had something simpler on their hands—a great sloshy romance like *Dr. Zhivago*, for instance, or at least a rollicking rip-off of olden times, like *Tom Jones*. Now Kubrick will help sell his picture. Among other things, he employs a bookkeeper to chart how films have played in the first-run houses of key cities, so his films can be booked into those with the best records. But the fact remains that his work habits are anything but helpful to publicists.

Multimillion dollar movies are usually open to the press as they are being made; their heavy tread can be heard clumping toward the theaters for a year prior to release. Kubrick's locations, however, were closed. Not a single publicity still emerged without the director's express approval, which was almost never granted. Thus the only word on *Barry Lyndon* came from actors and technicians, none of them privy to Kubrick's vision, and some were worried and literally sickened by his obsessive perfectionism.

At age forty-seven, he is the creator of one of the cinema's most varied and successful bodies of work: in addition to *2001*, it includes *Paths of Glory, Lolita, Doctor Strangelove,* and *A Clockwork Orange.* He enjoys the rare right to final cut of his film without stupid advice or interference. Warner executives were not permitted to see more than a few bits of it until the completed version—take it or leave it—was screened for them just three weeks ago. To put it mildly, it is hard for them to get a proper buildup going for their expensive property on such short notice.

FIFTH PARADOX: Stanley Kubrick himself. *Barry Lyndon* may be an austere epic, but an epic it surely is. Such works pose complex logistical and technical problems that must be solved along with the aesthetic questions that arise every time a new camera setup is chosen. Kubrick's basic cast and crew of one hundred seventy—augmented by hundreds of extras and supporting specialisists as needed—crawled from location to location across Ireland and England for eight and a half months. Normally, the commanders of cinematic operations on this scale are outgoing, not to say colorfully flamboyant characters.

That, however, is precisely what Kubrick is not. He is almost reclusively shy, "a demented perfectionist, according to the publicity mythology around me." This myth began building when he decided to stay on in England after shooting *Lolita* there in 1961. He found it "helpful not to be constantly exposed to the fear and anxiety that prevail in the film world." He lives and does all pre- and post-production work in a rambling manor house defended by two wooden walls and furnished in early nondescript. He rarely ventures forth even to London, less than an hour away. He prefers that the world—in controllable quantities—be brought to him via telex, telephone, television. All the books and movies this omnivorous reader-viewer requires are delivered to the retreat he shares with his third wife Christiane, his three daughters, three dogs, and six cats. He is, says his friend, film critic Alexander Walker, "like a medieval artist living above his workshop." According to an actress who once worked for him, he is also "a mole."

What has the mole wrought? Is the finished film worth the pains he has taken with it—and given to his associates over the long years of its creation? The answer is a resounding yes.

Kubrick does not know what drew him to this tale of a scoundrel's rise and fall. Beyond noting that he has always enjoyed Thackeray, he does not try to explain his choice: "It's like trying to say why you fell in love with your wife—it's meaningless."

Possibly, but Kubrick's curiosity was probably aroused by the chance to explore a character who is his antithesis. About his work Kubrick is the most self-conscious and rational of men. His eccentricities—secretiveness, a great need for privacy—are caused by his intense awareness of time's relentless passage. He wants to use time to "create a string of masterpieces," as an acquaintance puts it. Social status means nothing to him, money is simply a tool of his trade.

Barry, on the other hand, suffers a monstrous complacency. He betrays not the slightest moral or intellectual self-awareness. Born poor but with a modest claim to gentleman's rank, he never doubts his right to rise to the highest ranks of the nobility. Nor does he ever seem to question the various means by which he pursues his end: army desertion, card sharping, contracting a loveless marriage in order to acquire a fortune. As for time, it means nothing to him. He squanders it, as he does money, in pursuit of pleasure and the title he is desperate for.

In the novel, Thackeray used a torrent of words to demonstrate Barry's lack of self-knowledge. Narrating his own story, Barry so obviously exaggerates his claims to exemplary behavior that the reader perceives he is essentially a braggart and poltroon. Daringly, Kubrick uses silence to make the same point. "People like Barry are successful because they are not obvious—they don't announce themselves," says Kubrick. So it is mainly by the look in Ryan O'Neal's eyes—a sharp glint when he spies the main chance, a gaze of hurt befuddlement when things go awry—that we understand Barry's motives. And since he cannot see his own face, we can be certain he is not aware of these self-betrayals. According to Kubrick, Barry's silence also implies that "he is not very bright," he is an overreacher who "gets in over his head in situations he doesn't fully understand." Though a certain dimness makes him a less obviously comic figure than he is in the book, it also makes him a more believable one. And it permits Kubrick to demonstrate, without shattering the movie's tone, Barry's two nearly saving graces—physical gallantry and desperate love of his only child, whose death is the film's emotional high point and the tragedy that finally undoes Barry.

With the exception of Humbert Humbert in *Lolita,* this is the first time that Kubrick has moved beyond pop archetypes and taken the measure of a man with a novelist's sense of psychological nuance. Still, it is not as a study in character that *Barry Lyndon* will be ultimately remembered. The structure of the work is truly novel. In addition, Kubrick has assembled perhaps the most ravishing set of images ever printed on a single strip of celluloid. These virtues are related: the structure would not work without Kubrick's sustaining mastery of the camera, lighting, and composition; the images would not be so powerful if the director had not devised a narrative structure spacious enough for them to pile up with overwhelming impressiveness.

As a design, *Barry Lyndon* is marvelously simple. The first half offers something like a documentary of eighteenth century manners and morals. To be sure, a lot happens to Barry in this segment—first love, first duel, first wanderings, first military combat—but he remains pretty much a figure in the foreground, rather like those little paper cutouts architects place on their models to give a sense of scale. What matters to the director is the world beyond, the world Barry is so anxious to conquer.

And it is a great world, especially to the modern eye, accustomed as it is to cluttered industrialized landscapes, and architecture and décor that stress the purely functional. The recurring visual motif of the film—especially obvious in the first portion—is a stately pullback. Typically, it starts on some detail, like a closeup of an actor, then moves slowly back to reveal the simple beauty of the countryside that is as indifferent to the player's petty pursuits as he is impervious to its innocent charm. The lighting in all the outdoor sequences appears to be completely natural and patiently— expensively—waited for. Frequently, most of the emotional information for a scene may be found in the light, before anyone says a word. A superb

example of this occurs when Barry discovers his first love flirting in a garden with a man who is everything he is not—mature, wealthy, well born,
English, and an army officer to boot. The late afternoon sun, soft as the
lyric of a love ballad, literally dies along with Barry's hopes of romance.

Indoors, there are similar revelations, thanks in part to spaceage technology. Kubrick found a way to fit an incredibly fast (F 0.7) 50mm. still-camera
lens, developed by Zeiss, onto a motion-picture camera. It permitted him
to film night interiors using only the light available to inhabitants of the
eighteenth century. Some scenes are illuminated by just a single candle;
in others, hundreds gutter in the candelabra and chandeliers of great halls,
bathing the screen in a gentle, wonderfully moody orange glow that almost
no one now alive has ever experienced.

In the hands of another director, all this embellishment might seem
an idle exercise, perhaps even proof of the old movie adage that when a
director dies he becomes a cameraman. The first half of *Barry Lyndon* deliberately violates every rule of sound dramatic composition. Only a few of
the scenes end in powerful emotion or conflict, and there is no strong arc
to the overall design of the piece. And yet our attention never wanders:
such is Kubrick's gift for lighting and composing a scene, such is the
strength of his desire to prove that movies "haven't scratched the surface
of how to tell stories in their own terms."

The thought is not new. Everyone who has worked in or thought seriously about the cinema knows that the angle of a shot or the rhythm of a
scene's editing can impart information more economically than a long
stretch of dialogue. What is novel is that Kubrick has acted so firmly on
the basis of that nearly conventional wisdom in the film's first half—the
half that must catch and hold the attention of a mass audience (*The
Towering Inferno* crowd) if his picture is to succeed commercially.

It is a big risk, an act of the highest artistic confidence. Reassurance
comes in the strong melodrama of the film's second half. From the
moment Marisa Berenson, playing Lady Lyndon, appears and Barry's suit
for her hand succeeds, the film, without seeming to change its style or
gently enfolding pace, gathers tremendous dramatic force of a quite conventional sort. Barry's loveless use of her to further his ambitions has a
raw, shocking edge. His conflict with her son by her first marriage, culmi-
nating in what is surely the most gripping duel ever filmed, is full of angry

uncontrolled passion. Barry's innocent infatuation with his own child, "the hope of his family, the pride of his manhood," has a touching, redeeming warmth to it. His downfall, much more dramatically rendered by Kubrick than by Thackeray, has a tragic starkness and a moral correctness. In short, Kubrick has accomplished what amounts to a minor miracle—an uncompromised artistic vision, that also puts all of Warner Bros. money "on the screen," as Kubrick says, borrowing an old trade term. He feels he has done right by himself and "done right by the people who gave me the money," presenting them with the best possible chance to make it back with a profit on their investment.

Kubrick turned to *Barry Lyndon* after a projected biography of Napoleon proved too complex and expensive even for him. He reread the novel several times, "looking for traps, making sure it was do-able." With typically elaborate caution, he got Warners backing on the basis of an outline in which names, places, and dates were changed so no one could filch from him a story in the public domain. He then settled down to work on script and research. The latter may be, for him, the more important undertaking. "Stanley is voracious for information. He wants glorious choice," says his associate producer, Bernard Williams. Adds costume designer Milena Canonero: "He wants to see everything. He wants at his fingertips the knowledge, the feeling of the period."

Kubrick is a self-taught man with an autodidact's passion for facts and the process of gathering them. Son of a Bronx physician, he was an indifferent high school student. He experimented endlessly with cameras and at seventeen was hired by *Look* as a staff photographer. He learned something about people and a lot about photography, traveling the country shooting pictures for four and one half years. At twenty-one, he made his first short subject, three years later his first fictional feature—very low budget. He also audited Columbia University courses conducted by the likes of Lionel Trilling and Mark Van Doren, and became a tireless reader with catholic tastes. "I can become interested in anything," he says. "Delving into a subject, discovering facts and details—I find that easy and pleasurable."

It is also essential to his work. For one thing, he finds it impossible to invent an entirely original story, something drawn out of his own experience or fantasy life. Indeed, the creation of fiction awes him. "It is one of the most phenomenal human achievements," he says. "And I have never done it." Instead, he must do "detective work—find out about the things about which I have no direct experience." These, of course, offer metaphors in which to cloak such observations—they are never direct messages— that he cares to share with the world.

Research aids him in another way. Movie sets—even the cool, orderly ones Kubrick is famous for running—seethe with logistical, technical, and emotional problems. As Kubrick mildly puts it, "The atmosphere is inimical to making subtle aesthetic decisions." He is unable to determine how to shoot a scene until he sees a set fully dressed and lit. This is a moment of maximum risk. Says Ryan O'Neal, who plays Barry: "The toughest part of Stanley's day was finding the right first shot. Once he did that, other shots fell into place. But he agonized over that first one."

It is precisely then that Kubrick's memory bank, well stocked with odd details, comes into play. "Once, when he was really stymied, he began to search through a book of eighteenth century art reproductions," recalls O'Neal. "He found a painting—I don't remember which one—and posed Marissa and me exactly as if we were in that painting."

Most of his performers seem to worship Kubrick. One reason is that he is always willing to give their suggestions a trial run or two. He is also intelligent about not overdirecting them. "Stanley is a great believer in the man," says Murray Melvin, who is superb in the role of a snaky spiritual adviser to Lady Lyndon. "*You* have to do it." Adds Patrick Magee, who plays a gambler: "The catch-words on the set are 'Do it faster, do it slower, do it again.' Mostly, 'Do it again.'"

Melvin did one scene fifty times. "I knew he had seen something I had done. But because he was a good director, he wouldn't tell me what it was. Because if someone tells you you've done a good bit, then you know it and put it in parentheses and kill it. The better actor you were, the more he drew out of you."

There is no sadism in Kubrick's insistence on huge numbers of retakes. He did not press Berenson or the children in his cast, only the established professionals he knew could stand up under his search for the best they had to offer. "Actors who have worked a lot in movies," Kubrick says mildly, "don't really get a sense of intense excitement into their performances until there is film running through the camera." Moreover, the

"beady eye" that several insist was cast on them as they worked is merely
a sign of the mesmerizing concentration he brings to his work.

Originally Kubrick, who likes to sleep in his own bed and likes even more
to save the money it costs to house and feed a crew on location, had
hoped to shoot the entire picture within a ninety-minute range of home.
He dispatched photographers to all the great houses within that circle,
hoping to find the look he wanted. Impossible. He then decided to shoot
in Ireland, where the early sections of the book are set anyway. After a couple of months there, however, the I.R.A.—or someone using its name—
made telephone threats to the production. Kubrick decamped for rural
England, where he used rooms in at least four different stately homes, art-
fully cut together to give Hackton Castle, Lady Lyndon's digs, spaciousness
and richness. At Corsham Court, he was told that if he did not kill his
lights within thirty minutes, irreparable harm would be done to the price-
less paintings in the room where he was shooting. Similar incidents
sent the budget soaring, giving an extra twist to the pressures Kubrick
felt. Nerves produced a rash on his hands that did not disappear until the
film was wrapped, and though he had quit smoking, he started cadging
cigarettes.

　　Still, things could have been worse. Warner's production chief, John
Calley, was always tolerant. "It would make no sense to tell Kubrick, "O.K.,
fella, you've got one more week to finish the thing," he says. "What you
would get then is a mediocre film that cost say, $8 million, instead of a
masterpiece that cost $11 million. When somebody is spending a lot of
your money, you are wise to give him time to do the job right."

　　Calley admits he has no idea whether masterpieces are going to sell this
season. "The business is, at best, a crap shoot. The fact that Stanley thinks
the picture will gross in nine figures is very reassuring. He is never far
wrong about anything." If Kubrick is right, he will be rich. By the terms
of his deal with Warners, he receives forty percent of Barry Lyndon's profits.
Only one picture in history—Jaws—has made "nine figures"; it passed the
$100 million mark last week.

　　As for Kubrick, he is still working eighteen hours a day, overseeing the
final fine tuning of the soundtrack while keeping one compulsively atten-
tive eye on the orchestration of the publicity buildup. It is something he
feels he must do, just as he personally checked the first seventeen prints of

A Clockwork Orange before they went out to the theaters. "There is such a total sense of demoralization if you say you don't care. From start to finish on a film, the only limitations I observe are those imposed on me by the amount of money I have to spend and the amount of sleep I need. You either care or you don't, and I simply don't know where to draw the line between those two points."

He does not believe a single flop will cost him his ability to create independently, though he may occasionally think of a line in *The Killing*, his first major studio release in 1956. A thief muses that people romanticize gangsters and artists, but they are also eager to see them brought low.

Much more often, however, Stanley Kubrick is armored in the serene belief that whatever judgment the public passes on his new movie when it opens next week, he has fulfilled the director's basic ideal, which is to shoot "economically and with as much beauty and gracefulness as possible." Beyond that, he adds, "All you can do is either pose questions or make truthful observations about human behavior. The only morality is not to be dishonest." *Barry Lyndon* fulfills that ideal as well.

Not even the Brothers Grimm would have dared to write a fairy tale about a girl who started at the top and stayed there. But that is the story of Marisa Berenson, twenty-eight, the suffering heroine of *Barry Lyndon*. (The French fashion magazine *Elle* once called Marisa "the most beautiful girl in the world.") That is not precisely accurate (both the mouth and nose are a trifle too large), but it conveys the right idea.

La vita turned really *dolce* for Marisa in 1971, when Luchino Visconti signed her for her first film as the elegant young mother in *Death in Venice*. Bob Fosse then hired her to play the German-Jewish department store heiress in *Cabaret*. Both parts required Marisa to appear both remote and vulnerable. She is very good at it.

Today, trying to explain what he found in her, Stanley Kubrick says: "There is a sort of tragic sense about her." Actors do not always see their leading ladies as directors do, and Ryan O'Neal wondered why Kubrick had cast her. "Overbred, vacuous, giggly, and lazy," were Ryan's first impressions; as the filming progressed, O'Neal decided that the role called for Marisa to be just that. "She'll be nominated for an Oscar," he says. "But she's just being herself."

A bit churlish, that. Yet Marisa seems to sense that life with the trendies, where role playing is *de rigueur*, has locked her into an outgrown character. She concedes that in her younger days, her own shyness gave her a frantic need to be on the scene. Modeling gave her self-confidence, and acting "is a vent for my fantasies." Last week in Manhattan, cuddling her Shih Tzu, K.K. (short for King Kong), she reminisced about her most notable fantasy to date, Lady Lyndon. Done up like a portrait by Gainsborough, Marisa seems the model of eighteenth century English womanhood, even to the torrents of tears Lady Lyndon sheds at her son's death. "I could do nothing else but cry, looking at that sweet boy—I am quite good at crying," says Marisa. "Once I start, I can go on and on."

Ryan O'Neal has been unusually quiet lately. He finished his work on *Barry Lyndon* in July 1974 and, despite numerous offers, has avoided work since, so convinced is he that the film will radically change his image with the public and his standing in the movie business.

Not that there is anything especially wrong with either. Now thirty-four, he has had three hits in five years in romantic and light comic roles (*Love Story, What's Up, Doc?* and *Paper Moon,* in which his daughter stole the show). He is generally regarded by movie people as a hard-working actor and an agreeable off-the-set companion. It is just that in a career that began in early '60s television and got rolling with a five-year stint on *Peyton Place,* Ryan has never known anyone quite like Stanley Kubrick. "God, he works you hard," he wrote in the diary he kept all during the ten months he was before the cameras. "He moves you, pushes you, helps you, gets cross with you, but above all he teaches you the value of a good director."

Never having worked with a world-class director, O'Neal eagerly underwent something like a conversion. "Stanley brought out aspects of my personality and acting instincts that had been dormant. I had to deliver up everything he wanted, and he wanted just about everything I had."

Not only was the work demanding; it was also uncomfortable. It took O'Neal into the remoter corners of Ireland and England—not exactly the natural habitat of a fellow who does enjoy the occasional comforts of a bird and a *boite.* Nevertheless, he was sustained by "my strong suspicion that I was involved in something great."

Whether or not his patient faith in *Lyndon* will be rewarded is a nice question. There is no doubt that Kubrick permitted him to explore a wider range of emotions than he ever has on screen. There is no doubt either that his performance is technically expert. On the other hand, he has been carefully muted by the director. O'Neal, who has finally decided to go back to work in January with Tatum and Burt Reynolds in a new Peter Bogdanovitch film, could be disappointed in the response his hard work generates. "The real star of a Kubrick movie is Stanley Kubrick" is producer Ray Stark's shrewd comment, implying that O'Neal's hope for the role may be in vain.

If so, he will still have an improved talent and some warm memories to console him. Once, after days of effort, he finally managed to deliver exactly what Kubrick wanted in a difficult scene. "He found a way to walk past me, giving instructions to the crew—'Let's move on to thirty-two, move those lights into the foreground,' and so on—but as he passed me, he grabbed my hand and squeezed it. It was the most beautiful and appreciated gesture in my life. It was the greatest moment in my career."

Stanley Kubrick's Vietnam War

FRANCIS CLINES/1987

THE REASSURING THING ABOUT Stanley Kubrick is that after being deep as Yahweh in the creation of one movie for the last five years, he emerges gentle and curious on the seventh day, asking about beer commercials and envying silent filmmakers and recalling the pleasures of the Thalia Theater.

"Have you seen those Michelob commercials?" he asks as if they were samizdat, speaking of the thirty-second spots that came uninvited with the Giants football game videos that his sister sent the eminent director all last winter from New Jersey. Then, he had no time to spare for watching anything beyond his own work in progress and a weekly fix of football. "They're just boy-girl, night-fun, leading up to pouring the beer, all in thirty seconds, beautifully edited and photographed. Economy of statement is not something that films are noted for."

Sunday morning at Pinewood Studios in the London suburbs seems sepulchral in the empty executive offices, as quiet as HAL's deep-space murder scene in *2001*, an awful setting to encounter one of a kind. But Mr. Kubrick arrives rumpled and lone as the night watchman, offers a simple hello, accepts the fact that he cannot direct the phone to work properly, and settles down to discuss movies and imagination and his own new work, much as a carpenter would feel the grain of a cabinet. It is his newest making, perchance his best or at least another in his line.

From *The New York Times* 21 June 1987. Copyright © 1987 by the New York Times Co. Reprinted by permission.

"It starts with being excited by a story and finally it's telling the story on the screen," he says, speaking of the process of directing. "It goes from the most wonderful literary atmosphere to desperation. It can be as crude as standing up and writing on the back of an envelope when someone's just said something and it's four o'clock with the winter sun fading. You've got to shoot it and you're trying to exploit something that's just come up. It's like a quarterback calling an automatic play when he sees the defense he's up against."

His new movie, *Full Metal Jacket*, a story hinged on the trauma of the Tet offensive in the Vietnam War, is completed and opens in New York on Friday at neighborhood theaters. Beckton, an old 1930's-gasworks town abandoned on the Thames, has been destroyed by Mr. Kubrick's technical artists, all fiery and pocked as Hue, the Vietnamese city of the movie's climax. The two hundred palm trees flown in from Spain to make Vietnam of this sceptered isle have been returned to peacetime. Out on the downs, the Parris Island cadence counting has ceased along with all the lurid, ignoble, cynical and sadly mortal motion of characters directed onto film from the mind of Stanley Kubrick.

The movie is literally only hours old in Mr. Kubrick's finished, perfectionist version, and far from talking 1980s box office or 1960s jabberwocky about his personal agony through the nation's Vietnam experience, Mr. Kubrick is describing being true to the initial emotion that struck him when he first found this story. That was five years ago amid what is the hardest part of directing, he says, searching for a good tale that sustains the imagination.

"The sense of the story the first time you read it is the absolutely critical yardstick. I remember what I felt about the book, I remember what I felt in writing the script, and then I try to keep that alive in the very inappropriate circumstances that exist on a film set where you've got a hundred people standing around and nothing but particular problems, still trying to sustain a subjective sense of what it is emotionally—as well as what it is that pleases you."

Bearded and staring carefully as a question is asked, Mr. Kubrick speaks with his right hand rubbing his brow, often glancing down, like a man reciting the confiteor or handicapping the next race.

"That first impression is the most precious thing you've got, you can never have it again—the yardstick for any judgment that you have as you get deeper and deeper into the work because making a movie is a process of going into smaller and smaller detail and finally winding up in the minutiae of how does a footstep sound on the sound track when you're remixing the film."

No, he had no craving to make a signature movie about that war, he says. He was reading the *Virginia Kirkus Review*, as he usually does, looking for stirring fiction about something, anything that might promise a stunning translation to film and he came upon a novel, *"The Short-Timers."* He read a copy.

"I reread it almost immediately and I thought, 'This is very exciting, I better think about it for a few days.' But it was immediately apparent that it was a unique, absolutely wonderful book," he says about the novel, written by Gustav Hasford, an ex-Marine combat correspondent whose offering resembles a memoir of the pellucid and the ravaged as much as the naked and the dead. The screenplay is by Mr. Kubrick, Mr. Hasford, and Michael Herr, author of *Dispatches*, a memoir of the Vietnam War.

Full Metal Jacket is a reference in military bureaucratese to the rifle cartridge that is the field ammunition of the basic Marine Corps fighter-killer. The movie is blue with death and madness but also characteristically balletic at times with Mr. Kubrick's forensic eye, particularly in the initial boot camp scenes where men are shaved raw for war. The chorus-type character, Private Joker, played by Matthew Modine, traverses the war diagonally, encompassing the propaganda mill of the combat correspondents and the sudden, all-hands combat duty of the Tet offensive by the North Vietnamese. This is an event that shreds the jingoistic romance of the war and makes an unlikely killer of Joker.

Whether critics judge the film singularly good or bad—never an easy, predictable task for them by the director's track record—at a minimum the movie has been spare and ugly and beautiful by the time its dark sweep is completed from the Marine Hymn to the singing of M-I-C-K-E-Y M-O-U-S-E as Mr. Kubrick's Marines stagger beyond the Tet offensive into nowhere and houselights up.

Mr. Kubrick is such a loner in the film business, not only following the beat of a different drummer but more likely constructing his own drum, that it can only be purest coincidence that his movie has emerged now in the industry's sudden burst of special Vietnam films. It comes close after *Platoon*, the well acclaimed standout that he recently saw and liked very much, he says plainly as a fan who loved the Thalia's darkness, apparently devoid of professional envy. Mr. Kubrick shies from talking of what he hopes his movie says; he judges he was typically dubious and critical of the Vietnam War in its day, but he hardly seems the zealot-esthete now having his say about it. His worry about war in conversation is understandably technological from the man who made *Dr. Strangelove,* a doubt that nuclear weapons can ever be eliminated and a concern that there is too little negotiation to limit the chances of accidental missile war.

Mr. Kubrick works hermitlike for years on a single picture, searching out a story, writing a script, producing and directing all the way down to, lately, the search for good foreign writers, actors, and directors who might not spoil the work for him in the four main movie dubbing markets. His choice of subject matter for a new film is enough to fascinate buffs who have bounded with him across thirty eclectic years from *Paths of Glory* to *Spartacus,* from *Lolita* to *Dr. Strangelove,* from *2001: A Space Odyssey* to *A Clockwork Orange,* from *Barry Lyndon* to *The Shining.*

"I'm happy with the picture," he says in this period of pause when he will catch up on eighteen months of missed movies, good and bad, and read as ever with the hope of finding another story. "My films have all had varying critical opinion and it's always been subsequent critical reaction that settles the scores."

He talks of that more in puzzlement than vindication. "The only thing I can think of is that everybody's always expecting the last movie again, and they're sometimes angry — I mean some critics — often put off because they're expecting something else." He talks of trusting the "more democratic intelligence" of the public, a lesson he particularly learned after *2001:* "People who didn't have the responsibility of having to explain it or formulate clear statements about it two hours after they saw the film weren't troubled."

At age fifty-eight, Mr. Kubrick has been involved in making movies for thirty-five years, a physician's son who became a relative adventurer from the Bronx, dropping from formal education to become a photographer for *Look* magazine, then moving to motion pictures where he has mastered the basic phases from writing to financing and reigns as a bookish autodidact of unpredictable curiosities. He dislikes Los Angeles, feels New York is technically limited for filmmaking and so finds London the place to work and raise his family in satisfying privacy.

"Just keep at it," he says of his work habit of plunging into the making of each film, analyzing each approaching day's move well into the night before, much like the masters of Mr. Kubrick's beloved avocation, chess. "Chess is an analogy—it is a series of steps that you take one at a time and it's balancing resources against the problem, which in chess is time and in movies is time and money," he says.

Chess is less creative for him but teaches him not to get carried away with impulsive first ideas. "I've found over the long period of time which it takes to make a movie that your own sense of whether you think it's good or bad or how happy you are at a particular time is very unimportant, that the ideas just come and sometimes they seem to come out of some place that's got nothing to do with how you feel."

Mr. Kubrick talks of movies not as Ahab stalks the whale but as a physicist might toss and catch Newton's apple.

"I have a feeling that no one has yet really found the way to tell a story to utilize the greatest potential that films have," he says. "I think the silent movies come closest to it because they weren't trapped in having to present a scene which was essentially a stage type of scene; movies consist of little play scenes." He sounds gentle toned, as if he were not discussing the heart of his existence. "There's a gap between the guys who can actually write a story and someone who can visualize it, and that's a big gap because even the directors who write, like Woody Allen and Bergman, are very much bound up in the conventions of the stage."

As he talks, Mr. Kubrick suddenly puts his envy of the silents on a track parallel with his curiosity about the thirty-second Michelob spots. "The best TV commercials create a tremendously vivid sense of a mood, of a complex presentation of something."

"Some combination of the two might work," Mr. Kubrick says, braiding a fantasy that seems to twirl somewhere within. "I have a feeling that no one has begun to do what a movie could really do." His voice has a casual, New York mood, but his eyes reflect a terrible determination.

The director pictures a grainy old fade-in from the silents and he invents a title card: "Joe's cousin, Bill." "And you just see a shot of Bill doing something," he says as a listener lingers wishing that Stanley Kubrick would flesh out Bill. But Bill ceases to exist, with no time for mourning in the run of ideas, as Mr. Kubrick lovingly talks of "economy of structural statement, the nearest to silent film." This is a quality he savored in the

Vietnam book in his first reaction, he recalls, and one that in the film he has sought to transfer "quite literally because the dialogue is so almost poetic in its carved-out, stark quality."

But this movie is done, and Mr. Kubrick seems not so much depleted or doubting as waiting for the process to turn in his mind all over again, waiting for a story. "It's the most difficult thing," he says, "A good story is a miraculous discovery."

Even then he sounds more grateful than plaintive. "The structure making a movie imposes on your life when you're doing it again feels like it felt each time before," Mr. Kubrick says, smiling. "So there is a kind of wonderful suggestive timelessness about the structure. I'm doing exactly the same as I was doing when I was eighteen and making my first movie. It frees you from any other sense of time."

Candidly Kubrick

GENE SISKEL/1987

FIFTEEN YEARS AGO DURING the early release of his film *A Clockwork Orange,* a scruffy-looking Stanley Kubrick sat down in a restaurant near his suburban London home to talk about his masterful movie about a timid society dealing with evil in the streets.

Earlier this month an even scruffier-looking Kubrick agreed to talk about his latest film, *Full Metal Jacket,* a comedy-laced, horror show about another evil, the Vietnam war.

The setting this time was suburban London's Pinewood studio, inside its magisterial, wood-paneled boardroom, at a long table surrounded by two dozen chairs. Put some candles on the table, and it was a setting worthy of an eighteenth-century monarch.

But Kubrick, fifty-eight, arrived dressed as if he had just come from a camping trip, wearing a partially buttoned blue shirt and an ink-stained, brown corduroy jacket underneath a blue parka shell. His beard was a tangle, his wispy hair greasy. Only soft, brown eyes behind wire-frame glasses suggested an order beneath the mess.

In fact, Kubrick had been camping out — at his elaborate home studio, working day and night on the sound effects of the film's last reel.

He looked much the same as fifteen years ago. But in those fifteen years he had made only three films: *Barry Lyndon* (1975), *The Shining* (1980), and now *Full Metal Jacket.*

These are not the greatest Kubrick films. They fall short of his master-works: *Paths of Glory* (1957), *Dr. Strangelove* (1963) and *2001: A Space Odyssey* (1968).

Full Metal Jacket falters only near the end, leaving us wanting more, fol-lowing a tragic and savagely funny first act of Marines in training. Yet the humor in *Full Metal Jacket* is so raw, its horror so unflinching, that seeing it reminds one that Kubrick's near-best work is more adult, more complex and more audacious than the movies of virtually any other filmmaker today.

An American citizen who has lived in London for a quarter-century, Kubrick is the stuff of legend—the Howard Hughes of the cinema. By comparison, reclusive Woody Allen is a regular Pia Zadora in terms of accessibility, making a film each year and dining and performing in high-profile New York boîtes.

Meanwhile the Kubrick legend grows, fueled by few films and few pub-lic statements.

"There's so much misinformation about me," he said last week in his soft, rapid, New York-accented voice, often punctuated with him clearing his throat.

"The stories get more elaborate as they're repeated in the papers," he said. "I've read that I wear a football crash helmet in a car, and I don't allow my driver to go over thirty miles per hour. Well, I drive a white Porsche 928S. It's a lot of fun to drive. I don't wear a football helmet or any other helmet, and I don't have a driver. So the story is pretty inaccurate.

"Practically everything I read about me is grotesquely wrong. I read one story where a guy said that I hire a helicopter to spray my garden because I don't like mosquitos. Well, no. 1, there are no mosquitos, and no. 2, it's completely preposterous. The only 'story' about me that's true is that I don't like to fly.

"I'm not a recluse. I lead a relatively normal life, I think. But this stuff has been written and rewritten so often it takes on a life of its own."

What about Kubrick's London home, often described as a secretive com-pound.

"I don't live in any massively guarded compound," he said, "I live in a nice country house outside of London. It has about twenty-five rooms, fif-teen of which are devoted to filmmaking: editing rooms, screening rooms, and offices. The only gate I have is one four-feet high to keep our dogs from running out onto the road."

His living in London produced speculation that he may have purposely turned his back on America.

"There have been all sorts of stories about why I live in London but it's really very simple: In order to be at home some of the time I have to live in a production center, and there are only three places in the world that fulfill this requirement in a practical sense. If you want to make English-language movies, it has to be done in Los Angeles, New York, or London.

"I love New York City, though my wife doesn't. But it would rank third in the list of cities with the best production facilities, London being second. Hollywood of course has the best facilities, but I have never enjoyed living there (where he took over the direction of *Spartacus*, completed in 1960). I found the sense of insecurity and the whiff of malevolence that surrounds you there unsettling.

"So London seemed a very natural choice, though I cannot say a decision was ever reached. We had a lovely house there at the time I was making *2001*, which we returned to. I had three daughters who were growing up and who were by then involved in English schools, and I had a dog that I could not take out of England and bring back without putting it into quarantine for six months. So I would say it was more of a *de facto* kind of a thing than a decision." (The dog that played a role in the Kubrick legend was a West Highland terrier named Andy.)

With his daughters now adults and his third marriage—to painter Christiane Kubrick—firmly in place, Kubrick says of his lifestyle: "I generally go out to the theater and to dinner once or twice a week when I'm not making films."

For the last three years, however, he has been making *Full Metal Jacket*, based on Gustav's Hasford's *The Short-Timers*, a memoir/novel of Vietnam during the Tet offensive of 1968, when the North Vietnamese soldiers overran American troops in dozens of surprise raids, including ten days of fierce street fighting in the city of Hue. (The 1980 paperback will be re-released shortly by Bantam Books.)

"Since I have not written any original screenplays," Kubrick said, explaining how he chooses his subject material, "all the films I have made have started by my reading a book. Those books that have been made into films have almost always had some aspect about them which on first reading left me with the sense that, 'This is a fantastic story; is it possible to make it into a film?'

"I'm always suspicious when a book looks like too much of a sure thing. It usually means that it's too similar to other things, and your mind clicks into place too easily, understanding how it might be made into a film.

"The hardest thing for me to do," he said, "is finding the story. It's much harder than financing, writing the script, making the film, editing it, whatever.

"The fact that each of the last three films has taken about five years has been because it is so hard to find something I think is worth doing.

"I didn't set out to do a Vietnam film," he said. "I don't work that way. A good story suitable for making into a film is so rare, subject matter is secondary. I was just reading and reading. When I'm looking for a story, I read an average of about five hours each day, based on recommendations in newsletters and also reading at random.

"About five years ago I came across the novel *The Short-Timers*, and after the first few pages it was clear that this was an extraordinary work of originality. When I finished it I thought to myself that this might make a great film if it were possible to put it on film."

The specific appeal?

"Well of course the first thing was the writing, the dialogue, and its sense of uncompromising truth. The book offered no easy moral or political answers; it was neither pro-war nor antiwar. It seemed only concerned with the way things are. There is a tremendous economy of statement in the book, which I have tried to retain in the film. All of the 'mandatory' scenes, explaining who everybody is—that this guy had a drunken father and that that guy's wife is a . . . —are left out. What you find out about the characters all comes from the main action of the story.

"On the second page the drill sergeant says (to a wiseacre trainee he's about to tongue-lash), 'I like you. You can come over to my house and ---- my sister.'"

That vulgar, comic, contradictory line, which caught Kubrick's eye in *The Short-Timers*, sets much of the tone of *Full Metal Jacket*, which is wittier, colder and just as profound as *Platoon*.

"I saw *Platoon* only a month ago," Kubrick said. "I liked it. I thought it was very good."

But Kubrick said the screening had no effect on his film, "We weren't too happy about our M-16 rifle sound effects, and when I heard M-16s in *Platoon,* I thought they sounded about the same as ours.

"The strength of *Platoon,*" he continued, "is that it's the first of what I call a 'military procedural' that is really well done, where you really believe what's going on. I thought the acting was very good and that it was dramatically very well written.

"That's the key to its success: It's a good film. It certainly wasn't a success because it was about Vietnam.

"What never fails to surprise me about the people who finance pictures is that they think by packaging and market research they can avoid the (problems associated with) making a good film. They will try to assess the potential of a film with market research. They ask people whether they'd be interested in a film on a particular subject, with certain actors, and give them a pretty inadequate description of the movie—and from this they will often make very important decisions.

"With the exception of certain sequels to giant successes, I don't think the audience knows what it wants to see. It's pretty obvious they want to see a good film that entertains them.

"Only the ending of *Platoon,*" Kubrick said, "seemed a bit soft to me in the optimism of its narration." He was referring to the narrator's noble wish that the war's survivors recover and build a new life. Some Vietnam veterans have expressed the same skepticism about their ability to rebuild their lives.

There's nothing that soft in *Full Metal Jacket.* If *Platoon* warmly embraces the wounded Vietnam vet, *Full Metal Jacket* rudely confronts those who didn't fight with both the realities and ironies of that war, as well as with the perverse way the American establishment sold the war to soldier and citizen alike.

"One of the notable things about the Vietnam war was that it was manipulated in Washington by hawk intellectuals who tried to fine-tune reality like an advertising agency, constantly inventing new jargon like 'Kill ratios,' 'Hamlets pacified,' and so forth. The light was always at the end of the tunnel."

The film's leading light in *Full Metal Jacket* is a bright young man nick-named Joker (Matthew Modine), who, after basic training, is sent to

Vietnam to work for a Marine newspaper away from the fighting. Then he smarts off once too often and winds up in combat during the Tet offensive in rubblestrewn Hue City.

Full Metal Jacket sets its combat in harshly lit barracks and urban daylight, rather than in the lush, green-black, Southeast Asian jungle of most Vietnam films. The battle scenes, filled with haunting, burned-out, bullet-ridden buildings and naked walls on fire (including one shaped like the monolith in *2001*) were filmed at an abandoned gasworks in East London.

That visual choice, in addition to being true to the novel, is typical of Kubrick, who prefers the bright light of day—or brightly-illuminated interiors—to capture our attention.

"I just try to photograph things realistically," the former *Look* magazine photographer said. "I try to light them as they really would be lit. When inside, I use practical lights and windows and not any supplemental lights. I'm after a realistic, documentary-type look in the film, especially during the fighting. Even the Steadicam shots purposefully aren't very steady. We wanted a newsreel effect."

Over the years Kubrick has filmed many courageous and outrageous warriors, from Kirk Douglas crawling over the trenches under withering fire in *Paths of Glory*, to Slim Pickens whoopin' and hollerin' and riding an A-bomb to oblivion in *Dr. Strangelove*, to a most contradictory character called Animal Mother (Adam Baldwin) in *Full Metal Jacket*.

We find ourselves cheering Animal's bravery toward the end of the picture, even though we immediately despise the sight of him, covered in bandoliers of bullets, wearing a full metal jacket, you might say.

"Courage is appealing, isn't it?" Kubrick said, leaving us to wonder if a point being made with the title is that American boys were playing a deadly game "unclothed," without proper metal jackets.

Kubrick said he didn't use the book's original title, *The Short-Timers*, because it didn't seem strong enough. "Movie titles have a special problem in that most of your ads are just the title. I think a good title should not sound like any other film. It does not have to be descriptive but it should not be misleading and it should sound good when you say it.

"The title *Full Metal Jacket* refers to a type of bullet design where the lead bullet is copper-jacketed, to increase the reliability of bullet feeding up the ramp into the chamber, and, I believe, the FMJ is also regarded as more humane than lead bullets by the Geneva Convention on warfare. There are other types of bullets called 'lead round-nosed,' 'semi-wad cutter' and so forth."

A New York native, Kubrick said he learned about bullets when he owned and fired a .38-caliber pistol while working in Los Angeles making *Spartacus.* "I think I had a gun there because I was so amazed how easy it was to get one in California."

Affection for weapons is an often-repeated image in *Full Metal Jacket,* which begins brilliantly with the image of a seemingly benign instrument, an electric hair clipper, turned into a weapon of sorts. The image: Raw recruits being shorn like a parade of sheep to the tune of Tom T. Hall's wistful country-western song, "Hello Vietnam." It's a funny-but-chilling, typically Kubrick, cowboy-military melange.

Then the young Marines go through riotously comic and violent basic training as we meet Joker and most of the film's other major characters, including a simple Texan called Cowboy, a gentle photographer called Rafterman and a tubby, incompetent recruit nicknamed Pyle, as in Gomer Pyle.

The young soldiers are led—make that slapped, insulted, and kicked— through their paces by a drill sergeant played memorably by former Marine drill instructor and Vietnam vet Lee Ermey, hired first as a consultant to the film.

But Kubrick replaced the actor originally hired to play the drill instructor with Ermey, after seeing that the teacher was a better performer than the pupil ever could be. Shooting was stopped for five months, however, after Ermey suffered five broken ribs in a car accident. Kubrick has the power in the movie world to wait longer than most films take to shoot.

The central idea of *Full Metal Jacket,* according to Kubrick, is expressed about half-way into the movie, long after we have become accustomed to the character of Joker as a purposeful contradiction.

Joker is smart enough to have earned a student deferment, yet he's in Vietnam. In one moment he can be exceedingly kind to the misfit trainee Pyle; later, he can be coerced into pummelling the poor slob along with the rest of his company. He wears a peace button on his uniform, but his helmet reads "Born to Kill."

In Vietnam during Tet, Cpl. Joker is confronted by an old colonel who is confounded by the peace-symbol/born-to-kill contradiction on Joker's uniform.

Joker responds to the warhorse's persistent questioning, saying, "I suppose I was trying to say something about the duality of man."

"The what?" the colonel demands.

"The duality of man," Joker replies. "You know, sir, the Jungian thing."

To which the confused colonel can only reply, in the kind of dumb yet pointed dialog often spoken in Kubrick's films: "Well, which side are you on, boy?"

"If I'm forced to suggest something about the deeper meaning of the story," Kubrick said, "I would have to say that it has a lot to do with the Jungian idea of the duality of man: altruism and cooperation on one hand, and aggression and xenophobia on the other.

"I suppose the single improvement one might hope for in the world, which would have the greatest effect for good, would be an appreciation and acceptance of this Jungian view of man by those who see themselves as good and externalize all evil."

Viewed that way, *Full Metal Jacket* certainly fits neatly into the intellectual framework of Kubrick's great films.

He makes films about tools often run amok: the French rifles that ultimately kill French soldiers in *Paths of Glory*; the failed, fail-safe systems of the military loonies in *Dr. Strangelove*; the apes' bones and the scientists' computer in *2001*; the doctor's violent treatment for pacification in *A Clockwork Orange*.

Tools, Kubrick is saying, can be used for good and for evil—to communicate, to destroy. What he is trying to show us in *Full Metal Jacket,* as in so much of his work, is that man himself is such a tool, created by a toolmaker who has given us the ability to create and destroy ourselves and our world.

Tools abound in *Full Metal Jacket,* the most prominent being rifles. But it's how they're used that counts.

"Yes," Kubrick said, "it's like the drill sergeant says to the recruits: 'Your rifle is only a tool. It is a hard heart that kills.'"

Yet to view *Full Metal Jacket* as an antiwar film is too simplistic, Kubrick said. "I guess that's what the producer of *Platoon* said in his Oscar speech—that he hoped they had made a film to end all wars.

"But there may be a fallacy in antiwar films that showing people war is bad will make them less willing to fight a war," Kubrick said. *"Full Metal Jacket* suggests that there is more to say about war than it is just bad.

"The Vietnam war was, of course, horribly wrong from the start, but I think it may have taught us something valuable. We would probably be fighting now in Nicaragua had it not been for Vietnam. I think the message has certainly gotten through that you don't even begin to think about fighting a war unless your survival depends upon it. Fancy theories about falling dominoes won't do in the future."

Kubrick is well-known for being plugged into all manner of information through his voracious reading and extensive computer system, and he was asked to speculate on other subjects. After all, as much as any artist of his time, he has pondered the beginning, future, and end of mankind.

Fifteen years ago he was asked how he saw the world ending. He answered then in the spirit of *A Clockwork Orange*: "I think the danger is not that authority will collapse," he said, "but that, finally, in order to preserve itself, authority will become very repressive."

This day, Kubrick is more optimistic, encouraged he said by developments in Russia, but also possibly in keeping with the character of Joker who, Kubrick said, is no longer simply a joker at the end of *Full Metal Jacket,* but a positive life force.

"Of course the worst danger in the world today is still nuclear war," Kubrick said. "But I think the only way this could happen now is by some inadvertent use of nuclear weapons by accident, miscalculation, or madness. I wish there were more public discussion about the problem of communication in a crisis.

"Both of the superpowers want to reduce the amount of money they spend on weapons. That's true, but I don't think that in the coming arms talks they should be focusing on how many missiles each has. That seems less of a threat than failure of communication in a crisis, like the episode with the Korean airliner [that the Soviets destroyed when it crossed their boundary]. And I think that young man was able to land his plane in Red Square because the Russians didn't want to repeat what happened over Korea.

"Their command and control system is probably even more liable than ours to confusion and misunderstanding due to inadequate communication," said the director of *Dr. Strangelove.*

"I wish there was more open disclosure by both sides as to the actual possibilities of communicating in a crisis. There is no reason why either side should be secretive about that."

More worrisome right now than The Bomb, according to Kubrick, is a meltdown of the world's monetary system.

"A more likely threat is the social upheaval that would be caused by an economic catastrophe triggered by the failure of the largest banks in America, which are presently carrying huge Third World loans that can never be repaid as assets. Most of the ten major banks in the United States are technically bankrupt. It's really 'the emperor's new clothes.' They would be legally bankrupt if they were honest and stopped treating these loans as assets.

"Government treasury bills and bonds are the safest and most liquid investments. I would certainly not put any substantial funds in any bank today."

Kubrick proved to be equally tough in his thinking when confronted with the statements of other well-known directors about men and war.

He disputed François Truffaut's assertion that you can't make an antiwar film if you show bombs going off because, Truffaut maintained, film always romanticizes everything it shows.

"That's clever because you can't fault it, but I'm not sure what it means," Kubrick said. "There are obviously elements in a war film that involve visual spectacle, courage, loyalty, affection, self-sacrifice, and adventure, and these things tend to complicate any anti-war message.

"War memoirs show us that many of the men who aren't destroyed by the horror and stresses of combat, at least in retrospect, view their participation in the war as the greatest moments of their lives. Didn't Gen. Robert E. Lee say, 'It is fortunate that war is so terrible or we should grow very fond of it.'?"

Kubrick himself, however, has never been in combat. "I was very lucky," he said. "I slipped through the cracks each time. I was seventeen when World War II ended and was married when the Korean war began. I wouldn't have volunteered."

The son of a Bronx physician, Kubrick was a teenage prodigy with a camera and was hired by *Look* magazine as a staff photographer at age seventeen. After four years on the road he filmed his first short subject, and three years later he made his first fictional feature. At the same time he

audited literature courses at Columbia University, nurturing his continuing passion for reading.

As for *Star Wars* creator George Lucas's notion that you can divide directors based on their films into those who basically like people and those
who don't, Kubrick, often called a misanthrope, said in rebuttal, "I like
some people; I don't like others. If I had to make a draw between the two
options Lucas gives, I'd say I like people. But I think it's a silly notion.

"You don't have to make Frank Capra movies to like people," Kubrick
said. "Capra presents a view of life as we all wish it really were. But I think
you can still present a darker picture of life without disliking the human
race. And I think Frank Capra movies are wonderful. And I wish life were
like most any one of them. And I wish everybody were like Jimmy Stewart.
But they're not."

Fifteen years ago, he said it was inappropriate to talk about the characters in *A Clockwork Orange* as heroes and villains. The film was satire, he
said.

Similarly, he also resisted a good-evil analysis of the men in *Full Metal
Jacket.*

"I don't see the characters in the story in terms of good or evil, but in
terms of good *and* evil. The only character who seems absolutely beyond
the pale is the helicopter door-gunner who, when asked how he can shoot
women and children, says, 'Easy, you just don't lead 'em so much.' I don't
blame the grunts for their cynical view of the war or for their failure to
communicate on any human level with the Vietnamese.

"They were unprepared culturally for the situation they were put into,
and the language barrier didn't help. Neither did the fact that every man
and woman and child might have been a V.C.

"When they got there," Kubrick said, "they quickly realized the war was
hopeless, that the people back home were being given a false picture of the
war. There is no question in my mind that their innocence and courage
was misused.

"The war was evil, and the soldiers and civilians were its victims."

That view is similar to Kubrick's portrayal of the French generals who
sell out their trench soldiers for their own self-interest in *Paths of Glory.*

As for his fascination with warriors and war in so many of his films,
Kubrick said, "It obviously is emotionally intense and offers great visual
possibilities. And it's full of irony, depending on the war. In this film, for

example, you have this tremendous preoccupation with being hard and learning to kill, as represented by the drill instructor's speeches.

"It all seems so simple—what the drill instructor says—but it's not so simple in the field."

One point Kubrick wanted to stress is that he didn't see the film as anti-American. He did not want to be portrayed as an expatriate in London taking potshots at the United States during the bicentennial of its Constitution.

"Living away from America, I see virtues you may not see living there," he said. "Compared with other countries, I see the United States as a good place. I don't think Ronald Reagan is a good President, but I still see the American people as hard-working, as wanting to do the right thing."

Many times during the discussion, Kubrick said that he wasn't very good giving interviews, especially tape-recorded ones.

True to his perfectionist standards and desire for control, he asked—as he had fifteen years ago—to be able to read his quotes that would be used in the article and to have the privilege to rewrite them. Such permission was granted.

"I write better than I speak off-the-cuff," he said. "In fact the only two ways journalists can screw me up is to misquote me or quote me accurately. Not only can I usually write the answer better, but I might avoid unfairly attacking someone."

By acknowledging his strengths and weaknesses, however, Kubrick would appear to be in touch with his own yin and yang—you know, "the Jungian thing."

Even so, as one left him in the light rain at Pinewood studio, thoughts about his intense but slow work pattern crossed the mind. Based upon his current pace and life-expectancy, Stanley Kubrick has only four more films to give us.

The *Rolling Stone* Interview: Stanley Kubrick

TIM CAHILL/1987

HE DIDN'T BUSTLE INTO the room, and he didn't wander in. Truth, as he would reiterate several times, is multifaceted, and it would be fair to say that Stanley Kubrick entered the executive suite at Pinewood Studios, outside London, in a multifaceted manner. He was at once happy to have found the place after a twenty-minute search, apologetic about being late and apprehensive about the torture he might be about to endure. Stanley Kubrick, I had been told, hates interviews.

It's hard to know what to expect of the man if you've only seen his films. One senses in those films painstaking craftsmanship, a furious intellect at work, a single-minded devotion. His movies don't lend themselves to easy analysis; this may account for the turgid nature of some of the books that have been written about his art. Take this example: "And while Kubrick feels strongly that the visual powers of film make ambiguity an inevitability as well as a virtue, he would not share Bazin's mystical belief that the better filmmakers are those who sacrifice their personal perspectives to a 'fleeting crystallization of a reality [of] whose environing presence one is ceaselessly aware.'"

One feels that an interview conducted on this level would be pretentious bullshit. Kubrick, however, seemed entirely unpretentious. He was wearing running shoes and an old corduroy jacket. There was an ink stain just below the pocket where some ball point pen had bled to death.

"What is this place?" Kubrick asked.

"It's called the executive suite," I said. "I think they put big shots up here."

Kubrick looked around at the dark wood-paneled walls, the chandeliers, the leather couches and chairs. "Is there a bathroom?" he asked, with some urgency.

"Across the hall," I said.

The director excused himself and went looking for the facility. I reviewed my notes. Kubrick was born in the Bronx in 1928. He was an undistinguished student whose passions were tournament-level chess and photography. After graduation from Taft High School at the age of seventeen, he landed a prestigious job as a photographer for *Look* magazine, which he quit after four years in order to make his first film. *Day of the Fight* (1950) was a documentary about the middleweight boxer Walter Cartier. After a second documentary, *Flying Padre* (1951), Kubrick borrowed $10,000 from relatives to make *Fear and Desire* (1953), his first feature, an arty film that he now finds "embarrassing." Kubrick, his first wife, and two friends were the entire crew for the film. By necessity, Kubrick was director, cameraman, lighting engineer, makeup man, administrator, propman, and unit chauffeur. Later in his career, he would take on some of these duties again, for reasons other than necessity.

Kubrick's breakthrough film was *Paths of Glory* (1957). During the filming, he met an actress, Christiane Harlan, whom he eventually married. Christiane sings a song at the end of the film in a scene that, on four separate viewings, has brought tears to my eyes.

Kubrick's next film was *Spartacus* (1960), a work he finds disappointing. He was brought in to direct after the star, Kirk Douglas, had a fallingout with the original director, Anthony Mann. Kubrick was not given control of the script, which he felt was full of easy moralizing. He was used to making his own films his own way, and the experience chafed. He has never again relinquished control over any aspect of his films.

And he has taken some extraordinary and audacious chances with those works. The mere decision to film Vladimir Nabokov's *Lolita* (1962) was enough to send some censorious sorts into a spittle-spewing rage. *Dr. Strangelove* (1964), based on the novel *Red Alert*, was conceived as a tense thriller about the possibility of accidental nuclear war. As Kubrick worked on the script, however, he kept bumping up against the realization that the scenes he was writing were funny in the darkest possible way. It was a matter of slipping on a banana peel and annihilating the human race. Stanley Kubrick went with his gut feeling: he directed *Dr. Strangelove* as a black comedy. The film is routinely described as a masterpiece.

Most critics also use that word to describe the two features that followed, *2001: A Space Odyssey* (1968) and *A Clockwork Orange* (1971). Some reviewers see a subtle falling off of quality in his *Barry Lyndon* (1975) and *The Shining* (1980), though there is a critical reevaluation of the two films in process. This seems to be typical of his critical reception.

Kubrick moved to England in 1961. He lives outside of London with Christiane (now a successful painter), three golden retrievers and a mutt he found wandering forlornly along the road. He has three grown daughters. Some who know him say he can be "difficult" and "exacting."

He had agreed to meet and talk about his latest movie, *Full Metal Jacket,* a film about the Vietnam War that he produced and directed. He also co-wrote the screenplay with Michael Herr, the author of *Dispatches,* and Gustav Hasford, who wrote *The Short-Timers,* the novel on which the film is based. *Full Metal Jacket* is Kubrick's first feature in seven years.

The difficult and exacting director returned from the bathroom looking a little perplexed. "I think you're right," he said. "I think this is a place where people stay. I looked around a little, opened a door, and there was this guy sitting on the edge of a bed."

"Who was he?" I asked.

"I don't know," he replied.

"What did he say?"

"Nothing. He just looked at me, and I left."

There was a long silence while we pondered the inevitable ambiguity of reality, specifically in relation to some guy sitting on a bed across the hall. Then Stanley Kubrick began the interview:

I'm not going to be asked any conceptualizing questions, right?

All the books, most of the articles I read about you — It's all conceptualizing.
Yeah, but not by me.

I thought I had to ask those kinds of questions.
No. Hell, no. That's my... [*He shudders.*] It's the thing I hate the worst.

Really? I've got all these questions written down in a form I thought you might require. They all sound like essay questions for the finals in a graduate philosophy seminar.

The truth is that I've always felt trapped and pinned down and harried by those questions.

Questions like [reading from notes] "Your first feature, Fear and Desire, in 1953, concerned a group of soldiers lost behind enemy lines in an unnamed war; Spartacus contained some battle scenes; Paths of Glory was an indictment of war and, more specifically, of the generals who wage it; and Dr. Strangelove was the blackest of comedies about accidental nuclear war. How does Full Metal Jacket complete your examination of the subject of war? Or does it?"

Those kinds of questions.

You feel the real question lurking behind all the verbiage is "What does this new movie mean?"

Exactly. And that's almost impossible to answer, especially when you've been so deeply inside the film for so long. Some people demand a five-line capsule summary. Something you'd read in a magazine. They want you to say, "This is the story of the duality of man and the duplicity of governments." [A pretty good description of the subtext that informs *Full Metal Jacket,* actually.] I hear people try to do it—give the five-line summary—but if a film has any substance or subtlety, whatever you say is never complete, it's usually wrong, and it's necessarily simplistic: truth is too multifaceted to be contained in a five-line summary. If the work is good, what you say about it is usually irrelevant.

I don't know. Perhaps it's vanity, this idea that the work is bigger than one's capacity to describe it. Some people can do interviews. They're very slick, and they neatly evade this hateful conceptualizing. Fellini is good; his interviews are very amusing. He just makes jokes and says preposterous things that you know he can't possibly mean.

I mean, I'm doing interviews to help the film, and I think they do help the film, so I can't complain. But it isn't . . . it's . . . it's difficult.

So let's talk about the music in Full Metal Jacket. I was surprised by some of the choices, stuff like "These Boots Are Made for Walkin'," by Nancy Sinatra. What does that song mean?

It was the music of the period. The Tet offensive was in '68. Unless we were careless, none of the music is post-'68.

I'm not saying it's anachronistic. It's just that the music that occurs to me in that context is more, oh, Jimi Hendrix, Jim Morrison.
The music really depended on the scene. We checked through *Billboard's* list of Top 100 hits for each year from 1962 to 1968. We were looking for interesting material that played well with a scene. We tried a lot of songs. Sometimes the dynamic range of the music was too great, and we couldn't work in dialogue. The music has to come up under speech at some point, and if all you hear is the bass, it's not going to work in the context of the movie.

Why? Don't you like "These Boots Are Made for Walkin' "?

Of the music in the film, I'd have to say I'm more partial to Sam the Sham's "Wooly Bully," which is one of the great party records of all time. And "Surfin' Bird."
An amazing piece, isn't it?

"Surfin' Bird" comes in during the aftermath of a battle, as the marines are passing a medevac helicopter. The scene reminded me of Dr. Strangelove, *where the plane is being refueled in midair with that long, suggestive tube, and the music in the background is "Try a Little Tenderness." Or the cosmic waltz in 2001, where the spacecraft is slowly cartwheeling through space in time to* The Blue Danube. *And now you have the chopper and the "Bird."*
What I love about the music in that scene is that it suggests postcombat euphoria—which you see in the marine's face when he fires at the men running out of the building: he misses the first four, waits a beat, then hits the next two. And that great look on his face, that look of euphoric pleasure, the pleasure one has read described in so many accounts of combat. So he's got this look on his face, and suddenly the music starts and the tanks are rolling and the marines are mopping up. The choices weren't arbitrary.

You seem to have skirted the issue of drugs in Full Metal Jacket.
It didn't seem relevant. Undoubtedly, marines took drugs in Vietnam. But this drug thing, it seems to suggest that all marines were out of control,

when in fact they weren't. It's a little thing, but check out the pictures taken during the battle of Hue: you see marines in fully fastened flak jackets. Well, people hated wearing them. They were heavy and hot, and sometimes people wore them but didn't fasten them. Disciplined troops wore them, and they wore them fastened.

People always look at directors, and you in particular, in the context of a body of work. I couldn't help but notice some resonance with Paths of Glory *at the end of* Full Metal Jacket: *a woman surrounded by enemy soldiers, the odd, ambiguous gesture that ties these people together....*
That resonance is an accident. The scene comes straight out of Gustav Hasford's book.

So your purpose wasn't to poke the viewer in the ribs, point out certain similarities...
Oh, God, no. I'm trying to be true to the material. You know, there's another extraordinary accident. Cowboy is dying, and in the background there's something that looks very much like the monolith in *2001*. And it just happened to be there.

The whole area of combat was one complete area — it actually exists. One of the things I tried to do was give you a sense of where you were, where everything else was. Which, in war movies, is something you frequently don't get. The terrain of small-unit action is really the story of the action. And this is something we tried to make beautifully clear: there's a low wall, there's the building space. And once you get in there, everything is exactly where it actually was. No cutting away, no cheating. So it came down to where the sniper would be and where the marines were. When Cowboy is shot, they carry him around the corner — to the very most logical shelter. And there, in the background was this thing, this monolith. I'm sure some people will think that there was some calculated reference to *2001*, but honestly, it was just there.

You don't think you're going to get away with that, do you?
[*Laughs*] I know it's an amazing coincidence.

Where were those scenes filmed?
We worked from still photographs of Hue in 1968. And we found an area that had the same 1930s functionalist architecture. Now, not every bit of it

was right, but some of the buildings were absolute carbon copies of the outer industrial areas of Hue.

Where was it?
Here. Near London. It had been owned by British Gas, and it was scheduled to be demolished. So they allowed us to blow up the buildings. We had demolition guys in there for a week, laying charges. One Sunday, all the executives from British Gas brought their families down to watch us blow the place up. It was spectacular. Then we had a wrecking ball there for two months, with the art director telling the operator which hole to knock in which building.

Art direction with a wrecking ball.
I don't think anybody's ever had a set like that. It's beyond any kind of economic possibility. To make that kind of three-dimensional rubble, you'd have to have everything done by plasterers, modeled, and you couldn't build that if you spent $80 million and had five years to do it. You couldn't duplicate, oh, all those twisted bits of reinforcement. And to make rubble, you'd have to go find some real rubble and copy it. It's the only way. If you're going to make a tree, for instance, you have to copy a real tree. No one can "make up" a tree, because every tree has an inherent logic in the way it branches. And I've discovered that no one can make up a rock. I found that out in *Paths of Glory*. We had to copy rocks, but every rock also has an inherent logic you're not aware of until you see a fake rock. Every detail looks right, but something's wrong.

So we had real rubble. We brought in palm trees from Spain and a hundred thousand plastic tropical plants from Hong Kong. We did little things, details people don't notice right away, that add to the illusion. All in all, a tremendous set dressing and rubble job.

How do you choose your material?
I read. I order books from the States. I literally go into bookstores, close my eyes and take things off the shelf. If I don't like the book after a bit, I don't finish it. But I like to be surprised.

Full Metal Jacket *is based on Gustav Hasford's book* The Short-Timers.
It's a very short, very beautifully and economically written book, which, like the film, leaves out all the mandatory scenes of character develop-

ment: the scene where the guy talks about his father, who's an alcoholic, his girlfriend—all that stuff that bogs down and seems so arbitrarily inserted into every war story.

What I like about not writing original material—which I'm not even certain I could do—is that you have this tremendous advantage of reading something for the first time. You never have this experience again with the story. You have a reaction to it: it's a kind of falling-in-love reaction.

That's the first thing. Then it becomes almost a matter of code breaking, of breaking the work down into a structure that is truthful, that doesn't lose the ideas or the content or the feeling of the book. And fitting it all into the much more limited time frame of a movie.

And as long as you possibly can, you retain your emotional attitude, whatever it was that made you fall in love in the first place. You judge a scene by asking yourself, "Am I still responding to what's there?" The process is both analytical and emotional. You're trying to balance calculating analysis against feeling. And it's almost never a question of "What does this scene mean?" It's "Is this truthful, or does something about it feel false?" It's "Is this scene interesting? Will it make me feel the way I felt when I first fell in love with the material?" It's an intuitive process, the way I imagine writing music is intuitive. It's not a matter of structuring an argument.

You said something almost exactly the opposite once.
Did I?

Someone had asked you if there was any analogy between chess and filmmaking. You said that the process of making decisions was very analytical in both cases. You said that depending on intuition was a losing proposition.
I suspect I might have said that in another context. The part of the film that involves telling the story works pretty much the way I said. In the actual making of the movie, the chess analogy becomes more valid. It has to do with tournament chess, where you have a clock and you have to make a certain number of moves in a certain time. If you don't, you forfeit, even if you're a queen ahead. You'll see a grandmaster, the guy has three minutes on the clock and ten moves left. And he'll spend two minutes on one move, because he knows that if he doesn't get that one right,

the game will be lost. And then he makes the last nine moves in a minute. And he may have done the right thing.

Well, in filmmaking, you always have decisions like that. You are always pitting time and resources against quality and ideas.

You have a reputation for having your finger on every aspect of each film you make, from inception right on down to the première and beyond. How is it that you're allowed such an extraordinary amount of control over your films?
I'd like to think it's because my films have a quality that holds up on second, third, and fourth viewing. Realistically, it's because my budgets are within reasonable limits and the films do well. The only one that did poorly from the studio's point of view was *Barry Lyndon*. So, since my films don't cost that much, I find a way to spend a little extra time in order to get the quality on the screen.

Full Metal Jacket *seemed a long time in the making.*
Well, we had a couple of severe accidents. The guy who plays the drill instructor, Lee Ermey, had an auto accident in the middle of shooting. It was about 1:00 in the morning, and his car skidded off the road. He broke all his ribs on one side, just tremendous injuries, and he probably would have died, except he was conscious and kept flashing his lights. A motorist stopped. It was in a place called Epping Forest, where the police are always finding bodies. Not the sort of place you get out of your car at 1:30 in the morning and go see why someone's flashing their lights. Anyway, Lee was out for four and a half months.

He had actually been a marine drill instructor?
Parris Island.

How much of his part comes out of that experience?
I'd say fifty percent of Lee's dialogue, specifically the insult stuff, came from Lee. You see, in the course of hiring the marine recruits, we interviewed hundreds of guys. We lined them all up and did an improvisation of the first meeting with the drill instructor. They didn't know what he was going to say, and we could see how they reacted. Lee came up with, I don't know, one hundred fifty pages of insults. Off the wall stuff: "I don't like the name Lawrence. Lawrence is for faggots and sailors."

Aside from the insults, though, virtually every serious thing he says is basically true. When he says, "A rifle is only a tool, it's a hard heart that kills," you know it's true. Unless you're living in a world that doesn't need fighting men, you can't fault him. Except maybe for a certain lack of subtlety in his behavior. And I don't think the United States Marine Corps is in the market for subtle drill instructors.

This is a different drill instructor than the one Lou Gosset played in An Officer and a Gentlemen.
I think Lou Gosset's performance was wonderful, but he had to do what he was given in the story. The film clearly wants to ingratiate itself with the audience. So many films do that. You show the drill instructor really has a heart of gold—the mandatory scene where he sits in his office, eyes swimming with pride about the boys and so forth. I suppose he actually is proud, but there's a danger of falling into what amounts to so much sentimental bullshit.

So you distrust sentimentality.
I don't mistrust sentiment and emotion, no. The question becomes, are you giving them something to make them a little happier, or are you putting in something that is inherently true to the material? Are people behaving the way we all really behave, or are they behaving the way we would like them to behave? I mean, the world is not as it's presented in Frank Capra films. People love those films—which are beautifully made— but I wouldn't describe them as a true picture of life.

The questions are always, is it true? Is it interesting? To worry about those mandatory scenes that some people think make a picture is often just pandering to some conception of an audience. Some films try to outguess an audience. They try to ingratiate themselves, and it's not something you really have to do. Certainly audiences have flocked to see films that are not essentially true, but I don't think this prevents them from responding to the truth.

Books I've read on you seem to suggest that you consider editing the most important aspect of the filmmaker's art.
There are three equal things: the writing, slogging through the actual shooting and the editing.

You've quoted Pudovkin to the effect that editing is the only original and unique art form in film.
I think so. Everything else comes from something else. Writing, of course, is writing, acting comes from the theater, and cinematography comes from photography. Editing is unique to film. You can see something from different points of view almost simultaneously, and it creates a new experience.

Pudovkin gives an example: You see a guy hanging a picture on the wall. Suddenly you see his feet slip; you see the chair move; you see his hand go down and the picture fall off the wall. In that split second, a guy falls off a chair, and you see it in a way that you could not see it any other way except through editing.

TV commercials have figured that out. Leave content out of it, and some of the most spectacular examples of film art are in the best TV commercials.

Give me an example.
The Michelob commercials. I'm a pro-football fan, and I have videotapes of the games sent over to me, commercials and all. Last year Michelob did a series, just impressions of people having a good time—

The big city at night—
And the editing, the photography, was some of the most brilliant work I've ever seen. Forget what they're doing—selling beer—and it's visual poetry. Incredible eight-frame cuts. And you realize that in thirty seconds they've created an impression of something rather complex. If you could ever tell a story, something with some content, using that kind of visual poetry, you could handle vastly more complex and subtle material.

People spend millions of dollars and months' worth of work on these thirty seconds.
So it's a bit impractical. And I suppose there's really nothing that would substitute for the great dramatic moment, fully played out. Still, the stories we do on film are basically rooted in the theater. Even Woody Allen's movies, which are wonderful, are very traditional in their structure. Did I get the year right on those Michelob ads?

I think so.
Because occasionally I'll find myself watching a game from 1984.

It amazes me that you're a pro-football fan.
Why?

It doesn't fit my image of you.
Which is...

Stanley Kubrick is a monk, a man who lives for his work and virtually nothing else, certainly not pro football. And then there are those rumors—
I know what's coming.

You want both barrels?
Fire.

Stanley Kubrick is a perfectionist. He is consumed by mindless anxiety over every aspect of every film he makes. Kubrick is a hermit, an expatriate, a neurotic who is terrified of automobiles and who won't let his chauffeur drive more than thirty miles an hour.
Part of my problem is that I cannot dispel the myths that have somehow accumulated over the years. Somebody writes something, it's completely off the wall, but it gets filed and repeated until everyone believes it. For instance, I've read that I wear a football helmet in the car.

You won't let your driver go more than thirty miles an hour, and you wear a football helmet, just in case.
In fact, I don't have a chauffeur. I drive a Porsche 928S, and I sometimes drive it at eighty or ninety miles an hour on the motorway.

Your film editor says you still work on your old films. Isn't that neurotic perfectionism?
I'll tell you what he means. We discovered that the studio had lost the picture negative of *Dr. Strangelove*. And they also lost the magnetic master soundtrack. All the printing negatives were badly ripped dupes. The search went on for a year and a half. Finally, I had to try to reconstruct the picture from two not-too-good fine-grain positives, both of which were damaged already. If those fine-grains were ever torn, you could never make any more negatives.

Do you consider yourself an expatriate?
Because I direct films, I have to live in a major English-speaking production center. That narrows it down to three places: Los Angeles, New York, and London. I like New York, but it's inferior to London as a production center. Hollywood is best, but I don't like living there.

You read books or see films that depict people being corrupted by Hollywood, but it isn't that. It's this tremendous sense of insecurity. A lot of destructive competitiveness. In comparison, England seems very remote. I try to keep up, read the trade papers, but it's good to get it on paper and not have to hear it every place you go. I think it's good to just do the work and insulate yourself from that undercurrent of low-level malevolence.

I've heard rumors that you'll do a hundred takes for one scene.
It happens when actors are unprepared. You cannot act without knowing dialogue. If actors have to think about the words, they can't work on the emotion. So you end up doing thirty takes of something. And still you can see the concentration in their eyes; they don't know their lines. So you just shoot it and shoot it and hope you can get something out of it in pieces.

Now, if the actor is a nice guy, he goes home, he says, "Stanley's such a perfectionist, he does a hundred takes on every scene." So my thirty takes become a hundred. And I get this reputation.

If I did a hundred takes on every scene, I'd never finish a film. Lee Ermey, for instance, would spend every spare second with the dialogue coach, and he always knew his lines. I suppose Lee averaged eight or nine takes. He sometimes did it in three. Because he was prepared.

There's a rumor that you actually wanted to approve the theaters that show Full Metal Jacket. *Isn't that an example of mindless anxiety?*
Some people are amazed, but I worry about the theaters where the picture is being shown. They think that's some form of demented anxiety. But Lucas Films has a Theater Alignment Program. They went around and checked a lot of theaters and published the results in a [1985] report that virtually confirms all your worst suspicions. For instance, within one day, fifty percent of the prints are scratched. Something is usually broken. The amplifiers are no good, and the sound is bad. The lights are uneven. . . .

Is that why so many films I've seen lately seem too dark? Why you don't really see people in the shadows when clearly the director wants you to see them?
Well, theaters try to put in a screen that's larger than the light source they paid for. If you buy a 2000-watt projector, it may give you a decent picture twenty feet wide. And let's say that theater makes the picture forty feet wide by putting it in a wider-angle projector. In fact, then you're getting 200 percent less light. It's an inverse law of squares. But they want a biggest picture, so it's dark.

Many exhibitors are terribly guilty of ignoring minimum standards of picture quality. For instance, you now have theaters where all the reels are run in one continuous string. And they never clean the aperture gate. You get one little piece of gritty dust in there, and every time the film runs, it gets bigger. After a couple of days, it starts to put a scratch on the film. The scratch goes from one end of the film to the other. You've seen it, I'm sure.

That thing you see, it looks like a hair dangling down from the top of the frame, sort of wiggling there through the whole film?
That's one manifestation, yeah. The Lucas report found that after fifteen days, most films should be junked. [The report says that after seventeen days, most films are damaged.] Now, is it an unreal concern if I want to make sure that on the press shows or on key city openings, everything in the theater is going to run smoothly? You just send someone to check the place out three or four days ahead of time. Make sure nothing's broken. It's really only a phone call or two, pressuring some people to fix things. I mean, is this a legitimate concern, or is this mindless anxiety?

Initial reviews of most of your films are sometimes inexplicably hostile. Then there's a reevaluation. Critics seem to like you better in retrospect.
That's true. The first reviews of *2001* were insulting, let alone bad. An important Los Angeles critic faulted *Paths of Glory* because the actors didn't speak with French accents. When *Dr. Strangelove* came out, a New York paper ran a review under the head MOSCOW COULD NOT BUY MORE HARM TO AMERICA. Something like that. But critical opinion on my films has always been salvaged by what I would call subsequent critical opinion. Which is why I think audiences are more reliable than critics, at least initially. Audiences tend not to bring all that critical baggage with them to each film.

And I really think that a few critics come to my films expecting to see the last film. They're waiting to see something that never happens. I imagine it must be something like standing in the batter's box waiting for a fast ball, and the pitcher throws a change-up. The batter swings and misses. He thinks, "Shit, he threw me the wrong pitch." I think this accounts for some of the initial hostility.

Well, you don't make it easy on viewers or critics. You've said you want an audience to react emotionally. You create strong feelings, but you won't give us any easy answers.
That's because I don't have any easy answers.

INDEX